A Butterfly LIFE

A Butterfly LIFE

4 Keys to More Happiness, Better Health and Letting Your True Self Shine

Kristi Bowman

FOUR
Directions

Four Directions
San Francisco, California
www.sacredmovement.org/fourdirections

A Butterfly Life : 4 Keys to More Happiness, Better Health and Letting Your True Self Shine

ISBN-13: 978-0692059395 (softcover)
ISBN-10: 0692059393

Cover art by Kristi Bowman

Dedicated to you.
May you shine to your fullest.

Contents

Acknowledgments

Deep gratitude to my dearest love – my partner, best friend and tree-climbing companion. Your support has always come with such sweetness, patience and trust. You make my heart sing every day! Thank you to my family (and extended family) who is making this journey with me, with special thanks to Marci and Cody Zoller, Ryan and Jennifer Royal, Layne and Brenda Bowman, and the Conti clan. I love you, and I am so grateful for your unconditional love and support. Mom, my love for books and storytelling began when you gently read to me *The Gingerbread Man* over and over at my request. My deepest thanks. Dad, you are missed, though I still feel your presence and support. To Duane and Carol Jones, thank you for providing a most wonderful environment for this butterfly to unfold. Heartfelt gratitude to my students and participants from classes, workshops and other adventures. You inspire me to keep walking the path. Friends, teachers, mentors, many of you have had such a big, beautiful influence in my life. Rather than a sentence or two here, I've chosen to recognize and honor you in the pages that follow, for this story is for all of us.

Author's Note

I have adopted fictitious names for many of the people and places mentioned in order to protect privacy. No attempt has been made to create complete characterizations of the individuals, only to portray them as they relate to the story.

At times, you will find various kinds of animals have been capitalized. This is out of respect for the Native American tradition how each animal, indeed every living thing, is considered a teacher. There is much to be gained from a deeper relationship with the natural world.

Preface

The butterfly can be a powerful symbol for our own personal journeys. Change happens, and we can go through it kicking and screaming, or we can embrace it. Times of change are often challenging, no doubt – such as a relationship breakup, job loss or being diagnosed with a serious health issue. Or we may *want* things to be different, but it feels a little scary or overwhelming. The butterfly shows us change can be beautiful, even necessary, in order to realize our full potential and live our best life.

I would often get asked by individuals who read my first book, my memoir, *Journey to One: A Woman's Story of Emotional Healing and Spiritual Awakening*, "But *how* did you get from there to here?" In other words, how did I get from those dark, despairing beginnings to my current state of happiness and well-being? Though I included a few concepts that may be beneficial for others in their own journey of healing and self-discovery, *Journey to One* was not designed as a guidebook. It was primarily a documentation of how and where things began for me. My intention was to share my personal story in order to help others who may have had similar difficult life experiences and to reflect what is possible – that despite the circumstances, we can transform our lives and thrive. So in response to the inquiries, I would assure them another book was on the way.

A Butterfly Life was born from a desire to share teachings, tools and perspectives that I have found immensely beneficial and support as many individuals as possible in enjoying happy, healthy, fulfilling lives. In essence, isn't that what most of us want? We desire to feel good, have more energy, live our best life and feel like we're doing something meaningful.

I believe the secret lies within our own transformation. It's about doing our inner work. The more we learn and grow as individuals, the more we will be able to experience happiness and satisfaction in love, work and daily life. There is a ripple effect.

In the Native American spiritual tradition it is believed that animals carry medicine, gifts or teachings that can benefit us all. I feel a strong connection with the animals. Maybe it's because of the trace amount of Cherokee blood that runs through my veins, or because I grew up in the country, or simply because of my deep love for nature. Regardless, you will find animal symbolism woven throughout the book, most notably the butterfly. The butterfly is about transformation.

This book is organized into 4 sections, or stages: Egg, Caterpillar, Cocoon and Butterfly. As you move through the 4 stages of a butterfly's life, you can use the gifts found within each stage to positively transform your own life.

A Butterfly Life is part personal story, part guidebook. For thousands of years indigenous cultures have used storytelling, not only to entertain, but to pass along valuable life lessons. I have the heart of a storyteller. I enjoy drawing from this tradition and using story as a way of conveying helpful teachings. So through the first 3 stages of *A Butterfly Life* I share my story, particularly in regard to work and love, including the struggles and successes. Lessons are woven throughout, and these personal experiences also lay the foundation for the 4 Keys.

In addition to Native wisdom, I've included transformative teachings from yoga and leading-edge practices in the field of health and wellness. *A Butterfly Life* is designed to activate the potential for growth and positive change in each of our lives.

The fourth and final stage of *A Butterfly Life* contains tips and practical tools for achieving greater happiness in relationships, finding more satisfaction in work, enjoying increased health and well-being, and experiencing more peace and joy in daily living. Each of these tools are designed to support you in shining to your fullest. It is within the chapters of the Butterfly stage that you will find the 4 Keys. Briefly, they are:

4 Keys

1   Power of Words

Words affect how we relate to others, how we view ourselves and our beliefs. Through raising awareness in how we communicate with others and applying the techniques of "Listen First," we can reduce frustration and conflict and create more loving and satisfying relationships. By increasing awareness of our thoughts — the words we tell ourselves — we can change how we feel and achieve greater happiness and success.

2   Embodiment

This is about tuning into our bodies and practicing simple ways to support our health and well-being through movement, including walking and yoga, and what we eat. There are a plethora of exercise programs and diets already out there. How is a person supposed to know where to start? Rather than offer yet another program, the focus is on raising awareness and gaining a deeper connection with our bodies, which can lead to making choices that support greater wellness in body, mind and spirit.

3   Be Do Have

This 3rd Key reveals how satisfying work is possible. Frequently, we're not happy doing what we're doing and/or we feel like we don't know which direction to go. It starts with connecting with our core self, *being* who we are — strong, creative, worthy, loving, free, powerful, wise, beautiful beings. Discussed are four factors that play an important role in raising our level of satisfaction and enjoying meaningful work.

4   Remember Love

More than anything else, love has the power to transform lives in beautiful and profound ways. This is true individually, in relationship, with family, friends, community and globally. When we connect with love, we feel better about ourselves, we're able to make choices that support our own and others' growth, and we enjoy a greater level of happiness and fulfillment in life.

The tools in *A Butterfly Life* have proven to be helpful, not only personally, but in my work with others. For more than a decade, I've had the privilege of coaching and supporting people in a variety of settings, including business executives working to create organizational change, couples desiring less frustration and more joy in their relationships, and individuals wanting to get healthier and feel better about themselves.

This book also provides an opportunity for me to highlight and pay tribute to some of the people and experiences – from martial arts, to the Y, to yoga, to Native wisdom – that have helped shape and influence how I engage with others as a teacher and perpetual student of life.

Finally, there is something very special about Butterfly. Her stages of transformation are offered as a gift and example to us for our personal growth and evolution. Butterfly reminds us change doesn't have to be overwhelming or scary. Rather, transformation can be a beautiful and amazing process, rewarding and life-affirming. She is the true teacher in this story. She takes our hand and gently guides us along the journey, revealing how each of us can live a butterfly life.

Part I: Egg

She wriggles in her cocoon.
It feels snug on all sides.
She has grown so much recently
and has changed in unexpected ways.

She takes the opportunity to reflect on her life so far.
She remembers being close to the earth,
inching her way in search of food, always food.
She remembers feeling drawn to stay on the move
and how natural it felt to propel herself along,
her body bending and flexing with ease,
her movement a wave carrying her forward.

Not much is recalled prior to this time, though.
At times she experiences something
that can only be described as an echo from an earlier state,
like when you first blink your eyes awake
and can recollect only a flash of a dream you were having.
You know there was much more to the dream,
and that it went on for some time,
but all you hold now is a single, brief residual image.
The echo she experiences every now and then is simply a feeling,
that of being held safe,
and that of beginnings.

Chapter 1

Movement Happens

J sit poolside at my apartment complex, letting my toes dangle into the cool water on a sizzling August afternoon in 2009. The 2-story building encircles the pool, and the handful of palm trees and tasteful landscaping remind me of something off of the 90's show *Beverly Hills, 90210*, though perhaps not quite as upscale. Northern California is different from southern California. There are more mountains. It's greener. We get more rain, even snow. Rather than palm trees and Hollywood, we have redwoods and beautiful, rocky coastal shores. It feels more grounded. I have lived in northern California my whole life. I've lived here in this apartment 3 years, 8 months and some odd days.

These last few years have been chock full of memorable experiences. It is while living here that I remembered and reconnected with my love of nature with the help of nearby Diego Park. It is here that I first experienced the depth and joy of yoga, transforming my living room several days a week into a personal yoga studio watching my Shiva Rea DVDs. Here at the apartment I spent countless hours with individuals I was dating, through laughter and tears, and experienced relationships end and new ones begin.

A soft, warm breeze blows across my skin as I continue my reverie. This apartment is where I wrote my first book, *Journey to One*. All those years of experiences spilled over into words, and there was integration, completion.

Writing the book is one thing. Making it available for others to read is something altogether different, I soon realized. The lessons I learned, or perhaps I should say, the gifts gained, through the process of getting *Journey to One* published feel significant enough to share with you in more detail, for it seems to have less to do with writing and publishing, and more to do with perception, how we look at things, and how we potentially can hold ourselves back.

Upon completing the writing of the manuscript, I, like many other emerging writers, no doubt, was confident a publishing company would be eager to help me get the story out to the world. I did my homework, researching literary agents and publishers that seemed in alignment with the subject matter I was presenting. But as one rejection letter came after another, I realized it was going to be a bit of a challenge. The first couple letters I received stung a little, despite their attempts at a gentle let down. However, I kept my chin up, knowing there have been a whole slew of now well-known writers who bared the brunt of multiple rejections before succeeding in getting their work published – J. K. Rowling, Alice Walker, James Patterson.... Each letter affected me less and less until I would simply glance at it, sigh, and add it to the growing pile. I yearned to have *Journey to One* published, and soon, but things did not seem to be progressing as I hoped.

I was driving into town one morning on my way to work at the local YMCA, thinking about my book and feeling a little frustrated. Winding my way through the backstreets so as to avoid traffic, I started daydreaming about what it would be like to be a published author. I began to question myself. How would my life look differently? I envisioned not having to work so much at the Y, and instead spending more time writing, and perhaps also traveling and teaching. I dreamed of being able to move from my one bedroom apartment and having a place out in the country.

Then I further explored what it would *feel* like to be a published author, to be living my dream. I began to feel a strength and confidence well up within me. I felt a lightness and joy fill my whole body. Gripping the steering wheel, I sat up a little straighter in my seat, and I felt a smile spread across my face. And *that* is when the realization struck: Well, I can feel that NOW, BE that NOW! Though I continued to drive to work and carry out the usual and necessary daily activities, from that moment on, things were different. I walked a little taller and had a spring in my step. I let the strength, confidence and joy become part of me.

I also released the burden of want. It is not the desire itself that felt to be weighing on me, for I feel there must be desire in order for any goal to be accomplished. Rather, it was the belief that I would be happy, successful, and confident only once I got published.

It reminds me of some words of wisdom from Mahatma Gandhi. He said how only the person who is utterly dedicated and utterly detached is free to enjoy life. I felt utterly dedicated, but I was very much attached. I was making my happiness dependent on an outcome, rather than simply *being* happy.

Once I realized what I was doing, I decided, okay, I will just enjoy life now. I will make my future reality my reality NOW. I strengthened my intention to get published, knowing that no matter the results, everything was going to be alright. I set a deadline for myself to publish the book by the end of 2009.

I put my heart and soul into 7 more publisher proposal packages. I got bolder in my attempt to catch someone's eye. I made passionate pleas. "I understand how you might think you would be taking a risk on me, but it is often risks that move us forward." I would remind them how someone believed we could go to the moon when that once may have sounded preposterous. But, for whatever reason, the publishers didn't see taking on my manuscript as equivalent to the bold leap of humanity walking on the moon. I had hopes. But after 7 more attempts, I received 7 more rejection letters.

At this point I could have given up. I could have stood there dumbfounded, simply staring at the multiple roadblocks. I could have lost focus and listened to the fear and doubt that crept into my mind: *Maybe I'm not a good enough writer... What if people really aren't interested in reading the story? I thought getting this book out to the world was part of my purpose in life... If I'm not a writer, what the heck am I? Oh, no, what if... How will I...* I had done enough personal work by then to know this was just the empty chattering of my mind. It had no substance, and it did not reflect how I truly felt. With that acknowledgment, my mind grew more quiet, and I heard a deeper part of me whisper words of comfort and support. *Everything is going to be fine. Just trust the process.*

I maintained my focus and persisted. From past experiences I've realized the magic often comes when we choose to *hold* focus and energy toward a particular goal. It is similar to when you take a magnifying glass to a piece of paper on a hot, sunny day. Catching a ray of sun through the magnifying glass, you can see a bright spot on the piece of paper. If you move the glass all over the paper, staying for only a brief moment here and there, nothing happens. However, when you hold the magnifying glass steady, keeping the brilliant light focused, you soon see a brown patch form. Continuing to hold steady, it turns darker until the intensity of the light burns a hole through the paper. That is the power of focused intention.

I pondered my situation more deeply. I asked, *Why do I want my book to go to a large publisher? What is my reason? Is it so that it will get into more people's hands, to help others, or is it my ego wanting recognition?* I let the questions sink down into my heart.

Then I thought about how I had been trying and trying to get my book published, to no avail. Then, I saw it. Ah ha! The wise words of Yoda this time echoed in my ears. (From Gandhi to Star Wars, helpful teachings can come from all manner of sources!) "Do or do not, there is no try."

I've found when we fluctuate in our intention, where there is doubt, it acts the same as moving the magnifying glass around; the light and energy are scattered, unable to focus. I realized it was time to let go of doubt, let go of any fear, let go of *trying*, and just get it done!

After all the ponderings, rather than continue to seek out agents and traditional publishing companies, I decided to self-publish. After a little over a year of things feeling in a state of stagnation, this choice helped the book project get moving again. I felt fluid, flowing around the obstacles and continuing forward with my goals. With self-publishing, the story would finally be available for others to read.

Over the years, I have discovered it is during these times when you persevere through challenges that you find your limit is not where you originally believed it to be, and with each new challenge, finding nothing can stop you but you yourself. If we are dedicated to something, it's important to be open to possibilities and creative in achieving a solution. There are always alternate paths toward a destination.

So as I dip my toes in and out of the water, there is the sense that a chapter of my life is coming to completion. *Journey to One* is now in production. As I prepare to begin this next phase, I'm feeling it is time to move.

To be more specific, I would like a home closer to the ground, rather than living on the second floor. I want to be able to walk out my door and feel my bare feet touch the earth. I want more space, particularly a big yard where I can dig my hands in the dirt, plant some flowers, a few veggies, and have friends over for barbeques.

The apartment has served me well. I deeply appreciate this space that has allowed for such creativity and learning. However, I'm sensing increased growth accompanying this next phase. Like a chick growing too big for her egg, it feels time to have a place where I can live beyond the walls.

I begin to search Craigslist for a place to rent. Over the next several weeks, I look at half a dozen places. Each of them has its good points but is not quite what I want.

Then I see a notice for a property just down the street about a half mile from my apartment. It is advertised as having been recently remodeled, large bedrooms and a big backyard. In addition, just like my current place, it is walking distance to Diego Park, which intrigues me. I love the local park, and it would be ideal to stay so close to it. I decide to check it out. I drive down the hill a ways, into the valley, assess the neighborhood and pull up to the place. It's a cream-colored duplex with a single-car garage. The unit is towards the back, away from the road. It looks cute from the outside. There's a young maple tree out front, and also a couple flowering plants, bordered with river stones.

I peek through the front windows and see a large living room and 2 bedrooms with fresh paint and new carpet. I walk through the open gate at the rear of the property to continue my self-guided tour. I find an immense backyard. Maybe it just seems so large because I currently have zero yard space, but I can instantly see it being perfect for BBQs, gardening and all-around lounging.

I walk over to the back patio and look through the sliding glass door to see a dining area and large kitchen with oak cabinets. The only thing I can't see through the windows is the bathroom, but so far everything about it feels open and light. I breathe in and feel a sense of serenity here.

I see copies of the rental application sitting on the kitchen counter, and I call the number from the Craigslist ad from my cell so I can get a walk-through and fill out the form. We schedule a time to meet.

Once inside, I'm able to get a closer look. The living room and bedrooms are painted a soft beige and have light brown carpet. It's not incredibly imaginative, but it feels warm and welcoming and is a nice canvas on which to accent a variety of colors. The bedrooms have large, mirrored closet doors. As I stand looking at myself, I think how infrequently it has been that I've seen my whole self in reflection. The bathroom is a crisp, clean white, is spacious, and has charming, new fixtures. There's room for a washer and dryer off the dining area, and the garage has been freshly painted, so there is not even one speck of dirt or grease in it. Inside and out, the place feels perfect.

I fill out the rental application and chat with the owner. He tells me about his wife and himself and shares how he recently retired from being

CEO of the credit union to which I happen to belong. "That's nice," I say, "I've been a member of the credit union for several years." I open my checkbook and begin to write a check for the credit check fee, and I look down to see I'm writing with one of the credit union pens. Both of us notice at the same time, and we look at each other and chuckle. I've learned to not take for granted such serendipitous moments.

The following day, I get a call from the owner. "Well, everything checks out," he says, "so I want to offer you the place." I accept and give my current property manager notice.

I've observed how the fall season, for the last several years, has been a time of big transition for me. Relationship changes have taken place in the fall. A powerful, life-changing journey to Teotihuacán, Mexico took place in the fall. My beloved grandmother passed in the fall. My move into the apartment was in the fall. It's been almost 4 years to the day. Now, as October winds down, I'm preparing to move again.

During the time of living in my apartment, it feels like I found myself. I know who I am. I know my passions. I feel whole, complete. Now I will venture onward, in a new environment. I'm curious to know what life events, what growth opportunities, await me there.

On a cool Saturday morning in November, five minutes before the alarm is to ring, my eyes pop open. *Today is moving day.*

Chapter 2

From A to Y

When I first walked into the local YMCA for an interview in January of 2001, I was 24 years old and excited at the prospect of a Monday through Friday, 8 to 5 job. I had been working split shifts, starting at 6am and finishing out the workday at 10pm, with graduate school classes and a 3-hour commute in between. I was enrolled in a doctorate program for Clinical Psychology until I decided it was time for a detour. I was working in a residential treatment facility for adults with developmental disabilities. It was educational and enjoyable in many aspects, and it served well as an internship for school. But now, I hoped to find a full-time job to pay the bills, including the student loans that were now due, and with "regular" hours so I could catch up on some sleep.

I had no previous experience with the Y. There was no Y where I grew up as a child, so I never took swimming lessons there or went to summer camp. I later learned YMCAs all over the U.S. provide a number of great services for their communities in the areas of health and wellness, youth programs and social services. But at the time, I didn't know it was a place where you could work out. I didn't know it offered childcare programs. I didn't know it was a place where you could learn about nutrition or take a CPR class or volunteer. I had no clue that the Y was one of the largest and most well-known charitable organizations in the country.

I knew nothing about the Y other than the Winowa County YMCA had an Administrative Assistant position available with my name on it. I figured I would do that for a while until it became clear what I wanted to do as a career.

I dressed in black slacks, a black and white, sleeveless blouse with lace along the neckline, black blazer, and black flats. My hair was cropped short, in a boyish style, and I wore very little make-up. I felt professional and comfortable.

My interviews with Ellen Adler, the Director of Administrative Services, and later John Smith, the CEO, went well, and I was offered the job. My new role included assisting the CEO and providing general administrative support.

Ellen, who was my immediate supervisor, was a tall, strong-boned woman in her 50s with curly, brown, shoulder-length hair. She was meticulously detailed and organized, and these qualities served her well in her role.

In a Y facility that housed two pools, a fitness center, basketball court, group exercise studio, child watch room and several offices, the Admin Office was centrally located. If the Y were a machine, the Admin Office would be its inner workings. With her oversight, Ellen ensured the gears continued to operate smoothly, which then extended to most other aspects of the Y's functioning. Located towards the back of the Admin area was Ellen's office. She was the wizard behind the curtain.

With her many years of service and experience, she seemed to have all the answers. She held a wealth of knowledge and knew the history behind most everything Y-related. Support staff and directors alike would come to her when they needed to find out where a file was located or how to proceed with a task, or simply when looking for advice. She was the motherly figure of the Y. I found her to be kind, fair and always professional.

I quickly became friends with my officemate, Judy, who was responsible for the technology of the Y. She was in her 40s with a sturdy build and short, dark, curly hair graying around the temples. If Ellen were the mother, Judy was the cool, eccentric aunt. Standing less than 5 feet tall, she was a petite woman, but she was surely a big, colorful presence. She had a prolific collection of Beanie Babies lining the shelves of her desk, humorous pictures posted on her file cabinet, including the one of a frazzled-looking cat in need of its cup of coffee in the morning, and chocolate usually tucked away in her drawer (pieces generously handed out whenever one was in need of a pick-me-up). She was loved by all, especially kids and younger staff.

I was intrigued by Judy's stories of when she was younger, her saucy tales of living in San Francisco and the unique, loveable characters she encountered. She was the only person I knew who got married in full regalia at a Renaissance Faire. She wore her emotions on her sleeve and never held back in saying what she thought. She was someone others felt comfortable talking to about their personal lives. Having also been with the Y for well over a decade, she knew much about the workings of the organization, as well as personal details on just about everyone.

Ellen, Judy and others at the Y quickly became like family to me. Only 6 months prior to being hired, I had been cut off from several members of my biological family due to differing beliefs and my sexuality. At the Y, I felt immediately welcomed and accepted by my coworkers for who I was.

It was at the Y where I first dressed up for Halloween (not having celebrated it prior to this). Staff often came up with a theme, and that year it was, appropriately, the Village People. Ellen was the Construction Worker. Judy was the Cop. We had an Army recruit, and a couple Chiefs. Most of us dressing up were women. I was the Biker gal. My costume was complete with black leather jacket, boots, riding gloves and black leather motorcycle chaps. We took photos and shared a lot of laughs.

When my partner at the time and I decided to have a commitment ceremony, a few staff members threw a shower at the Y for the brides-to-be. Later, several Y friends came to our ceremony. Being the recipient of such kindness and acceptance, I began to understand that the Y wasn't actually about group exercise classes or youth sports, it was about *people.*

Perhaps certain people and specific work circumstances come into our lives for a reason. I like to believe they do. Or maybe, in looking back, I am simply feeling appreciative of the experience. In either case, little did I know then that I would be embarking on a lengthy career with the YMCA.

Over the years, I continued to grow personally and professionally, due in part to my love of learning, but also due to several positive role models at the Y. My understanding about the Y grew, and I enjoyed having a part in a non-profit, human-service organization. Human service was turning into a recurring theme in my work.

After a couple years, my role shifted into Administrative Coordinator and I took on some additional responsibilities, including supervision of a dozen or so front-line staff. About a year after that, the newness and excitement of the new position was starting to fade. Perhaps it's indicative of us Generation X-ers, but I felt I had many skills and qualities that I could not utilize in my current role, and I dabbled with the idea of finding a different job. I submitted my resume to a few places and had a couple job interviews, but nothing panned out.

Then, quite unexpectedly, a management position opened up at the Y. The Director of Membership & Communications just packed up her personal belongings one day and walked out. There were whispers around the office about what happened, but who really knew for sure? It seemed odd, and a little sad, but interesting timing, nonetheless.

It was exactly the type of position that I felt ready to move into, and I thought I would be able to contribute a lot to it. It looked like it would be a good fit with my skill level, educational background, personality and experience. It would have its challenges, though. If I were to get the promotion, I would have very little training in the responsibilities of the position because of the abrupt departure of the director. There would be a lot of things to figure out on my own initially. It would also be challenging because the Y was preparing for a large expansion and remodel project. It would be a high priority to retain and increase membership during and after the construction. I surmised that it would take some innovative and strategic thinking. I enjoy a challenge and felt up to the task.

I had a strong working relationship with several individuals on the management team, and when I expressed my interest in the position, I received a great deal of encouragement and support from almost everyone. John Smith, the CEO, was the only one who did not seem supportive. He expressed that he didn't want to lose me as his "secretary." I felt his comment lacked understanding of my skills and what more I could offer the Y. Though he was initially in opposition, after some time of deliberation, I was hired as the Interim Director of Membership in June of 2004. There was some reorganization around the position, and it shifted from directly reporting to John to instead reporting to Amy Long, the Director of Operations. I was grateful for the reorganization. I had enough experience assisting John and getting an up-close view of his character and mode of operating to know that I'd rather have Amy as my direct supervisor.

John Smith was in his mid 40s, physically fit, and had thinning brown hair. He dressed in a stylish, professional manner, but was not necessarily known for his professional behavior.

When I worked as his assistant, there were times when I wondered what it was he actually *did*, for I would see that his time at the computer was frequently spent checking the scores on the latest ball game or surfing the internet. He also was on the phone a lot, frequently talking with one of his ex-wives and dealing with personal issues. I didn't spend too much time thinking about John, though. My interactions with him were minimal, and I just focused on my responsibilities at hand. He did his thing, and I did mine, and it was fine, except when it wasn't.

From early on, John stood out to me as different from the rest of the people with whom I worked. For one, he seemed to lack the emotional maturity that the other directors exemplified. One morning I was in John's office for our weekly meeting. I was there to take notes about items he wanted me to handle. He was having one of his irritable days and just finishing up a phone call. Maybe he and his ex-wife were arguing again,

I'm not sure, but it was apparent he was upset. John angrily slammed the phone down, then with a quick swipe of his hand scattered papers across the desk and onto the floor, and said a few choice words. After he settled down, we went over the weekly items.

When I returned to the Admin Office, Ellen and Judy were there. I couldn't help but say it out loud, "John is an emotional child." Ellen did one of her "mmm"s.

"What?" I asked.

"Careful," she said, as she strolled to her office. It was then I understood that though we all knew it, we were not to talk about it. It was the wisdom of the long-timers.

Shortly after I stepped into my new role as director, there was another memorable experience with Mr. Smith. My office was now adjacent to the Member Center where people stopped in to get information about the Y, join as a member, sign up for classes and the like. The Member Center was frequently the first point of contact individuals had with the Y. An important aspect of my job was to ensure they had a pleasant first experience. There were no blinds on my office window, so I had a clear view of the goings on in the Member Center. I was standing in this area one afternoon talking with a couple members of my staff when John came storming in with clenched jaw and furrowed brow. "Kristi, I need to speak to you!" he ordered, pointing to my office. I followed him into my office and closed the door. It wasn't unusual for him to start conversations in such a way. It was familiar, but I would still get a queasy feeling in the pit of my stomach and a flushed face.

Once inside my office, he demanded to know how a specific error occurred on a postcard mailer. I had designed a postcard at his request to send to the members, got his approval and emailed it to the offsite printer. I reviewed the proof from the printer and let them know they could proceed. Last minute, John instructed me to add more information. Last minute demands were familiar as well. I called the printing company and asked them to add the info. Being relatively new to my position, and new to marketing responsibilities in general, I didn't request a second

FROM A TO Y

proof before it went to print and instead relied on the printer to ensure it was correct. The additional wording caused the phone number to not be visible on the printed card.

I sat down at my desk and calmly explained to him what happened. John was furious, "Do you know how this makes me look?!" he yelled and flung the postcard towards me. It whizzed by my ear and landed on the counter behind me. I wondered momentarily if he intended to hit me with it. It was another one of John's tantrums. I looked at the card, looked at him, then glanced out my office window, hoping no one was seeing it. Thankfully, no customers or members were in the office at the time, but there were a few staff members witness to his behavior. He continued to rant and yell for some time.

Most days, however, passed without incident. In my new role, I enjoyed getting better acquainted with the staff in the Membership Department. I had known them for 3 years, since I first started, but now I was able to get to know them better working directly with them. The staff person I worked with most closely now was Maureen, the Member Services Coordinator. She was the direct supervisor of the front-line membership staff. Though I was Maureen's supervisor, I felt we both played a key role in leading the department, and together we maintained a courteous, positive and efficient team.

Maureen was about 15 years older than I and was easily recognized by her long, straight, brown hair that hung down to her waist. She was extremely hard working and always positive, despite a list of challenging life situations. She held a lot of knowledge and experience as well, as she had been with the Y well over 20 years. I liked Maureen. She was patient, caring, smarter than she gave herself credit for, funny, creative, and when she wasn't at work, she was probably riding her Harley. We worked well together.

I felt a close connection with several staff members. At the Y, the lines often blurred. Coworkers turned into friends, friends became like family. It is these coworkers and friends that often kept me motivated to come to work, particularly on the challenging days. When I walked into work at the

Y, there was always someone with a smiling face to help the day go by a little easier. Sometimes there was even a little surprise treat or good-hearted practical joke left on my desk, which brought a smile.

In the months and years after taking on the director role, I sought out a number of training courses. After first attending a couple classes and enjoying the experience, I decided to work towards becoming a certified YMCA Senior Director. With the Bachelor's degree I already held, there were about 8-10 training courses to complete in order to meet the requirements. The training was designed to provide a strong foundation in non-profit leadership. Senior Director was the highest director level one could achieve in the Y structure, and it opened up opportunities for increased responsibility in the organization.

I found the trainings, offered by YMCA of the USA (Y-USA), the headquarters based in Chicago, to be extremely valuable and of the highest quality. The instructors and presenters were primarily made up of top leaders from Ys around the country, Y-USA staff and leadership development consultants. I gained knowledge and experience in supervision, fiscal management, diversity and inclusion, member engagement, effectively leading others and more. The courses were educational, people-centered and often delightfully encouraged creativity and innovation. The trainings also offered a broader perspective of the Y. I met staff from all over the country and learned the principles, practices and personalities that made up the organization. I knew these skills would be very useful for my work at the Y, as well as any future work I might do. In any case, the Y seemed like an organization that supported growth on all levels.

There were a couple simple points that really stuck with me from some of these courses. The first point was a saying by the instructor of a course on member engagement, "If you don't feed your staff, they'll eat the members." The second was from a training on supervision and leadership: how important, and how much more effective, it is to lead by example. I took these teachings to heart and made a deliberate effort to demonstrate to the staff that they were appreciated, and to set a positive example.

One day rolled into the next. Month followed month, and year followed year. My thoughts about the Y being just a stop-over until I figured out what I wanted to do as a career faded away. This *was* my career. I successfully managed a $2 million/year department and juggled the duties of being a Y director. I enjoyed working with staff and volunteers on multiples levels – from individuals on the front lines to members of the Board of Directors. I appreciated the level of responsibility and having the opportunity to play a key role in ensuring the Y continued to operate effectively. I also felt great satisfaction in having a part in helping to increase the health and well-being of members of our local community. Overall, I enjoyed the work.

Some days, though, were more challenging than others. John continued to stand out as different from the other directors in the leadership team. Everyone else seemed to pull their own weight. John was known to use his title and pull rank so that the rules did not apply to him. In simple and complex ways, this became steeped into the culture of the Y. He lacked professionalism. I'd observe him staring at the breasts of one of my young, female staff members. It wasn't even subtle. He'd just chat and stare, smile charmingly, and chat and stare some more.

"It's like I'm not respected around here," John once said.

It was true. John wasn't respected. He was tolerated and obeyed, but not respected. What he did not seem to realize is respect is not afforded simply because of title or position. Respect is earned.

With my close relationships with several staff, both support level and management level, I heard many stories about John over the years, his bullying tactics, temper, inappropriate comments, distasteful jokes and more.

As appropriate, I would share the information with my supervisor, Amy, the Director of Operations. She was all too familiar with such accounts. During her many years working for the Y, she no doubt heard more complaints than I regarding John.

Amy had been with the Y over 15 years. She was in her late 30s, petite, athletic and warm-hearted. She was likable, a hard worker and on all accounts was dedicated to the Y. She was also a person with whom staff felt comfortable talking honestly. As I shared the latest with Amy, she would kindly listen and commiserate, but there was always a sense of "that's just how things are." He's the CEO, after all, what were we to do? I think Amy was simply trying to keep the peace and carry out her responsibilities. I believe she did not wish to rock the boat and instead work to just keep it afloat.

I found myself adopting the same attitude. There seemed to be an unspoken consensus that as long as there were no blatant, illegal activities, we were to simply shrug our shoulders, tolerate John's behavior, and carry on.

It was important to stay on John's good side, because if one challenged his view or methods, he or she would likely become a target. We were being molded into a group of Yes Men and Women. Those who were strong enough and vocal enough to challenge his view, or simply offer a different perspective, were often phased out of their responsibilities or no longer with the Y altogether. Those of us who remained learned how to stay on good terms and keep our jobs. That meant agreeing with John or keeping our mouths shut. In large part, I chose to be a quiet observer.

In time, I found myself beginning to take work stress home with me. While I would be cooking dinner or doing laundry, or trying to write, thoughts of the Y would fill my mind. It was not the kind of thoughts like, "I need to make sure I finish my reports tomorrow," or, "Oh, I have to remember to pick up those items for the member event on Thursday." It was thoughts about Mr. Smith. It gnawed at me how he showed one face to the Board of Directors while revealing a very different face to the staff members. I would think about how his behavior affected morale and was impacting the environment of the Y.

By the end of 2007, I felt the need to have some kind of change in my work. It was a time in my life when things were already shifting a great deal. Just a year prior I had taken a transformative journey to Teotihuacán. I was in the thick of writing *Journey to One*, and I was opening to greater possibilities as a whole.

That year I finished the last course needed for the YMCA Senior Director certification. The last step was to get a recommendation letter from my supervisor to make it official.

As 2008 unfolded, in blew the winds of change.

Chapter 3

Year of Alignment

*W*ith the arrival of moving day, I crawl out of my sleeping bag, which I placed on my bare mattress the night before, ensuring a quick and easy way to pack up the bedding this morning and break down the bed. I enjoy being efficient. I walk to the bathroom, passing boxes upon boxes of my stuff. I feel like I live fairly simply, yet seeing all the boxes reminds me of how much I truly have. I have friends coming at 1 o'clock to help me move, and I've yet to finish packing the kitchen and bathroom.

Before diving into my tasks, I feel the need to just take a moment and be grateful. I am thankful to have found the duplex down the street. I was clear about what features I wanted in a new place. I set the intention, and now it's coming to fruition. It reminds me how powerful it is to set intentions. As I begin to wrap up plates and bowls with newspaper, my mind drifts and I revisit the road of reminiscing.

It was at the beginning of 2008 when I started setting an intention for the coming year. Many of us do something similar at the beginning of a calendar year or around our birthdays. We set goals or New Year's resolutions.

The words "goal" and "intention" are often used interchangeably to represent something we want to do or achieve. In some ways, I feel the word intention has more power behind it. I've found when we have a goal, any goal, such as "lose weight" or "spend more quality time with my kids," it can be easy to find ourselves simply sitting back and waiting for it to happen. It doesn't always become fully internalized. When we have an intention, on the other hand, the objective or purpose is held in mind, and there is drive to move towards it. When I *intend* to do something, I know it is up to me to make it happen. The desire is strong, and there's dedication. In language, the difference between a goal and an intention may be illustrated as, "I would like to lose weight" versus, "I *will* lose weight."

Deepak Chopra, M.D. states that an intention is a directed impulse of consciousness that contains the seed form of that which you aim to create. I wanted to identify an intention for 2008, and focus that intention down to one potent word. I called this my Seed of Intention exercise. With the year before me, I wanted my work to be more in alignment with my passions and purpose. My "purpose" was still unfolding, parts of it unclear, but I felt there was more to it than working as the Membership Director at the Winowa County YMCA. Though there were many positive aspects about my position at the Y, I felt there were parts of me that were not able to fully grow or express in that role. The word for 2008 came to me easily: alignment.

The word is the seed. When we plant a literal seed, such as a vegetable or flower seed, we know the environment is crucial for the seed's outcome. So we make sure the dirt has the needed nutrients and is prepared loosely, so the sprouts can easily push through the soil. We also ensure the seed receives the necessary amounts of water and light. As time passes, we regularly maintain the environment. The rest takes care of itself. For the most part, with a nurturing environment, the seed will follow its natural course, sprout and grow.

I wanted to make sure the environment surrounding my Seed of Intention was one that allowed for growth. I did that by keeping an open mind and being open to change. It also meant being okay with not knowing *exactly* how this alignment was going to take place, but keeping the purpose in mind.

I took out a piece of paper, drew two columns and identified one column "Things I enjoy about my current job at the Y." The second column was for "Things I would like to be doing (or doing more of)." I wrote down items in the first column. Then, in the second column, I listed items like yoga, writing and spending time in nature. I felt a lot more excitement as I wrote down this second list. I used this excitement as an indicator; this was the direction to be heading.

It started very simply. In addition to my management responsibilities, I volunteered to lead a hiking group through the Y, starting in January. It was a free program to Y members, as well as outside participants. Once a month we hit the trail and hiked through one of the many beautiful, local parks. The hiking program was successful with several participants enjoying the treks. Individuals were able to get some fresh air, exercise and have a chance to socialize and meet new people. Leading the group allowed me to not only spend more time in nature, but to share this enriching experience with others, which felt very satisfying.

I also enrolled in a yoga teacher training with Shiva Rea. I had been doing yoga for about a year and a half. I fell in love with it and wanted to be able to teach others. I was first drawn to Shiva and her style of yoga through her instructional DVDs. I later learned she is a world-renowned yoga instructor. I eagerly anticipated the first of two 10-day intensive trainings in the spring.

Additionally, shortly after my seed was planted, a new endeavor through YMCA of the USA, known as "Activate America," came on the scene. In early 2008, my supervisor, Amy, and I met for our usual weekly meeting, and she introduced Activate America. It was something our Y recently signed on to, and she was the Project Manager, she explained. There were a number of other roles that she hoped some of the directors would want to assume. Like most other initiatives at the Y, it would require a dedicated team effort to be successful.

I was interested in being a part of Activate America, even though I had a very limited understanding of what it involved. I always enjoyed the opportunity to gain more knowledge, experience and responsibility. There were 6 different areas of focus in Activate America, and a "Point Person" was needed to lead each of these components. Amy gave me some information, said I could look it over and let her know the following week what area I was most interested in exploring.

Out of the 6 areas of focus, I chose the one involving strengthening relationships with members. It seemed to be the best fit with my personal interests and also made the most sense in my role as Membership Director. The qualifications of the Point Person resonated with me, as well, which included "a passion for relationship building as demonstrated through natural empathy and listening, and have the respect of and influence with other staff members, especially the management team." I certainly did have a passion for building relationships, and I felt I was respected by the staff and management. I let Amy know my choice. She remarked that she thought the Relationship Point Person was the best fit for me, too, and was hoping I'd choose that one. We both smiled, pleased to be moving forward together in this new Y venture.

Within just a couple months of setting my intention, things were beginning to move into place. I was pleased how quickly it was happening. There were aspects of my Seed of Intention where I put deliberate effort – such as starting the hiking group and signing up for the yoga teacher training – and there was unexpected alignment occurring, as well, with the introduction of Activate America.

As the days progressed, I continued to nurture the environment surrounding my little seed. Then I watched and waited to see what might grow.

In March, I headed south to Venice Beach for my first 10-day yoga teacher training with Shiva Rea. Shiva grew up in southern California surfing the waves and looks the part. She is strong, beautiful, blue-eyed, blond, laid-back and always sporting a healthy tan. She is one of the most well known and respected teachers in the global yoga community. After enjoying her DVDs, I knew I wanted to learn from her. She offered a high-quality training, and I appreciated how she also incorporates dance, creative movement and other activities into her yoga trainings and classes. There were students in the program from around the world, women and men from Europe, South America, Australia, and all across the U.S. We all came to learn from one of the best. As our training began, I recognized immediately how Shiva is an excellent teacher who, through yoga, helps guide others to their own potential, and she does it with such power, humility, playfulness and grace.

By the eighth day of the yoga training, all of us students were buzzing with energy, a little sore and feeling blissed out after a week of yoga, positivity, and warm, sunny weather. That morning, we were in the thick of a new sequence, which Shiva named Agni Namaskar. Agni means fire. Namaskar refers to the sequence, and is a way to acknowledge or show respect. Just like it sounds, it's a very active, strong, firey sequence. In addition to being challenging, strength-building and invigorating, it is designed to help ignite one's life passions and creativity, and align with the energy needed to turn our dreams into reality. Yoga teachers like Shiva are known to work with multiple aspects of a person – physical, mental, emotional, spiritual.

There were 50 to 60 of us moving together, sharing the same breath rhythm, glistening with sweat, and yet each of us was also riding the waves of her or his personal experience. I focused on my own practice and felt the intensity of the movements fuel my desire to create what it is I dream. It had happened to me several times already during this training, but here again, as Shiva was motivating us and guiding us through the sequence, she seemed to be speaking directly to me. "If I wanted to create a change in my work, I'd be doing Agni Namaskar..." her voice weaving around the room. "If I had written a book and wanted it published, I'd be doing Agni Namaskar." *How does she know?* as I exhaled my way through another chaturanga, or yoga pushup.

When I returned from that trip, I felt a deepening of my personal yoga practice and had a realization that yoga was going to take on more of a role in the upcoming stages of my life. As soon as possible, I wanted to share the tools and benefits of this practice with others.

In mid spring I started teaching a free yoga class at Diego Park on Sunday mornings. I couldn't think of a better way to start offering yoga than to have it free and outdoors. I scouted out a flat, grassy spot under a large oak tree that seemed like a perfect location. Every week loyal students showed up. It was a small but committed group. It was a class for individuals to increase their wellness and find greater peace of mind. We worked with breath and moved through poses and sequences amidst the squirrels that scurried from tree to tree, the occasional spider that would crawl across the mat, and the gentle drumming of the woodpeckers. It was sweet beginnings.

All through the summer I walked the ¾ mile distance from my apartment to the park every Sunday with yoga mat in hand. The walk took me past an elementary school, a small park, a church, and through the local neighborhood before arriving at the larger park and our beloved yoga spot. For me, the yoga class began when I stepped out my front door and started walking. I enjoyed the rhythmic sound my steps made on the pavement. I took notice of the cool, moist air against my skin on the mornings the coastal fog rolled into the valley. It was a time of tuning in, as well as appreciation and contemplation about the simple things of life. As I strolled past the church, watching the men and women in their suits and dresses heading up the walk towards the entrance, I wondered, *When was it we started believing the divine was to be found indoors?* I found yoga in the park to be a most enjoyable and deeply fulfilling experience.

With the hikes and yoga classes taking root, I could feel the alignment occurring more and more. A few hours of my time were being devoted to activities that I was passionate about, and it felt purposeful. Things were continuing to grow regarding my Activate America work at the Y, as well.

In time, what Activate America was became clearer. I learned it was a strategy developed by Y-USA in response to the growing health crisis in the U.S. This crisis is evidenced by the escalating rates of obesity and chronic diseases, such as type 2 diabetes and cancer. Activate America was a plan and set of resources designed to support YMCA's across the country in increasing the health and well-being of adults and families in their communities. Activate America was quite comprehensive. It offered strategies to assist Y's in transforming how they operate in order to better position them to be leaders in chronic disease prevention.

The first step for our local Y was to familiarize all the Y staff with Activate America using DVD presentations and discussions. The initial area of focus was around gaining a better understanding of individuals who seek to improve their health and looking at the concept of well-being. As the Activate America Project Manager at our Y, Amy took on this task, which continued over the course of several weeks. She first shared the information with the management team and Board of Directors and then brought the information to the staff in all the departments. This helped lay the groundwork and provided everyone a better understanding of the nation's health crisis and what the Y was doing in an effort to make a positive impact.

I began to get a glimpse of the scale of the work. It was big-picture stuff, and I found it exciting! We were only at the beginning of a long-range plan. Each of the 6 components was going to take weeks, months, or even years of work. A phrase put forth by Y-USA regarding Activate America summed it up well, and was rather comforting, "It's a marathon, not a sprint." This level of organizational change takes a while. The important thing was to just take one step at a time and keep moving forward.

After Amy completed the first step, we began to focus on the relationship-building work. Amy and I attended a "Listen First Institute" in Phoenix, Arizona. At the institute we learned the key communication skills of Listen First. These skills were designed to provide an environment which was most effective for supporting others in achieving greater health and well-being. Then we learned how to facilitate Listen First workshops for the employees back at our local Y, so it could ripple out and these staff could apply the skills with the members and others.

This institute struck a chord with me. The specific skills were not necessarily new; I had learned similar communication techniques from my earlier psychological counseling coursework in college. But it was a fresh approach and had new ways to apply the skills. It was also a powerful reminder how relationships are the essence of our human service work, and how these relationships are built on genuine care for others and a desire to support others' well-being and personal growth. *This is what I want to be doing*, I thought to myself. I had been working for the Y 7 ½ years by this time, and was involved in a variety of aspects of Y operations, but it was here in communication and strengthening relationships that I felt I truly found my niche. (In the Listen First chapter later in this book, you will find an adapted version of these helpful communication tools that you can use to enjoy more satisfying relationships with the people in your life.)

Upon returning from the institute, I mapped out a plan for our Y to roll out the workshops to all the staff. It was suggested by Y-USA to start at the top, first facilitating the workshop for the senior leaders, so that is where we began.

At the end of August 2008, Amy and I co-facilitated the first Listen First workshop with the senior leaders, including the CEO, CFO, and a dozen or so other directors. I felt more comfortable facilitating that workshop than any previous workshop or training I had conducted. I was very familiar with the material, but it was more than that. It just felt natural.

When we asked the workshop participants to break off into pairs to practice a few communication techniques, everyone was teaming up, and it was looking like John, the CEO, was going to be the odd man out. I took the initiative to be John's partner in the exercises. I hoped he, more than anyone else, perhaps, would gain the tools from this workshop and utilize them in his daily interactions, for he seemed to have considerable room for growth in this area. I wanted to put my all into the workshop for the best possible chance that each participant would find it of value and utilize the tools.

After the workshop was over, one of the directors, Eric, chatted with me a while, and expressed his appreciation for the course and how it was facilitated. I found Eric to naturally use effective communication skills in his interactions with others, and I valued his input. "Even when someone obviously didn't get it, and they said something totally out of left field, you were able to pull the gem from what they said, and bring it back around, allowing that person to feel good while still getting the points across. You were always positive," he said, "and that takes some skill." I thanked him. My intention was to meet everyone where they were, help them feel comfortable with the material, and offer some alternative and effective ways to communicate. I'm glad it played out as intended. I thoroughly enjoyed the whole experience, and it helped reassure me of my budding role as a teacher.

I was so excited about Activate America, and Listen First in particular, that I wanted to play a part in carrying out the skills and concepts on an even larger scale. I wanted to see if I could do some relationship-building work for the national Y, such as lead a Listen First Institute, like the one I attended in Phoenix.

That was my intention, but I didn't know where to begin. So I started at the top. I gathered my thoughts and picked up the phone one day and dialed the number for Paul Stevens, President and CEO of YMCA of the USA.

It actually wasn't the first time I contacted Mr. Stevens. The first was about 10 months prior. I had heard Paul speak in person at a conference on diversity and inclusion, as well as at a YMCA Key Leaders' conference, where I introduced myself to him. I admired him as a person and as a leader. I later wrote him with some thoughts and a proposal of sorts to be an "Environmental Consultant." I thought I might be able to provide support towards national trainings and conferences being more eco-friendly. He wrote back, expressing appreciation for my letter, and let me know about his shared passion for the environment, as evidenced by his creating an environmental program for youth when he was CEO of the Y in Seattle. However, that was not one of the primary initiatives of the Y at the current time. His response was kind and professional.

Here I was at it again, this time regarding something that *was* a primary initiative of the Y. I got Paul's voicemail, and I left a rather lengthy message about how, after these 7 years at the Y, I finally found my niche and how I felt Activate America and all its components was the most important work the Y was currently doing. Feeling comfortable jabbering away, I continued, "I feel I want to focus more of my time and energy in Listen First and Activate America, for it is here that we are genuinely connecting with people. It is about building relationships and supporting growth. These relationships, these authentic human connections, are what life is about. I would like to have a role in carrying out Activate America or Listen First on a larger scale, working for the national Y. I'm calling you to ask how that might happen."

Within 24 hours, I got a return call from Paul, and he put me in contact with Aaron Rothenberg, Vice President for Health Strategy & Innovation at Y-USA. When I connected with Aaron, I again shared my enthusiasm about Listen First and Activate America. Aaron said he appreciated my enthusiasm and remarked, "That's what we need, people who are passionate!" He suggested I send in my resume and follow-up with the national Activate America Project Manager, Jennifer Martin. Aaron also let me know they weren't in need of anyone immediately but I should call back in a couple months. I was pleased at the prospect.

After the initial Listen First workshop with the senior leaders, other workshops followed. I also worked with a few directors and key staff, teaching them how to facilitate the workshops so we could introduce Listen First to the over 200 staff across departments in a reasonable amount of time. It was no small undertaking, but I was indeed passionate about it and kept the momentum going. Of course, the communication would only be as effective as the directors and supervisors were in modeling the skills themselves. Several directors, including Amy, Eric, Ellen and others, strived to set a positive example. Many found the skills useful in relating and communicating with their staff and Y members, and some even found the skills quite helpful outside of work, with family and friends. A minority of directors dismissed Listen First as not important or not applying to them, though I observed they often were the directors whose staff had the most complaints about their management. Indeed, they were the ones who could most benefit from the skills.

The process of integrating this new way of communicating into the daily operations of the Y had an unexpected benefit. It demonstrated to the employees that the Y cared. Their ideas, opinions and experiences mattered. Listen First was helping to create a more welcoming environment where staff could feel heard.

I was already someone both members and staff frequently came to talk to, but after the Listen First workshops were in full swing, I became even more of a go-to person, especially for a few of the other Y directors. These directors were sometimes looking for advice, but more often than not, a listening ear. It seemed my psychology education came full circle, and I often felt like the in-house therapist.

Y-USA leaders identified Activate America as part of a larger "culture change" that was taking place within the organization nationwide. Some Ys around the country seemed to have lost focus or perspective and were looking like your general, for-profit fitness club. As one of the largest nonprofit, charitable organizations, the Y is so much more, not just in the programs and services offered, but in how it operates. The vision of Activate America really highlighted again how the Y is about *people,* not dollars.

Since I first started working at the Y, I felt a fondness for it. I often thought about our Y as an example of how we could be as a larger community. The people of the Y, staff and members, were made up of different political beliefs, religious beliefs, cultures, sexual orientations, ages, educational backgrounds and income levels. It was inclusive and harmonious. I felt I came to a greater acceptance of myself through the acceptance and kindness from my friends at the Y. Though there may have been differences, we shared a common goal, based on the organization's mission – to help others grow in spirit, mind and body.

I noticed many employees had been with the Y for 10, 20, 30+ years. They would remark that they stayed because of the people and because of the non-profit's mission. It felt good to be part of the Y. With the Y, you're part of something bigger, part of a force for positive change.

As an organization, the Y also allows *itself* to grow, understanding the necessity and benefits of evolving. The Y has lasted nearly 160 years. Worldwide, it serves more than 45 million people in 119 countries. One of the reasons it has lasted so long and touches so many lives is because it is constantly looking at the needs of the community and adapting to meet those needs. It supports personal growth and social change. Activate America and the culture change that was taking place in YMCAs across the U.S. was part of this natural evolution.

Change, evolution, growth – in work and in life. I kept my Seed of Intention in mind as the year progressed. Here it was, delightfully sprouting in multiple ways.

With summer over, the weather was getting cooler, and I discontinued the yoga at the park and started teaching a couple beginner classes per week at a local yoga studio. I showed up to teach my first indoor class, and one person showed up, a man named Tony. I also started to teach an intermediate class at the Y after work on Friday evenings on a volunteer basis.

The available hours at the yoga studio were not what I had hoped. After just a couple weeks, I decided to make a change and instead rent a studio space in a physical therapy building. I appreciated the independence this particular space provided. I could set my own prices at an affordable rate and have my desired class times. It didn't come without its challenges, though. As it was not a dedicated yoga studio or gym setting, I would need to do all of my own marketing to grow the classes. I was starting from scratch, except for those dedicated few who enjoyed the classes in the park, and Tony. I was experienced and comfortable marketing for a good cause, though, and decided to head up the challenge.

The new studio space was beautiful. Its bamboo flooring, blue walls, large golden Buddha wall-hanging, and wooden vaulted ceiling created a warm, welcoming environment that supported well-being. It also just happened to be 2 blocks from my home. How convenient! It was just where I wanted to be.

In early November '08, as the year wound down, I returned to southern California for the second 10-day yoga teacher training with Shiva Rea. For this trip, I hoped to have an opportunity to speak with her individually. I had some questions and felt like I needed some guidance.

Each day was filled with movement, opportunities for introspection and meditation, learning ways to impart the benefits of yoga to others, and a feeling of community. I was receiving so much.

Shiva is generally a woman on the go, and when she isn't teaching, she is often heading off to her next commitment. She remarked to the class, though, how she would set aside some time for meeting one on one at the end of the training.

On day 9 our group would be taking part in a Native sweat lodge ceremony. I appreciate how Shiva incorporates a number of different experiences into her trainings and how she has a fondness for nature and indigenous traditions. This would be my first time in a sweat lodge, and I was looking forward to it.

Carpooling was organized, and we caravanned out of Santa Monica, driving north along the coastal highway, then into the hills to arrive at the location of the sweat lodge. After about an hour we pulled up to our destination. My attention was first drawn to a large Native American medicine wheel made with rocks on the property. The wheel was at least 25 feet across, a circle of 12 stones with two perpendicular lines, one aligned north-south and the other east-west, with a small empty circle in the center. The stones ranged in size from grapefruit to basketball, with the larger rocks placed at the four directions. Upon getting out of the car, I headed immediately over to the wheel. I sat down in the center, right on the dirt, closed my eyes, and simply meditated for a few moments.

There was some time before the sweat lodge would be ready, so our group milled about and walked around the property. I stood overlooking the Pacific Ocean. The surrounding grass-covered hills were brown and dotted with scrub brush and interesting rock formations. It was dry, yet the fullness of the sea lapped against the land.

There was a time, not that many years ago, when I would have stood on that bluff contemplating leaping off, tumbling down, bumping against the many rocks, and ending the life that resides in this body. But here I felt only the *fullness* of life and grateful for each breath.

As our yoga training group was large, we separated into 2 smaller groups for the sweat ceremony. I was in the first group. The sweat lodge was a dome structure covered with several layers of tarps and heavy blankets. There was one flap door through which to enter and exit, with a height of about 3 ½ feet. After changing into our bathing suits, sarongs and other modern-day sweat lodge attire, we crawled in, one after the other. We circled our way around a small pit in the center which housed some hot volcanic rocks. There were scraps of heavy fabric to sit on, and we also had our towels. The group sat in 2 layers. The smaller circle closer to the rocks would experience more of the heat, while those sitting behind in the outer circle might enjoy the ceremony a couple degrees cooler.

I was feeling fired up and wanted to send as much energy as I could to get my book out to the world. I chose to sit on the inner ring to bring more fire to that intention. We all sat very close in order to fit, with our legs crossed or tucked up in front of us, feeling our arms pressing into the arms of those on either side. The group was made up of mostly women and a couple men. Once the two dozen or so of us got settled in, we were introduced to our guide. He was in his early 60s, with graying hair and an ample belly. Our guide explained some of the practicalities of the sweat lodge, as well as how he would be singing a number of songs and chants in the Native language.

Then the flap was closed. Complete darkness filled the space. *Just like a womb. What will be birthed from here?* Our guide began saying a few words in a Native language and pouring water on the rocks. I heard a sizzling sound, and the steam rose and spread out, filling the lodge. This continued for several minutes, songs and steam and heat. Though it was pitch black, not a single speck of light, it felt far from empty. The darkness was filled with song, words and prayers that had been passed down for generations. It wasn't long before I understood why it's called a sweat ceremony. I was dripping. The waters of condensed steam and sweat blended, and I felt pleasure in feeling the droplets drip off the end of my nose and run like little rivers down my chest.

Before experiencing a sweat ceremony personally, I imagined it might be unbearably hot. It was hotter than anything I had experienced to date, but surprisingly I didn't feel stifled or fearful. Through the heat, I simply breathed, and as the heat gathered and intensified, I returned to my breath.

I was sitting snugly in the womb, feeling comforted and also energized by it, when the flap flew open. Light seemed to blind us momentarily. We looked around at each other. Everyone was flushed and glistening, our clothes sticking to our skin. Some of us were smiling ear to ear while others seemed more reflective, with eyes cast downward, looking within. It was time for a break, a cool down.

An assistant brought in some more hot rocks with a pitch fork, and the flap was shut again. We returned to the darkness for 3 more cycles. We had a few sips of cool water half-way through. Each time in the darkness, chanting filled the air... and we sweat.

In the final cycle, our 4th round, an image appeared to me in the darkness. I'm not sure if it was my imagination or a vision. I saw a Native woman, hovering in the vastness of that dark space that had no boundaries or end. She wore white animal skin clothes and had long, dark, shiny hair.

She smiled and identified herself as White Buffalo Woman. I didn't know what it meant, but I clearly got the sense her appearance was a message that it's time for positive change. Not just for me individually, but for everyone. I felt comforted and hopeful.

I was not aware of the legend of White Buffalo Woman at the time of the sweat lodge. But I later learned the legend is believed to be more than 2,000 years old and is central to many Plains Indian tribes. The legend states how a woman of supernatural origin came to the Lakota from the west when they were on the verge of starvation. She brought gifts, including the sacred pipe, and taught them how to pray. She taught the men and women and children of the Lakota nation about gratitude, balance and harmony. When she finished sharing her gifts and teachings, she departed, walking towards the red ball of the setting sun. She then stopped, rolled over on the ground and turned into a black buffalo. As she went, she stopped and rolled over 4 times. The second time she turned into a brown buffalo. The third time, a red one. Finally, the fourth time, she rolled over and turned into a white buffalo. As soon as she disappeared over the horizon, buffalo in great herds appeared. These buffalo furnished the Lakota with everything they needed to survive – meat for food, skins for clothing and tipis, bones for tools and more. It signaled a time of abundance.

The following day was the last day of our yoga teacher training. We were scheduled for a morning session, then all of us student-teachers would be off, scattering in multiple directions, to make the return trip home.

I was lying on my belly on my yoga mat at the training studio. I heard an ocean of sound around me. There were pods of students in groups of two, three and four, talking, laughing, crying and finding closure in these last few moments of our time together. Soon we would be returning to our regular, day-to-day lives, no longer embraced by the love and familiarity of this yoga community. I laid there in silence, taking it all in, jotting a few notes in my journal and feeling full. The life journey is incredible, no matter where it goes, no matter what it looks like, no matter how it feels. It is utterly amazing to be alive. Letting out a big, contented sigh, I then rose up, joined in the pods, exchanged contact information with new friends and shared in goodbye hugs.

There were 4 of us who wished to speak one on one with Shiva. The studio space where we trained was getting occupied by another class, so we waited outside the back door on the sidewalk. My stuff was propped against the wall — rolled up yoga mat, backpack, suitcase, and yoga accessories bag. My flight was not for another 3 hours, and LAX was only ½ hour away by shuttle. I was in no hurry.

Shiva emerged from the studio, came over and put her arm around me. She picked up and carried my backpack and yoga bag. I was reminded of the inherent humility in truly great teachers. As we walked next door where she had arranged a place to chat, she said she would meet with me first.

I began by thanking her for the opportunity to meet. After a few moments of idle chit-chat, I started reading to her from my journal. I had written down a few "Questions for Shiva." The "questions" filled two journal pages. As I started reading, I began realizing that what I was reading simply needed to be said out loud. All sorts of things came tumbling out. I shared how I wanted to support the evolution of consciousness and help others remember their strength and inner light. I was going on about philosophical matters, as well as some deep spiritual inquiries that my mind was trying to wrap itself around. I was presenting all this to Shiva as if she held the answers to all the mysteries of the universe. When I got about ¾ of the way through reading the first page, Shiva interrupted and asked, "Are you a writer?"

I looked up at her blue eyes, a reflection of mine. "Yes!" I said with an exasperated sigh. I then began to chuckle, realizing how I was rambling on and so thankful she was able to pull the gem from the interaction.

"Imagining we don't have the time to dive into all this right now, how can I support you?"she asked, giving me the opportunity to get to the point. "Are you writing a book?" she asked.

"I wrote a book," I replied. I gave her a brief synopsis of *Journey to One*. Everything shifted, and I realized that I wanted to meet with Shiva, not to talk spirituality or philosophy, but to ask her practical questions. Shiva was also a writer. I knew she had written numerous articles for widely-distributed publications, such as *Yoga Journal*. I hoped she would be able to offer me a couple helpful tips.

"As a fellow writer," I continued, "do you have any suggestions about getting my book published?" We chatted for a few minutes, exchanging ideas.

Shiva proceeded to tell me how she has sat in a "pregnant pause" on a project which lasted 1-2 years before things started moving. I appreciated her sharing that, a reminder that there are times of dormancy, when seemingly nothing is happening... and then there are times of movement and growth.

Shiva may not have shared with me the answers to all of life's questions, but I received exactly what I needed. We wrapped up our discussion. I thanked her again and began walking towards the door. I stopped and turned around to face her. "*Journey to One*, it is not just my story. It is about *all* of our stories." For some reason, I wanted to be clear that my book wasn't about ego or self-serving interests.

"It comes from spanda," Shiva reassured me and smiled. In the yogic tradition, spanda is creative energy, the spark of inspiration that drives us. It is the energy that transforms creative potential into something tangible. A project that comes only from ego has no substance. A project that comes from the creative spark of spanda has depth and unlimited potentiality.

I crawled into the shuttle heading to LAX. The driver, with a heavy Indian accent, said out of nowhere, "I get the sense you're a writer."

I laughed in disbelief. Here I was in my yoga outfit, lugging around my yoga mat and yoga bag, which visibly contained yoga music CDs, yoga training course binders and other clearly-yoga paraphernalia, my hair was a little tousled, sweat still drying, and he asks if I'm a writer! "I am a writer," I replied. "What gave you that sense?"

"Oh, just something that came into my thoughts," he said. He was a jovial, talkative fellow. He weaved his way through traffic, and we talked a little about writing. Then he proceeded to tell me about his ex-wife, kids and work. As he chatted away, I was reminded how interconnected and intuitive we all are. Life is truly magical.

I didn't wish to head back into "normal" life the following day, returning to work and the usual activities. There was something lying dormant inside of me, and I knew it would not stay hidden for long. It had a force behind it, and a purpose. Eventually it would break out. I gazed at the road ahead, the passing cars and street signs just a blur. I felt aligned with something larger than myself, and deeply connected with creative energy. When I looked ahead, I didn't simply see the road home... I saw an extraordinary life.

Chapter 4

The Dance

*"I want to know if you will risk looking like a fool for love,
for your dream, for the adventure of being alive."*
– Oriah Mountain Dreamer

*T*he year of 2008 felt very powerful and transformative, working with the intention of alignment. I decided to close the year by hosting a winter solstice yoga event and then diving into a week of silence. Some of my friends and coworkers had asked why I was planning to be silent. I didn't know for sure. I could only answer that I wanted some time for reflection and writing. I didn't expect any grand epiphanies. I had never spent any extended time in silence and simply felt the desire to do so around this time of the solstice. It was something new for me, and I believe we grow when we allow ourselves to explore new things.

I went to the grocery store to fill my empty fridge. I made my way through the challenge of finding parking during the holiday season and through crowded store isles to stock up on food in preparation for my upcoming hibernation. I wasn't planning to be out and about much. The weather forecast predicted rain, and I decided I'd mostly stay around home and the park.

I also decided on a couple rules for myself. I would only allow for journal writing; no speaking or written correspondence. Sounds that emerged through emotion were allowed, such as laughter or crying.

On Dec. 21st I began my week of silence. The first couple days were subtle. As I watched the rain pour outside one afternoon, I asked myself, *Am I being silent, or am I just alone in my apartment?* Then I thought, *Ha! That could be a Zen koan, like if a tree falls in the forest and no one is around, does it make a sound?* I found myself just carrying out usual daily activities, hearing the seemingly endless chattering of my inquisitive mind... and dancing a lot. Sometimes I'd dance to music. Other times, I simply danced to a rhythm that came from within me. I danced in the living room. I danced in the shower. I would sit still to reflect or meditate, and my body just wanted to move, as if it had a mind of its own. I just followed it and enjoyed the dance.

I would awaken in the morning from a dream-filled sleep. In many of my dreams I was silent... and often dancing, moving. In one dream, I was in a studio with a number of yoga students. I was doing yoga, flowing through the sequences, immersed in the movement, and feeling like I was connecting with each student, without words. This was teaching.

As the days progressed, I went deeper. Through this time of turning inward, I felt I got better acquainted with certain aspects of myself. I came to a greater understanding of the teachings and tools I have to share. The time of silence managed to be profound after all. By the end of the 7 days, it became apparent that I had retreated into the silence in order to find my voice. I felt more tuned into my strength and direction in life, and I was excited to continue the journey.

I enjoyed working with the Seed of Intention, seeing it unfold throughout the year. I decided to repeat the exercise. Just like it did in 2008, my Seed of Intention for 2009 came easily. This time it was "abundance." I was open for abundance in all forms to come to me – particularly in the area of relationship, but also monetarily.

At the beginning of the calendar year, I took some time to reflect on my romantic relationships and attempt to gain some clarity in that aspect of my life. After the 5-year relationship with my partner, Lisa, ended a few years back, I had an on-again-off-again relationship with another woman for a couple of years. Then I dated a man for a while, then back to the previous woman, and finally spent some time alone. I don't find labels particularly helpful for me personally, so I don't identify as bi, gay or straight. I am simply Kristi. I didn't know if I would eventually share my life with a woman or a man. I figured it would just depend on the person.

One thing was clear. I knew I wanted a relationship where there was no push-pull energy, the power struggles, the yanking back and forth. I wanted a relationship where the two energies, the two souls, simply danced, a beautiful dance... and loved.

In my previous relationship experiences, I was always the one to do the leaving. After one such instance, my now ex-boyfriend told me over the phone one evening as we were finding closure, that I needed to fall madly, head over heels in love with someone and then have that person leave. He said it would give me a new perspective. He was feeling sad and hurt, but he said it with love and sincerity, not out of bitterness or anger. It is true. I had not experienced "falling in love" or the heartbreak from that person leaving. Perhaps it *would* give me a new perspective, but it was not something I was looking to have happen, at least the heartbreak part.

Then I met Kali, pronounced Käli, like the Hindu goddess. It wasn't the name she was born with, but is the name she chose to use. She said she felt like Käli sometimes.

Out of all the Hindu deities, Käli truly stands out. She is often illustrated in a downright frightening manner. There are many different illustrations, but she is most often portrayed brandishing various weapons with her multiple arms, and wearing a necklace made of human skulls. She has serious anger-management issues and is usually on a rampage. She has a black complexion, signifying she is "beyond time" or before there was light. She has been known as the Goddess of Time, the Goddess of Change, Power, Creation, Preservation and Destruction. Käli is also known to slay a demon or two and other evil forces. There are occasions when Käli's appearance is more beautiful, and she is shown to be benevolent and compassionate.

In the Hindu tradition, she is known as a destroyer, a destroyer of the illusory ego. Käli helps people confront and dissolve their ego in order to achieve "moksha," or ultimate freedom, liberation from reincarnation and suffering. Though she may appear frightening, she is believed to play an important role in one's life journey.

Käli is the female counterpart to the male, Shiva, meaning "Auspicious One." Shiva is one of the three main deities of Hinduism and is also known as "the Destroyer," or "the Transformer." In essence, Käli is a representation of the divine feminine, sometimes known as Shakti. Shiva is a representation of the divine masculine. Together, they help dissolve the illusion of ego and support transformation.

In a nutshell, I had a feeling this girl was going to be intense. I first met Kali at a community event at a local park. She was not hard to notice. She had a pretty face without layers of makeup. Her skin was tan from time in the sun. Defying the standards of much of society, Kali wore her hair in dreadlocks. They weren't unkempt dreads, as some can be. Instead they were thin, well-maintained dreads that hung almost to her waist. Most were the dark brown of her natural hair color, but a few strands were died fuchsia, purple, blue, and tan. Kali had a trim build and wore a shimmery, loose-fitting, gold-colored dress that went down to her ankles, followed by sandals. The best word to describe her is – earthy.

I was interested in meeting this woman and decided to strike up a conversation. We chatted about yoga and, interestingly, about communication. I noticed immediately how she made eye contact and was very present and engaged while we talked. When I looked into her eyes, I was utterly mesmerized. Perhaps it was light reflecting off of her dress, but her eyes looked golden, like a cat's eyes. As I gazed into those golden disks, I imagined her facial features beginning to transform and look like those of a cat – a large cat. I saw a lioness. I blinked a few times as I returned my attention to Kali's words, and the image faded. She seemed kind and sincere, and a little mysterious.

Kali was different from the two women with whom I'd previously been in a relationship. She was more feminine and more earthy. I was a little taken aback at the attraction I felt. I found myself, to my surprise, stepping into the pursuer role, more traditionally associated with the masculine. A couple days after the picnic, I gathered my courage and decided to give her a call, hoping to get to know her better.

Over the following weeks and months, we met for tea, went on walks, and shared in conversation, talking about everything from gardening to sexuality to spirituality. Sometimes we'd talk on the phone for an hour or two, until our ears hurt from holding the phone to it for so long, and exchange emails that would span pages. There was such closeness and intimacy through words.

A frequent topic of conversation of ours was relationships. Both of us were at a point in our lives when we were re-evaluating what "relationship" meant. On one occasion she shared a short story with me. I don't know if she originated it, or if she heard it from someone else, but its message struck a chord, and I thought it was beautifully told. I'm summarizing the story here and calling it "The Tree & the River."

> *Relating is like a river. There is flow, movement. The river passes by a tree along its edge, saying hello, nourishing the roots, giving water to the tree, and it moves on, dances on. It does not cling to the tree, and the tree does not say, "Where are you going? We are married! And before you can leave me you will need a break up, a separation, a divorce, and a little pain. Where are you going!? And if you were going to leave me, why did you dance so beautifully around me? Why did you nourish me in the first place?" No. The tree showers its blossoms and flowers on the river with deep appreciation, and the river moves on. The wind comes and dances around the tree and moves on. And the tree gives its fragrance to the wind. There is no possession, no attachment, only a dance.*

After a couple months of knowing Kali, I went over to her house for the first time to bring her some cough medicine that she wanted, as she was dealing with a cold. Kali was, by her own account, "a dread-headed hippie who lived in a shack." She felt compelled to prepare me prior to my visit, and described her home in detail. I assured her I would not judge her for where she lived.

As I pulled into the driveway, I couldn't help but think of that game M.A.S.H. my friends and I use to play in elementary school. Maybe you remember it. The game consists of different categories, such as the vehicle, the home, number of kids, type of pet, job, and spouse. You'd play the game to predict your future. M.A.S.H. stands for Mansion, Apartment, Shack or House. In the spouse category, you would write names of some of your classmates. Being the pre-teen girls that we were, that meant the boys you liked, and also a boy or two you didn't like, to make it interesting. In the vehicle category, you'd write down things like, Ferrari, Jeep, or the much less desirable Moped. For number of children, you might have 3, 12, 0, or something totally crazy like 8,362,104. You'd then draw a spiral until your friend said "stop." The number of rings in the spiral determined how many rotations in the round. Through a well-formulated process, items would be slowly crossed out from each category until you ended with one answer per category, determining what your so-called future was going to look like. Needless to say, it often caused unending fits of laughter, particularly when you ended up with the boy you *really* didn't like.

Kali must have ended up with the shack, I thought to myself. Her home was originally an old chicken coup out in the country that was converted into a living space approximately 20 years earlier. It apparently was part of a ranch that operated 80+ years ago that raised several hundred chickens. From the outside, it now looked like a small, narrow house with aged wood siding and a couple large windows that had been installed in the renovation. Upon first entering the building from one side, there was a room used primarily for storage. A swing door would lead you into the kitchen, which had the basic necessities – gas oven and stove, sink, fridge. There were no kitchen cabinets, just a few shelves covered by cloth curtains for food storage. Past the kitchen was a small dining area with a 4 foot, round table, mismatched chairs, a couple houseplants and a medium-sized window that overlooked the front yard. From here you could watch deer that frequented the property, nibbling on apples that fell from the trees. Kali had also hung a hummingbird feeder and planted a few flowers that attracted butterflies outside the dining room window.

To the left of the dining room was a small living area with a propane heater, an old couch and desk. Turning left again, one entered the bedroom and bathroom. The sleeping area consisted of a full-sized loft bed with a ladder to get up to it, and bookshelves and a storage area for clothes underneath. The bathroom was simply a compost toilet off to the side. When you wanted to take a shower or use a flush toilet, you'd walk next door to the main house, an old Victorian.

On the walls, Kali had posted inspirational quotes, collages, other artwork and colorful scarves, making it as homey as possible. If you looked up, you might find some pieces of scrap wood covering the insulation in the ceiling. It appeared to have everything to meet one's basic needs for shelter and warmth, but it was most definitely – a shack.

I wondered if the universe was presenting me with some sort of test or lesson that I needed to learn. In previous relationships, the topic of money arose frequently. My last girlfriend and I entertained the idea of living together at one point. My income was higher than hers at the time, and I held some resentment over how I would have to be responsible for more of the living expenses, and how we'd be able to afford a nicer place if she had a "regular" job and worked full time like I did. It's ironic, because when I was with my earlier partner, the tables were turned and my partner made quite a bit more money than I did. In both cases, the issue of finances and what it could provide, or not provide, carried with it some sour feelings.

So here I was, somewhat getting involved with this woman. Would I feel myself better, more important, more successful than Kali because she lived in a shack and I didn't? Would I look down at her for her compost toilet? No. I had no judgment towards her. By this point in my life, I didn't feel any resentment or inequality or pride or anything of the sort. Instead, I simply accepted things for what they were. Kali lived in a shack, she was a beautiful person, and that was that.

One of the things I enjoyed most about being around Kali is she *heard* me. In previous relationships, it sometimes felt like I was in an environment where I wasn't fully heard or accepted, and I then felt I couldn't be completely open. I would share only certain parts of myself. I wanted a different way of relating. I wanted to be vulnerable, fearless, and able to express the deeper aspects. As I now felt heard, I experienced an incredible comfort with Kali, and I could feel my heart opening more and more, like petals unfolding.

I felt I heard her as well. It was mutual. We both highly valued open, honest communication at all times. Our interactions were full of unconditional love, acceptance and respect. I felt a sense of freedom and lightness, not weighed down by expectation, judgment or fear. I thought to myself, *this is what a relationship is supposed to feel like.*

From this place of freedom and openness, I bared my soul. I wrote Kali love poems. I danced for her. I felt inspired to design yoga sequences for her, sing, compile mixed music CDs, and engage in numerous other creative endeavors. She was my muse.

Time spent with Kali was deep. As we got to know each other more and more, I couldn't help but sense we had some sort of cosmic connection. Yes, it sounds very California of me to say that, but I frequently envisioned the two of us – Shakti and Shiva – engaged in a dance among the stars and galaxies, a dance that spanned time and space. It felt like we had crossed paths and shared amazing connections in multiple lifetimes before, and here we were now simply stopping by to say hello and greet each other with a warm smile and a familiar hug. It didn't really matter what happened in this life, we already had that.

All of this was new and unknown territory for me, yet I decided to take each step boldly. I was determined to enjoy the dance for however long it lasted.

I had intended to be with Kali without attachment to the outcome. From the start, I knew this woman was not likely to be my life partner. Neither of us had made any commitment to only be with one another. It was more of an experiment in relating. Yet, I soon found myself wanting the dance to last. I adored Kali. I loved her on so many levels. I loved how she embodied the feminine, I loved our friendship, I loved our soul connection, our openness and acceptance. The feelings I had for her were intense. There was no question about it. It happened. I had fallen in love.

It seems just as soon as it happened, my heart felt like it was breaking. I always felt I had more interest in Kali than she did in me. I was the pursuer. I was the one who desired our connection to go deeper. We both seemed to be enjoying the dance, but then one afternoon she revealed to me how she wanted to be with someone else. I didn't expect to feel so hurt.

It was nearing fall of 2009, and I was awake at 1:00am in my bed, after spending the previous few hours dreaming about Kali and floating in a sea of confusion. Floating, floating, floating, trying to figure where I would settle and come to rest. I cried for hours, feeling an intense sadness and ache where my heart lies within my chest.

I wanted to make sense of it, tried to wrap my head around it. *Am I feeling left out? Am I feeling jealous? Why have I made the choices I've made with Kali? It feels like it is because of love. Well, what choices do I make today or tomorrow in regard to her? What do I desire? Do I desire a committed relationship? Do I wish for someone to share only certain aspects of herself or himself with me and me alone?*

Despite a lot of unanswered questions, I eventually fell back to sleep. I awoke later in the morning and cried some more. Afterwards, I felt a little more refreshed and had a clearer perspective. I decided to get out my *Medicine Cards* book and accompanying card deck written by Jaime Sams and John Carson. Sams is an artist, author of several books, and is of Cherokee, Seneca and French descent. Carson is of Choctaw descent. The wisdom found in the book and cards are based on Native American spiritual traditions. On each card an animal is pictured, and the book describes the medicine, gifts or teachings that each animal offers. I have found the book and cards to be a powerful tool for personal growth over the years. I drew a card. It was Frog. "Frog medicine is akin to water energy," it stated. "Frog teaches us to honor our tears, for they cleanse the soul." It said Frog can signify a time to replenish ourselves, cleansing ourselves from any person, place or thing that does not contribute to our serenity. The cards always seem to know what I need when I need it most.

For several weeks, I moved through the difficult experience of this separation. When heartache occurs, there is often a tendency to want to draw in, contract and guard the heart for fear of future pain. There were moments when I felt myself want to draw in, moments when I desired to erect some protective walls. During those times, I told myself, encouraged myself, *challenged* myself, "Stay open, Kristi, and open your heart even more."

Kali headed out of town to spend some time up north at a place that had special significance for her. After some time away, she returned to town for a day or two. Our connection no longer felt as deep as it once had. She then headed out again. I could feel her moving on, just like a river – flowing, dancing and nourishing the roots of other trees for a time, as rivers do.

Though there was pain, I was grateful to Kali for providing such an abundance of experiences in the area of relationships and helping guide me to some beautiful and important realizations. I learned how attachment and love are not synonymous. I had experienced an emotional intensity that I'd never felt before. I also gained greater clarity as to what I wanted in a relationship.

A dream provided an illustration of what I was truly seeking. It was a brief and simple dream: Kali and I were lying on a bed like a couple of school girls, chatting and laughing as friends do. We were in a place that looked like an unfinished house. Only the cement foundation and framework of the house had been built. The floor was bare plywood, and 2x4s made up the frame. There were no solid walls, nothing to prohibit things or people from passing through.

The dream revealed to me how I did not wish to live in a house simply made up of a foundation and framework. Though freedom of movement is there, what happens when the weather turns cold and the rain comes? I wanted a house with a roof and actual walls. The walls need to have windows and doors, of course, which allow for light and coming and going, but there is a more solid structure in place.

Through the dance of Shiva and Shakti, a few things became apparent. I desired open, honest communication. I wanted an environment in which I could be fully, fearlessly me. There needed to be unconditional love and acceptance. I wanted a relationship that felt balanced and where I could comfortably express my own "masculine" and "feminine" qualities in a balanced way, for I *am* strong and logical, as well as gentle and intuitive. I am assertive and also yielding, organized as well as creative. I also desired stability, commitment, and a solid structure... for winter was coming.

Kali later moved out of the area. I cherished the gifts I had received and welcomed continued abundance in this area. Perhaps it was necessary for Kali to leave in order for there to be space for something, or someone, new.

Dream, Aug 2009

I have picked up some food for dinner and I'm driving home. After some time, I realize I've missed my turn, and I am close to the coast. I decide to continue driving forward to view the ocean, as the sun is beginning to set.

I follow a road to its end, and there is a short walking path that goes over a sandy dune. I walk over the dune, and I see the ocean in all its expansiveness. There are dozens of people on a small beach. The water looks very clear and warm, and many are swimming in it.

It feels too crowded for me, so I don't even proceed down to the water. I turn and make my way back up the sandy hill. It's a little difficult, because I'm carrying a bag with my food in it. There is a woman who emerges over the hill, and I ask if she can hold the bag while I come up.

She does. At the top of the hill, she points toward the water and asks me, "What bridge is that?"

I turn and look and see a bridge and some other structures. I look to see if it's the Golden Gate, but it is not. "I'm not sure," I tell her. Then I ask if she's been to any of the other beaches, which are much larger and more open than this one. She says no, this is her first time seeing the ocean.

I'm now walking towards my car, and from a distance I see what I think are dolphins in the water next to the road. There are several people around, and I point out the dolphins. I'm excited to see them! I walk closer and look from the road. The dolphins are playing. I look to see if there is a way down to the water to get an even closer look. From the road to the water it's steep and sandy, but it's just 10-12 feet in distance.

I close my eyes, and I can feel the presence of the dolphins. I wonder if they can feel my presence. I open my eyes and see some dolphins have swum up close and seem to be beckoning me to play with them. I've never petted a dolphin before and am thrilled at the opportunity. I notice a place where I can walk down to the water, and I start heading down. I'm just 2 feet from being able to touch a dolphin when somebody calls to me from behind.

It's a man. He's in his 30s and seems to be a park ranger or something of the sort. He asks that I do not touch the dolphins. I don't understand why he doesn't want me to do this, as I know dolphins like humans. But I turn away from the dolphins and walk back up the short, sandy hill and sit next to the ranger.

I caress the palm of his left hand with a single fingertip of my right hand and then interlace all fingers. It feels nice. I look out and now see children petting and playing with the dolphins, yet the ranger is not saying anything to deter them.

We sit together for some time, enjoying each other's company and the coastal view. Dream ends.

Part II: Caterpillar

Resting snugly,
she recalls feeling the coolness of the ground beneath her,
the gentle breeze,
the warmth of the sun,
and the pull of gravity on her rounded, plump body
as she would inch her way up a vertical plant stalk.
A chuckle escapes her as she remembers the excitement of
arriving at a fresh, green leaf
with an aroma and texture that irresistibly drives her to eat.
She clearly remembers the sound created by her own
munch munch munching.

She recalls getting bigger,
and the sensation of shedding her skin again and again.
There were moments when things began to feel
uncomfortable, constricted.
Then, it would happen, naturally,
with hardly any effort on her part.
Each time it felt like she was breaking out. It was so freeing!
A rebirthing, necessary for continued growth.
This is how her days passed back then.
She was content to be her caterpillar self
having her caterpillar experiences…
for a while.

Chapter 5

Growing Full

*I*n addition to the area of relationship, the abundance of 2009 also revealed itself in my work. As I fully engaged in the Activate America efforts at the Y, my understanding of the vision and goals of the organization as a whole became clearer. In addition, because the goals of the Y felt to be in such harmony with my personal values, my dedication to the organization grew stronger. The more I worked on this national initiative, the more I desired to play an increased role in helping the Y move forward.

I had completed years of leadership training, and early in the new year I obtained my Senior Director certification. In order to work directly with YMCA of the USA on the Activate America endeavor, it was necessary to have achieved this level of leadership. So I was thankful when I received my certificate in the mail. It gave me a sense of completion. I put it in a frame and hung it on the wall in my office. It was a symbol of my growing commitment to the work of the Y.

My friend and co-worker, Maureen, immediately noticed it when she came to my office and congratulated me on the accomplishment. Amy also shared her congratulations. Not everyone, though, was so supportive. When John came to my office to discuss something, the framed certificate caught his eye, as it was something new on the wall. He did a double-take, and read it over for a couple seconds, then quickly averted his eyes toward the floor and acted as if he hadn't seen it. He didn't say anything about it, and I wasn't expecting him to.

In January of 2009 I attended a YMCA Key Leaders' conference in Monterey, California. Those in attendance were primarily Board members, CEOs and senior-level staff from our region. As I sat in my business casual attire, listening with one ear to the speaker and with the other ear to the voice within, I looked around the room, and my thoughts drifted: *Am I in the right place? I feel I want to be helping people directly, but I seem a bit disconnected in my current role. I know I can fit in anywhere, but at the end of the day, I am most comfortable in a pair of yoga pants. What more can I do? How else can I share my passions and goals with others?*

I suppose it all boiled down to the fact that I wanted to help change the world, to somehow play a part in making it a better place during my lifetime, if at all possible, and the Y felt to be one avenue where I could make a difference. I gathered that most people's hearts were sincere, coming from a place of kindness, even if not expressed in so many words, and in that I felt like I fit.

But there was also a sense of imbalance in the room. Most of the 175 or so attendees were middle-aged, Caucasian males. One of the amazing things I see about the Y is how it attracts and accepts people from all walks of life. Staff in support positions, and those at the mid-management level, are primarily women and vary in ethnicity, age, sexual orientation and ability. But in these senior rankings, the Y looks similar to most other corporations in America.

Then I started to feel frustrated. I was thinking about how just two months prior there was serious discussion at the management meeting about whether or not to have a staff holiday party. The concern was that it was "too costly." Times were tight, and no staff had received raises for the last 2 years and morale was going downhill. John and the CFO were arguing against having the party. Others of us were fighting to have it. Staff looked forward to it every year. I felt we needed it to give a little boost to morale, and I also believed staff should be appreciated and reminded that the service they provide the Y every day is invaluable. There ended up being enough of us fighting for it that it was decided to go ahead and have the party.

Here we were just a few weeks later at this conference. Generally 3-5 leaders from our Y would attend the annual Key Leaders' Conference. This year it was arranged for 10 people to attend, with the Y paying for the cost of the seminars, as well as putting everyone up in a very nice hotel, complete with bell hops and deep, delectable bathtubs. The cost of the conference was well beyond the cost of the holiday party, and considerably more than we had spent in years past. Was it just me, or did anyone else find the situation a bit disconcerting?

I could have continued with my internal tirade, but all of a sudden my attention shifted back to the speaker. Cal Jensen, Executive Vice President and COO for YMCA of the USA, was saying he wanted to share a quote by Marianne Williamson called "Our Deepest Fear" from her book *Return to Love.* He began to read:

> "Our deepest fear is not that we are inadequate. Our deepest fear is that we are powerful beyond measure. It is our light, not our darkness that most frightens us. We ask ourselves, 'Who am I to be brilliant, gorgeous, talented, fabulous?' Actually, who are you not to be? You are a child of God. Your playing small does not serve the world. There is nothing enlightened about shrinking so that other people won't feel insecure around you. We are all meant to shine, as children do. We were born to make manifest the glory of God that is within us. It's not just in some of us; it's in everyone. And as we let our own light shine, we unconsciously give other people permission to do the same. As we are liberated from our own fear, our presence automatically liberates others."

I scribbled the name Marianne Williamson and "Our Deepest Fear" on my note paper. These sentiments were powerful.

I remembered how I used to twinge at hearing the word "God." I had had so many negative associations with it. But by this time, I understood and respected that there are various perspectives. God can mean different things for different people. It might even be thought of as an aspect of ourselves, or all life. God is one of many words we use to try to understand life and creative energy.

I was captivated by this passage "... Your playing small does not serve the world. There is nothing enlightened about shrinking... as we let our own light shine, we unconsciously give other people permission to do the same. As we are liberated from our own fear..." It was just what I needed.

The sharing of this quote, by a middle-aged Caucasian male, no less, told me that the individuals at the very top of the organization, at the national level, had their hearts in the right place.

With the help of endeavors like Activate America, it was apparent the Y was putting forth genuine effort to move forward and grow. The Activate America guidebook, which gave an overview of it, stated, "The work of Activate America is transformational on a personal, professional and organizational level," and it was calling on YMCAs to "go beyond traditional approaches to addressing the nation's health crisis to charting a bold new path in addressing individual and community well-being." With words like "bold" and "transformational" being used to describe the work of Activate America, I was chomping at the bit to get more involved.

I followed up with the Activate America Project Manager at YMCA of the USA, Jennifer Martin, as recommended earlier by Aaron. The next thing I knew she was inviting me to meet with her face-to-face to discuss the possibility of being an Activate America Facilitator, and I was on a plane to Chicago!

Jennifer was around my age. She had dark, shoulder-length hair and a warm, easy smile. Turns out we both had been working for the Y the same length of time. Jennifer was comfortable to talk with, as if we had run around on the playground together growing up or had been college classmates, and she was professional, competent and forward-thinking. She informed me about the role and shared about the direction the Y was heading as an organization. I talked about my experience and interest in the work. The meeting went well, and she felt I would be a good fit for the position.

When I had initially made the call to the President and CEO of Y-USA regarding Activate America, my thought was to hopefully have a part in leading Listen First Institutes around the country. Being an Activate America Facilitator was a position of even greater responsibility. In March, I was offered the role of Facilitator, and I returned to Chicago in just 12 days to attend the orientation session and meet my first cohort. Things were moving quickly.

Working as a facilitator was a part-time role with Y-USA. In that role, I provided guidance and support to a number of leaders at Ys across the country. I was still responsible for meeting my responsibilities as the Director of Membership & Communications at my local Y, as well. I had a foot in the national scene and a foot in supporting the local community.

Becoming an Activate America Facilitator increased my level of professionalism in the Y leadership structure. I was already a qualified Branch Leader, and now also an Organizational Leader, which is the highest level one can attain. It is the same leadership level afforded to CEOs. In addition, my new role provided an increase in my salary. I was now making more money than I ever had. Abundance was coming in all forms.

As the months progressed, I learned more and more what the Y was about as an organization through working with staff at Y-USA. Not only did it have a long history and deep legacy, it was an organization on the move. There was a vibrancy, passion and commitment apparent in the leaders, and they seemed to walk the talk. Innovation and creativity were encouraged. In communication, people truly *listened*, and alternate viewpoints were respected. The Y identified itself as a learning organization, constantly evolving to better meet the needs of those it served, and those not yet served. There was honesty, transparency, and egos appeared to be in check. There was a high level of professionalism. No one was going around slamming doors or yelling at their subordinate staff. I appreciated the environment, and felt I fit in well with those at Y-USA.

In this national work, I was one of 21 Activate America Facilitators. We were informed of, and tasked with, the responsibility of being "change agents." We were to support the YMCAs in our designated cohorts in the transformative endeavor that was Activate America. It was no small task. This work was part of an organization-wide culture change. It was going to require a great deal of effort to help educate Y leaders on what Activate America was, and people often balk at change.

On the Y-USA front, things were going well. There was movement and growth taking place personally, professionally and organizationally. I was getting a glimpse of the power behind a movement when there are dedicated, passionate people leading the way, inspiring others into action. It felt meaningful and fulfilling.

On the local Winowa County YMCA side, though, things were feeling less than satisfying, and even uncomfortably constrained. John Smith was the captain of our ship, but he seemed to have very little interest in steering the ship in the direction of the larger Y movement. Perhaps it was due to lack of understanding or lack of motivation. In general, it seemed like he had "checked out." For months John appeared disinterested during the weekly management meetings – daydreaming out the window, scribbling doodles on his notepaper, or running off to answer his cell. In regards to Activate America, he neglected to take advantage of the information and support Y-USA provided specifically for CEOs. Amy, in her role as Project Manager, worked diligently to keep the process moving. John, though, seemed out of touch, and his lack of interest and involvement restricted the potential for growth.

One of the most challenging things for me during this time when I had a foot in both worlds was seeing the potential of our Y from a national perspective, while also remaining true to my designated roles at the local Y. I had a unique perspective of Activate America work through my responsibilities as a Facilitator. YMCAs that had CEOs or Executive Directors who were engaged in the work were more likely to thrive. A number of Ys that were implementing the tools of Activate America were reporting greater staff satisfaction. They were creating beneficial collaborative partnerships with organizations in their communities. Ys were being awarded grant funding for new programs. Members were reporting they were feeling more supported in their health goals. These Ys were experiencing growth and positioning themselves for more growth. Y's who didn't have engaged, passionate leaders were often at a stand-still, or struggling.

As change agents, we were specifically asked how we could create a sense of urgency in those who have an influential role at YMCAs. Indeed the situation is urgent. The health of the nation is at crisis level. (There is more information about the state of health of individuals in the U.S. in chapter 17, along with tips for what we can do to achieve greater health and well-being personally.)

As mentioned earlier, the heart of this Activate America effort was personal connection, the relationships we build, how we communicate, our genuine care and concern for others. This personal aspect is the necessary foundation for being able to best support others in creating healthier habits. This thread of human connection runs all the way back to the origins of the Y, wanting to help young men stay off the street and out of trouble, and it continues to run through its operations today.

With all this focus on relationship-building, I felt it was vital that the individuals representing the organization communicate and interact with others in a manner that coincides with the values held by the organization, the values of caring, honesty, respect and responsibility.

What was nagging at me, however, was how, out of all the staff I knew, both locally and nationally, John Smith, the leader and CEO of our

Y, seemed to least embody these values. This weighed on me, particularly because several staff felt like nothing could be done to change the situation. Numerous complaints had been made over the years, but to my knowledge nothing regarding him had been documented. There was no change or improvement in his behavior. He was the CEO, the one in control. The environment created by John felt stagnant. It was not a place where open, honest communication could take place, which breeds expansion and growth. It was an environment that often stifled expression and led to people feeling uncomfortable, disempowered and dismayed.

As an agent of change, I thought long and hard about if there was anything I could do to improve the situation at our local Y and aid in its forward movement. Staff at various levels of responsibility experienced a side of John that the Board of Directors did not see. So one thing that I realized I could do was start getting documentation.

Another thing that I felt I could do to create a sense of urgency as a change agent is talk with the Board. I had discussed with Amy during our weekly meetings how I wanted to meet with a particular member of the Board, Joe Phillips, to share some concerns. This Board member had a long history with the Y. I observed Joe to be extremely well-spoken, a critical and strategic thinker, and he exuded compassion. That is what led me to speak with him the most, his compassion. He was also a highly respected attorney and member of the community. I was not the first staff person or director who had approached a Board member with concerns, and I knew I was not the first to approach this particular Board member, either. I figured one more voice sharing a concern might, at some point, lead to some sort of positive change. I was letting my heart lead the way, and it led me to his office.

He was gentle and kind as usual. I sat, albeit a bit nervously, with my page of notes in hand. I talked about the Y, shared a little about Activate America and my two roles – with the local Y and with YMCA of the USA. I also shared some thoughts about John, the reason for the visit. I was a bit cautious, though. I didn't feel it necessary to go into too much detail at this time. Perhaps I was testing the water. But I felt I said enough. At the end of our hour meeting, Joe asked if I was comfortable talking with the Board Chair. I said yes. The Board Chair position was in transition, however. The current one was leaving, and I figured it would take at least a couple months for the new one to get settled. But I felt comfortable talking with either of them. I believed they both had the best interests of the Y at heart.

In the latter part of 2009, I noticed John starting to realize that a culture shift was underway, spurred by leadership at the national level. John respected our Y's Resource Director, who was a liaison between Y-USA and our Y. He had many years of top-level leadership experience and had supported John and the rest of the management team with various projects and strategic planning over the previous couple of years. On his last visit, the Resource Director mentioned how *we*, as in Y-USA (and the Y as a whole), were working to create a different culture. I'm glad John was being made aware of this culture change from him, too, and not just Amy or me.

John made a remark during one of the weekly management meetings that caught my attention. He looked straight at me and said, "It's like you're trying to have a change in administration, only the people are the same." I figured when he referred to me, he was actually referring to Y-USA. It was an interesting way to look at it. In a sense, it did feel like the shift that we were creating was as significant as the change from one presidential administration to another. Y-USA was working to engage the existing CEOs and other leadership to head up this culture change, but there were also changes being made in the leadership itself. As CEO's were retiring or leaving through other means, the next generation of Y leaders was stepping into their places, and this included those who were passionate about Activate America.

What I realized at this time was how movements are more powerful than any one of us is as an individual. I could feel tremendous movement taking place, evolutionary waves of change. Like a wave building in the ocean, gathering energy, size and strength, and preparing to wash onto the sandy shore, there was passion and action and momentum pushing the culture shift forward. I recognized that even if there were Y leaders who didn't readily jump onto their surfboards and join the others in riding the wave, or leaders who deliberately back paddled, doing their best to work against it, the wave would simply be too large and the momentum too strong.

A situation soon arose with John that felt worthy of documentation. The incident involved questionable business practices and seemed a bit "shady," to use the word of another senior staff member who was involved. It caught the attention of a couple other directors, for I overheard whisperings about it in the hallway. I kept track of all the emails and correspondence and details of the situation. Then I filed away the experience to be added to any accounts of future incidences. The words of an instructor from a Y training that I attended years before rang in my ears. "It's all about documentation, documentation, documentation!"

Chapter 6

The Bear & the Butterfly

$\mathcal{M}$y friends came and helped me move that cool November day. Now I stand staring at the boxes and boxes of my stuff piled in my new place. It feels like a fresh start. Movement is happening on all levels.

I begin to contemplate the coming year and think about what my word, my Seed of Intention, might be for 2010. The last two years, I had such an incredible experience with planting the seeds and then receiving "alignment" and "abundance." What word will arise for this next cycle? Unlike the previous two years, nothing immediately comes to mind. I feel unsure. Is it "potential?" Is it "love?"

I head out to run some errands one morning. As I look along the tops of the surrounding mountain ridge, I am amazed at the clarity of the visibility. The air is crisp, and there is no hint of fog or haze. The outer world beautifully reflects the clarity I feel within. I'm settling into my new home. My book, *Journey to One*, is completed and at the publishers. I have recently come to a place of acceptance with Kali flowing on with her life. I know what it is I want in a relationship.

Fall will soon be turning into winter, and I feel not unlike a bear making preparations for the coming cold, dark months. That evening, as I lay reading in bed, I pause to glance over at the space next to me and feel the desire to have another bear hibernating with me in the cave. "Who is willing to be a bear with me this winter?" I ask the empty room.

An image of Tony flashes in my mind. *That's funny*, I think. Tony is a gentleman who showed up to my first indoor yoga class a little over a year ago.

I reach down to the floor next to the bed, where I keep the Medicine Cards. I pick them up, give them a good shuffle and then fan them facedown onto the comforter. I'm curious what may lie ahead as the seasons are changing. I choose two cards and turn them over. Bear and Armadillo. How very interesting that Bear makes an appearance after I was just thinking about it! Armadillo is about establishing appropriate boundaries, always a good reminder.

I remember when I first met Tony. A local chiropractor had recommended he try yoga for an ongoing back problem. He seemed nice, and he liked to talk.

During that time, I was making a concerted effort to use my Listen First communication skills in just about all my interactions with others. Through Listen First I had become better equipped to demonstrate my interest in and care for individuals, and how to communicate with them in a supportive manner.

Using these skills had some unexpected side-effects. In a period of about 2 weeks, I had 3 men ask me out on a date. I found it interesting how taking a little time and effort to truly listen to another person was often interpreted as romantic interest. However, it afforded me the opportunity to create some clear boundaries.

Tony was a regular attendee of my yoga classes from the start. We would often use the time before or after class to chat. He often shared about his work, feelings of stress and the issues he was confronting with his body. I listened intently as his yoga teacher and hoped I was effectively sharing some of the tools of yoga that could aid him on his journey to greater health and wellness.

He seemed to be a kind, gentle soul. It was obvious that he was a hard worker, and was also committed to getting his body to a healthier state.

He was attractive with his piercing blue eyes. I had never seen eyes as light and clear blue as his. His features revealed a strong brow, indicative of his Italian roots, and he shaved his head. From our chats, I learned that he had started going bald at a young age and decided to simply shave his head and keep it that way. It suited him well. He had a small, round nose, full, pink lips and there was a sweet innocence to his face. On most occasions, covering his cheeks and strong jaw were dark brown whiskers, interspersed with a few gray, salt and pepper, which suggested he carried some wisdom. His whiskers would often be grown out about a week or more and formed a full, perfect beard. Tony also had an athletic build. He showed natural strength and tone in most areas, no doubt kept physically active by his work.

One evening after class, a couple months or so after our first meeting, as I was gathering up my iPod, yoga mat and other items, Tony pulled out a hiking book. He flipped through the pages and asked me if I would be interested in going on a hike with him sometime. During the 2-second pause that followed his question, I couldn't help but think, *You know, for a guy to ask me out, that is certainly the best way to do it – standing in a yoga studio asking if I want to spend time in nature – my two loves.*

"I would be interested in going on a hike with you, *as a friend*," I replied. "I love nature, I love trees," I said.

"Me, too. I love trees so much I took a class on them at the Junior College!" Tony shared. I wondered if he was just trying to impress me.

"Really?" I asked.

"Yes, the class was called Native California Trees & Shrubs. I enjoyed it a lot," Tony responded. "For a while I thought I wanted to be a ranger and studied Forestry and Natural Resource Conservation."

I didn't have any romantic interest in him. At that time, I was still knee deep in the river of Kali. However, I always enjoyed having friends with whom to go hiking. We made a plan to go in a week.

I locked up the studio, and we walked through the dark night together to our vehicles, making idle chit-chat along the way. Our vehicles were parked next to each other, my silver Accord next to his silver Tacoma. As we unlocked our vehicles and prepared to leave, I said to him, "I feel it's important to be open and honest, and I want you to know that you seem very nice, but I do not generally date men. As I said earlier, 'I'm happy to go hiking and spend some time with you *as a friend*.'" I wanted to be clear.

"I appreciate your openness and honesty," Tony replied. "I, too, value those things. Yes, as friends." I felt relieved to have clearly communicated my intentions, and my truth. It was part of my new way of relating with others – upfront and not afraid to just be *me*.

Over the following months, he continued taking yoga classes with me. We enjoyed a few hikes together, as well as our chats before class. Though he was kind, I didn't find him very... interesting. But in all fairness, few would be as interesting as Kali. As the months progressed and Kali moved on, I found comfort in the fact that things were clear and simple with Tony. We spent time together, mostly in nature, hiking, or at the beach, and we talked. I found him to be an excellent listener and communicator, and over time I began to see there may be more to this man than I first realized.

Lying in bed, gazing at the Bear and Armadillo cards, I imagine how it would go if I picked up the phone and called Tony at 9:30pm to say, "Hi, do you wanna be a bear with me this winter?" The thought makes me laugh out loud. Boundaries, Kristi.

The Wednesday before Thanksgiving, there are only a few students in yoga class. Tony is one of them. By now, he has been doing yoga about a year. The small class size gives me the opportunity to go around frequently and offer some hands-on adjustments. As we near the end, with bodies tired and happy, the students are settling into that delicious peacefulness that accompanies a well-rounded yoga practice. I begin to make my way around the room.

"As you lie on your back, resting in our final pose, savasana, close your eyes and let yourself fully relax." In a gentle tone, I continue, "Lengthen out your legs, and allow your arms to rest out and away from your sides.... Allow the muscles in your brow and forehead to smooth out, and soften the muscles around your eyes, jaw and mouth…. Drawing in a couple deep breaths, see if you can relax even more…… releasing any tension you may be holding. Replenish yourself here in savasana." Following the theme of Thanksgiving, "Connect with your heart… feel something that you are grateful for, and rest into that peace…."

Bodies are melted onto the floor as I walk around to give adjustments. For one student, I slowly lift her feet into my hands and pull with care, providing some gentle traction, then softly lower her legs back to the floor. Then I walk up to her head and briefly massage the muscles in her neck as she sinks more and more into relaxation. They're considered yogic adjustments, but in savasana they are better recognized as delightful, blissful, healing experiences.

I then turn towards Tony. He is not in a traditional savasana pose. His eyes are open. His right leg is bent with his foot placed on the floor, and his arms are out at a 90 degree angle from his body. He often does his own thing these last few minutes of class. I figure it may be because he is still fairly new to yoga and hasn't yet experienced the benefits of fully sinking into this last pose. Other times, I think it may be a way to express that he is his own person, and he is being authentic to himself.

I take a few steps back towards my mat, feeling at first that I won't offer any adjustments to Tony, as he seems comfortable where he is. Then, on second thought, I decide I can provide some gentle adjustments for his head and neck. I lift his head into my hands and tilt it to the left. Holding his head with my one hand, I use my right hand to give him a brief massage down the right side of his neck and into his right shoulder, helping to lengthen and relax the muscles.

In the past, Tony has surrendered to similar adjustments, breathing and relaxing into them. But this time I notice he is not fully relaxed. As I tilt his head to the other side to massage, his left hand floats up, and with a single finger, he gently caresses my left hand. I have no feeling or thought whatsoever to take my hand away. I accept his soft caresses, receiving the touch from this gentle soul.

The following morning, Thanksgiving, Tony and I go for a walk at Diego Park, the park that I love so dearly, where I have spent countless afternoons exploring secret trails, sitting in trees, or laying out a blanket and enjoying some sun. Diego Park is one of Tony's favorite places, too. This is his hometown, and he knows the park even better than I do.

We decide to walk a nature trail that is a little over a mile in length, an opportunity for a nice stroll. As we walk, I notice how I often lead the way, setting the pace. I observe how there are also times when Tony will lead. From this vantage point, I get a chance to gaze at his firm, round butt and muscular calves. He is sure-footed and seems comfortable navigating the terrain, evidence of a life lived close to nature. It is a familiar feeling. We make our way along the dirt path, and there seems to be a natural flow in how we exchange the lead position. The ease with which we exchange leadership roles feels significant. It demonstrates to me that no one is trying to overpower the other. There is no struggle, but instead a mutual recognition of our equality. On a deeper level, it feels like a balance of strength and humility, and reveals an unspoken understanding about life in general: Sometimes we lead, sometimes we follow.

We stop at a small footbridge and gaze over the railing at the murky, stagnant water. The seasonal rains have not yet begun. I then look over at him and say, "You have amazing eyes." I pull out my digital camera to capture those clear, blue jewels. I take a picture of him, then hold the camera out in front to take a picture of the two of us together.

"I enjoy your eyes, too," Tony says. My eyes are more of a medium blue, whereas his are light.

"Nice. Our blue eyes can gaze at each other," I say with a playful smile, feeling a little flirtatious.

We come up to one of my favorite trees in the park, one that I refer to as the Grandmother Tree. The species is a coast live oak. It's at least a couple hundred years old, and its bark resembles the wrinkled skin of an old woman. When I visit this tree, I often have the same feeling as when I would visit my grandmother as a young girl. Sometimes I climb and sit in her branches as I used to sit in my grandmother's lap.

I approach the tree and touch my hand to her wrinkled skin, silently greeting her and connecting with the wisdom of her years. Then I turn, lean back against the rotund truck and face Tony. We look into each other's eyes, neither turning away. I feel open and receptive, perhaps on the verge of beckoning. Still, Tony holds some distance, respectful. He just smiles at me. I invite him in with my eyes. He walks closer, and we stand with bodies touching. He seems to be waiting, still respecting boundaries. "I'm wondering if you'll kiss me," I then say, being more verbal with my invitation. He gives me an intent look, and without hesitation, leans in and touches his soft lips to mine. Our tongues explore one another briefly before we part lips. We gaze into each other's eyes once again... and kiss some more.

"I'm excited to see this tree you've been telling me about," I say after some time. During our walk, Tony has been telling me about a tree that he visited a lot when he was young. Having spent so many hours at the park, exploring places off the beaten path, I can't imagine there is a trail that I haven't yet explored or a tree I haven't seen. Tony leads us to the start of a narrow, dirt trail. I am surprised at myself for not having taken this trail before, as it is just off one of the main trails and not at all hard to find.

"I thought I've showed you this tree before," Tony says. This is the first time we've spent time together in this park. A past life, perhaps.

"No, I've never been here," I assure him. We walk 50 yards or so into a wooded area. The trail then opens up into a shady grove consisting mostly of very young coast live oaks, a couple alder trees and some shrubs. But standing before us is an immense, old coast live oak, hundreds of years old. I let out a spontaneous "Awwwww..."

The tree has two large limbs, a couple dozen feet in length, extending from either side, appearing as arms outstretched, practically inviting people to climb up into its branches. Under the tree sits a picnic bench. It is clear this spot is a popular hangout for teenagers, and has been for a while. Both the bench and the tree have numerous carvings. On the bench I see typical things – everything from initials to hearts to a rough carving of a penis, which boys are so fascinated with when they're going through puberty.

As I walk around the large tree trunk looking at the various carvings, one catches my interest above the others. I step closer to get a better look. The carving is located on the trunk, about 3 feet taller than my head, just where the tree begins to fork and the lowest limbs branch out. It's about 10 inches wide and 18 inches tall. The carving is old and deep. I make out that it is a Native American medicine shield with three feathers hanging from it. On the round shield is a bear paw. "Wow, look at this carving!" I excitedly shout to Tony. "It's a medicine shield!"

Tony walks over to take a peek. "Yeah," he replies, "it looks like it has a bear paw, and there's the feathers hanging down." Bear has made an appearance once again, and each time it seems to be associated with Tony.

Tony talks about how he used to come to this tree as a child with his friends and climb on it. He says the brush in the area used to be very dense, and he would have to use his hands and arms to part branches and make his way to the big oak. I listen intently as he shares some of his playful childhood memories. Then, under the expansive canopy of limbs and leaves, he kisses me. A kiss under my tree. A kiss under his tree.

In the weeks that follow, we spend a great deal of time together, enjoying each other's company and enjoying intimate moments. We both have the week of Christmas off of work, so we make plans to go to Monterey for a couple nights. Tony comes over to my place, so we can talk more about the trip and pick out our hotel. Our "talk" ends up being more like rolling around on the floor of my living room, kissing, laughing and holding each other, like a couple of teenagers.

"You seem so delicate, so fragile," Tony says, as he inspects my small wrist with his hand, still getting familiar with each other, "but I know how you are very strong." He has been witness to my physical strength in our yoga classes. Indeed, I am thin framed, but by no means delicate. Having grown up in the country with three older brothers, riding bicycles and motorcycles, doing flips on the trampoline and otherwise being a die-hard tomboy, "fragile" was not in my vocabulary. But I see how I might look that way. "You're like a butterfly," Tony says. I feel the incredible sweetness in his statement.

As we continue to roll on the floor, there is one point where I am lying on my back and Tony is positioned over me with his knees straddling my thighs and his arms framed around my torso, resting on his elbows. I embrace him as his body rests lightly on mine. I always feel so comfortable and safe in his embrace. He is strong, yet gentle. As I soak in the enjoyment of this position, I have an image come to mind – a butterfly held ever-so-carefully in a strong hand. It reminds me of the scene in *Lord of the Rings* when Gandalf is trapped atop Saruman's tower, and he catches the moth. Gandalf clutches it with the lightness of a feather, causing it no harm, grasping only the outermost edges of its wings.

"You know how you say you see me as delicate?" I say to Tony. "How you're positioned right now," I share, "I see a butterfly held in a strong hand." I bring my two hands together to illustrate, just my fingertips touching, creating a gentle holding space. I continue, "The butterfly is held securely, but it is still able to move."

Tony looks at me, blinks a couple times and says nothing. A few minutes later, as we sit together on the couch, he says, "That's the nicest thing anyone's ever said to me."

I give him a quizzical look, as I have not said anything the last few moments. "What is?" I ask.

"The butterfly," he replies. I have a feeling, in his embrace, I will fly.

Chapter 7

Premonition

On December 3rd a package arrives for me at work. I know immediately what it is. I open the cardboard sleeve to find *Journey to One* in shiny, new book form, an advance copy sent to me from the publisher! It is real. All the years, all the thoughts and feelings, experiences and lessons that were once just in my mind or written across the pages of my journal, are now here in my hand. I hold this precious gift, squeal with glee, and then grasp the book close to my heart. Afterwards I pass it over to a couple of my coworkers to see and hold, like a newborn baby.

The year of 2009 turns into 2010. My seed word of intention still has not come to me. It doesn't seem to be "love" or "potential," as I first pondered. I have a desire to bring community together, so I wonder if it's "community." No, that's not it either. The days continue to pass. "Visioning," maybe that is it. No words stick. It has to feel 100% right. I figure something will eventually come, providing me a sense of direction for the coming year.

One afternoon I pack up a few things and walk through Diego Park, making my way out beyond the Grandmother Tree and onto a deer path. As I follow the path, I come to a hub of trails. Amidst the tall, brown grass in an open meadow are several clearly marked deer trails, distinguishable due to the significantly shorter, new green grass upon which numerous deer hooves have stepped. There are 8 trails set out like 8 spokes of a wheel. I stand for a few moments in the hub, where all the paths converge.

I hear a faint whispering of the word "convergence" as a possible Seed of Intention. I open my backpack and lay a couple towels onto the damp earth. I then pull out my meditation cushion, place it on the towels and seat myself in the hub. I look around and notice how there is blue everywhere. I am wearing a blue tank top that peaks out from underneath my ½ unzipped blue sweatshirt. There is a blue bath towel, followed by another blue towel, a slightly lighter shade. Also, I see my blue backpack, and in my hand, a blue pencil.

In yoga, blue is the color associated with the throat chakra, the communication center, how we speak, give voice, as well as listen. I have been drawn to blue as long as I can remember. When I was a young girl, blue was my favorite color, and I wore a lot of it. I close my eyes and sit quietly. I hear the word "teaching" surface. *Which path do I follow?* Eight paths, 8 like the symbol for infinity, all possibilities. The inner voice of wisdom responds, *Where all paths converge, there is nowhere to go but wherever you choose.* Where do I choose? Which path? Then it dawns on me that I have already chosen – to be a teacher.

I hear a song arise, fading into my awareness, "This little light of mine, I'm gonna let it shine…" I only know the first verse of this gospel tune. I hear it in my mind as it sounded in that movie, *Corrina Corrina,* starring Whoopie Goldberg and Ray Liotta. That was actually the first I heard the song altogether.

I love that movie. It's a story about a 7-year-old girl, Molly, whose mother had recently died. At first Molly does not speak. Her father, the character played by Ray Liotta, tries to deal with his own grief and that of hers. Whoopie plays a sassy, loveable nanny. Later, Ray Liotta's and Whoopie's characters begin to form a romantic relationship. Set in 1959, a bi-racial relationship was definitely taboo. The little girl spends a great deal of time with Whoopie's character, immersed in the love and expressiveness of her family and that of Black culture. Ultimately, it is a story of healing on multiple levels. At the very end of the movie, Molly, in her sweet voice, full of soul, is singing this song. Her grandmother, up to then, a rather closed-minded and rigid woman, joins the little girl, with her heavy Yiddish accent, in singing. It is a deep and special moment filled with hope. Perhaps this song will be my "word" for the year.

> This little light of mine, I'm gonna let it shine
> This little light of mine, I'm gonna let it shine
> This little light of mine, I'm gonna let it shine
> Let it shine, let it shine, let it shine!

I often use the second bedroom in my duplex, which I sometimes refer to as my energy room, for reflection, meditation and acts of creativity. At home, it is where I go when I need to recharge. The center of the room lies empty most of the time. Around the edges, hugging the walls, is a medium-sized bookshelf with a number of titles that support personal growth, and also a lamp, a guitar, an African djembe drum, and a couple cushions. I want to keep most of the space free of clutter so inspiration can pour in without distraction.

One evening, I feel inspired to go into the energy room and work with the Medicine Cards. I usually just lay them out and draw one or two cards and read about the teachings. This time, as I shuffle and prepare to lay them out, a new way of working with the cards comes to me. I feel I can receive guidance and support from different animals for each of the 4 seasons of 2010. I also have the image of a Native Medicine Wheel in mind and understand that I can use this as a learning tool, with each of the animals sitting in the four directions.

In a traditional Native Medicine Wheel, each of the four directions – east, south, west and north – are associated with one of four natural elements – air, fire, water and earth, respectively. The seasons, too, can be associated with these same four elements: air = fall, fire = summer, water = spring and earth = winter. I spread out the Medicine Cards face down and begin the process. Following my intuition, I begin by choosing an animal card to represent winter, the current season.

I quietly ask which animal wishes to share its guidance and support for winter. My hand hovers over the cards, and my finger touches down on two cards. Bear and Deer, not surprising. In addition to the Bear energy associated with Tony as of late, Bear is about introspection. Just like how it enters the cave and hibernates, Bear is about following instinct and going inward for answers. Deer is about gentleness. I put them both in the north position. I continue to pick another card for spring. It is Otter, associated with the medicine or gifts of women, specifically, as well as playfulness, according to Native tradition. Otter is comfortable on land and water, and can also be about finding balance, particularly balanced feminine energy. That is, not meek, not overbearing, but balanced. I place Otter in the west. For summer, I draw the Badger card. Badger feels shocking to me, as it is associated with aggressiveness, quite opposite of my usual nature. In all the years I have been working with the Medicine Cards, I have never drawn the Badger card... ever. *How can I possibly work with that aggressive energy?* I place it in the south, and figure I'll simply trust the process. I continue to draw one more card for fall, and it is Beaver, the builder. Beaver is placed in the east. It looks like the year is going to embrace everything from the gentleness of Deer, to the playfulness of Otter, to the fierce determination of Badger, to the construction of Beaver. It is all quite fascinating. I make a mental note to re-read the information for each of the animals as each season changes.

At this time in January, I am deep in Activate America work at the local Y. It is decided we'll have a presentation on Activate America for the Board of Directors, and I volunteer to create the PowerPoint. Each member of the Activate America leadership team, 6 of us total, contribute content as it relates to our area(s) of focus, whether it is the curriculum at the childcare sites, staffing practices, data collection, relationship building, the physical environment, etc. With my concurrent work with YMCA of the USA, I have a broad perspective of what Activate America involves and how it is interwoven into all aspects of operations. I gather information from the other team members and also incorporate relevant materials provided by Y-USA.

Amy, the Activate America team leader for our Y, wishes for each person to have a role and present his or her area of specialty. For the presentation, we will discuss what has been accomplished in that area to date, as well as how we are looking ahead to develop it further.

One morning, the Activate America leadership team meets to discuss the upcoming presentation. It is truly an amazing team, I feel. There are 2 directors who oversee childcare and camp programs, a Senior Director who oversees youth sports and other youth programs. We have the Fitness Director who oversees the fitness center and wellness programs and classes. I oversee membership, and we have Amy, the Director of Operations and Activate America Project Manager, our team leader. Each of us brings our dedication to the Y and our passion to help young and old to enjoy greater well-being.

After compiling all the information for the PowerPoint, it looks like the presentation will be quite long. The Board's primary focus is on policy and planning for the future of the Y, not necessarily on procedural details. The presentation, though, is full of finer details. Also, the Board meetings are at night and generally don't last more than an hour and a half, to allow people to get home, have dinner and rest after a long workday. There would be other items on the Board meeting agenda, and I feel, ideally, the presentation should last no more than 20 minutes to maintain interest and keep up the energy.

It feels like there is a lot riding on the presentation. It is an important opportunity for the Board to gain a deeper understanding of Activate America and the direction the Y is moving as an organization. It is a chance for our team to educate, inform, motivate and inspire, and for the

Board to "get on board," so to speak, to advance the effort even more. In addition, it is an opportunity for John Smith, our CEO, to continue to gain a greater perspective and understanding of Activate America. Perhaps he will be able to see just how comprehensive it is, as well as the importance of his involvement in leading the effort in order to make it a success.

With all the information in the PowerPoint, I estimate it will be 45 minutes or more. I suggest in the meeting that the presentation be simplified and shortened. It seems like it would lose some of its effectiveness at that length. I want to put some time in reworking the presentation. I keep thinking how this is an important and infrequent opportunity, one that we want to maximize to the fullest. However, Amy decides we will proceed as it is currently put together.

After the discussion concludes regarding the length of the presentation, I hear Eric, the Senior Director of youth programs, ask a couple questions concerning Activate America in its broader sense, while I scribble some notes. Up to this point, Amy generally responded to these types of questions, being the senior leader in the room and the Project Manager. In fact, there were many meetings over the years – management meetings, committee meetings, event planning meetings, fundraiser meetings – when questions were asked and no one seemed to know the answer or wish to give a response. Amy would then step up and respond. She always seemed to have an appropriate answer, and I respected that about her. At the end of Eric's questions, there is silence. The pause is unusually long. I expect to hear Amy's voice in reply. I finally look up from writing, only to find all eyes on me, waiting. For whatever reason, this feels like an important moment, and not one to take lightly. It seems like a matter of leadership. I could answer what was asked, but I do not wish to do so. It feels most appropriate for Amy to provide the answer. Something in my gut is telling me to tread cautiously and with great awareness regarding my multiple roles with the Y. I shift my eyes away from everyone's gaze and respond, perhaps a little too bluntly, "I'm not the leader here." Amy, picking up the ball, clears her throat and begins to answer.

I have a growing sense that John is starting to view me as some sort of threat, and I don't wish to add any ammunition. I've observed how there is often at least one person, generally a director or supervisor, whom John does not take kindly to, particularly if that person does not subscribe to being a Yes Man. Just recently one of the directors quit, and she had expressed to me that she felt forced to leave because of him. She was strong, voiced her perspectives, even when they didn't fall in line with his, and it was clear he wanted her gone. I hadn't challenged his views, necessarily, but he saw me growing stronger through gaining more professional experience. Particularly once I started working as the Activate America Facilitator with Y-USA, he appeared to carry some resentment towards it. Would I be his next target?

A few days later, I sit on my meditation cushion on the floor of my bedroom, positioning myself under the ceiling heating vent in an attempt to get warm. I am shaking like a leaf. I'm not sure if it is the cold or fear or what. I continue to think about the year ahead and contemplate how I might allow myself to grow and expand.

Then all of a sudden a wave of sadness comes over me. It enters my body and comes to rest as a heaviness in my heart. My eyes well up with tears. *Why am I feeling this? Where is it coming from?* It feels like a glimpse into the future, a premonition, an indication that there is mourning ahead regarding the Y. It is a short preview, but for those brief moments, I feel it in its intensity – the heavy heart, grief, sadness, and a sense of deep loss. As quickly as the feeling comes, it dissolves. There is nothing for me to do but take a deep breath.

Things around my work are intense at times, but my time with Tony feels nothing but sweet. Perhaps it is the fluttering, frenzied pheromones inherent in a new relationship, but whenever I'm around him, I just want to tear off all my clothes and press my naked body against his. I find him to be so beautiful, inside and out.

I lie down and snuggle next to him one evening and rest my head on his shoulder. He encircles me with his arm. From this vantage point, I admire his bare chest and gently caress his chest hairs, which I determine to be perfectly formed. They are not overly abundant, and by no means are they course or wiry. Rather, they are soft, like the feathers of a baby bird. They are predominantly brown with just a few gray near the neckline. I trace their growth pattern with my fingers, lightly brushing up and over his pectoral muscles, then down the center line, following the narrow path of perfect hairs toward his belly. About 3 inches above his navel, the hairs form a subtle spiral. The hairs from below grow upward while the hairs from above grow downward, and they meet, circling one another, a sweet swirl.

I shift my gaze to the whiskers on his face and begin petting those. I brush my fingers gently across his cheeks and chin as he looks at me with those blue eyes and perfectly-curved, soft, full, kissable lips. As our relationship grows, Tony reveals himself to be intelligent and loving, logical and intuitive, balanced in his own right. I appreciate how we both enjoy nature and how yoga is part of our lives. I also feel we walk the same path in life, which boils down to simply being kind. Also, when we are intimate, I love the non-verbal, natural, intuitive reading of each other's body, of each other's energy, riding the waves together, sharing love. He is a beautiful gem.

February is when the Activate America presentation with the Board takes place. As evening falls, each member of the Activate America Team takes his or her portion of the presentation. Amy facilitates the process, and we present our material. The clock ticks by, 20 minutes, 30 minutes … 40 minutes… 45… 50… I watch as John loses interest early in the presentation. He then gets fidgety and repeatedly looks at the clock, then looks around at the Board members. I rush through my portion a little, reading his body language. Some Board members get up to leave the meeting, stating they have to go. Some other Board members even fall asleep. It is the end of a long meeting at the end of a long Monday. When it comes to a close and the lights flick on, those who remain scramble to get out the door. Amanda Bennett, the Board Chair, looks to be the only member who is surprised at everyone, and she states, "Oh, I was finding it really interesting."

As Board members are shuffling and gathering up their things, John says, "Yeah, the Rotary makes us do this kind of thing once a year, too." He continues, "Probably the reason you haven't heard me talk much about Activate America is because it's a culture change, it's subtle…. But we've seen how it's not a program." It seems like his statement is more for himself than for the Board. It is apparent that he at last grasps how Activate America is not simply a new wellness program but is, indeed, part of a larger culture change.

I'm not sure that a culture change is subtle, however. There was one slide included in the PowerPoint that had a quote from Paul Stevens, President & CEO of Y-USA. It read, "We are changing the DNA of the YMCA." That's definitely not subtle. When this slide appeared, I saw John squint and get a closer look, appearing a little surprised to see it. Indeed, this change effort was not just coming from Amy or me or anyone else on the Activate America Team at our Y. It was coming from the top.

I feel some disappointment over the presentation. I wonder if we had lost *the* opportunity for John and the Board to be inspired and compelled into action. So many individuals had tuned out. The only action they seemed compelled to do was get out the door as quickly as possible. Up to this point, I felt John lacked clear understanding regarding what Activate America was all about. Though he was impatient and a bit irritated through the presentation, it seemed to be at least somewhat eye-opening for him, revealing the extensiveness of the culture change that was already in motion. Perhaps that was enough for now.

A couple days later, I decide to talk with John about the presentation to get his thoughts. I let him know I had put together the PowerPoint and also felt it could have been more effective. He agrees how it could have been more effective, and we talk about a couple ways it could have been so.

I do not intend to be disrespectful towards Amy or to make myself appear better in any way, but I can tell John mistakenly perceives my words that way. This is simply about a presentation and an opportunity to engage the Board in an important initiative.

"So this isn't insubordination," John says, with a tone that tells me he is looking for something, searching, "this is in the best interests of the Y."

There's that word. I think of previous directors who no longer work for the Y and wonder if the word "insubordination" exited John's lips in conversation with them. I am not disobeying authority or being "rebellious" or any other adjective that makes up the definition of insubordination. I deeply respect and admire Amy as a person and for all she does for the Y. She is an excellent supervisor, leader and role model to many.

"Yes, this is in the best interests of the Y," I confirm. In a way, I feel I *am* the Y. I am a representative of YMCA of the USA to Y's across the country. I am also passionate and dedicated to my work at the Winowa County YMCA. Yes, of course this is about the Y. It isn't about any individuals; it's bigger than that. It's a movement, and I hope there are further opportunities in which I might help our Y, and others, move forward.

"You want an opportunity to...... shine," John then says. I pause. *What an interesting choice of words.* I contemplate the consequences of my response. If I say no, would I not be diminishing myself? I am reminded of the Marianne Williamson quote: "There is nothing enlightened about shrinking so that other people won't feel insecure around you. We are all meant to shine..."

"Yes," I reply.

"Well, everybody's stayin' where they're stayin'," John concludes.

I am a little confused by his remark. It is not about position or power. I have no desire to take over Amy's or anyone else's job responsibilities. I *do* desire the opportunity to be myself, however, to shine, as it were. But after working under John Smith's leadership for 9 years, I understand the unspoken rule that shining is not allowed.

Chapter 8

It's About Change

If you do not change direction,
you may end up where you are heading.
— Lao-Tzu

*J*teach a yoga class later that evening. In yoga, teaching, I feel 100% me. There is no pressure to remain small or keep quiet so others won't feel insecure. There is no need to hide my light. I can bring all of me to the table, or to the mat, as it were. In doing so, I hope to inspire and encourage others to let their light shine.

After class, I head over to Tony's house, share in conversation with him, then slip into his hot tub. Tony joins me in the hot tub for a while then goes into the house, providing me the time and space to reflect on recent events.

I think about how I wish the Y were a democracy in which staff could vote and elect their leader. I believe Amy would make a much better CEO than John. I would nominate her. I think the majority would vote for her as well. She is a passionate and caring individual who leads by example. She works hard, is humble and embodies the core values of the Y. She has a big heart and demonstrates integrity. I have no doubt she would put the needs of the organization and community ahead of any self-serving interests.

John stops into my office and says to me one day, "It's not my job to care about the staff." I sometimes wonder if he hears himself. This person, who cares so little, stands at the helm of a human service organization. Even if one wants to look at it from a purely business perspective, staff are the first point of contact for potential members and existing members and program participants, which make up the bread and butter of the Y. Staff members are the ones who talk about the Y the most out in the community, with family, friends, sharing about both their positive experiences and, even more so, negative ones. These very same staff members are also frequent volunteers and annual donors, giving back to the organization. The staff are what keep the Y operating.

But even more so, on a strictly human level, why not simply care? It feels good personally, and it does good for others. It serves the cause. Caring builds people up, increases their well-being and helps create a more caring, responsible community.

"I wish you were in that position," I say to Amy at one of our meetings, feeling frustrated. I think about all the complaints I've heard about John over the years, and my personal experiences with him. Amy has heard innumerable complaints about him, also, during her many years at the Y. People talk. People especially talk about things that bother them, and John is bothersome.

Over the past few months, Amy has shared with me some accounts of her personal experiences with John. I have been a confidante for her, as she has been for me.

"I feel the need to go to the Board Chair," I say to her. "It feels important that the Board knows John is not always as he seems. He plays one face to them while revealing another, less savory face, to the rest of us. It seems the Board should at least be informed of the situation, and they can proceed as they see fit."

Amy likes to play devil's advocate, as she puts it. She will often take this position to try to unearth more options and gain understanding from multiple sides of an issue. This time, though, she seems to be playing devil's advocate out of fear. With my statement of going to the Board Chair, I see fear well up in her body. She abruptly breaks eye contact, spins her chair around to the side to face her computer, and closes off. I think I can see her hands shaking as they rest on her keyboard.

"I need time to digest this," she replies. "I mean, you're talking about a person's standard of living." I'm not sure who she is referring to – her own, mine or John's. I know I am one at great risk for loss, likely the greatest risk. I respect Amy's need to think it over more fully, and we wrap up the meeting.

I am reminded of an article from the *Harvard Business Review* that was given to all the Activate America Facilitators to read in Chicago. The article is called "Managing Yourself: A Survival Guide for Leaders," by Ronald A. Heifetz and Marty Linsky. In the opening paragraph it brings attention to "people spearheading significant change initiatives in their organizations who have suddenly found themselves out of a job." It says, "Let's face it, to lead is to live dangerously" and talks about how there is a dark side to leading change: "the inevitable attempts to take you out of the game." The article continues to state how risks are especially high because change that truly transforms an organization requires that people give up familiar ways of doing things, daily habits and ways of thinking. Individuals often want to stay in their comfort zones, and they attempt to undercut the change agent in one way or another, attacking him or her rather than addressing the initiative.

"I have a prediction!" Tony announces one evening as we discuss dinner options. I'm listening. "In the next 6 months, you'll either be fired, you'll quit, or you'll be CEO," he says.

"I don't want to be CEO," I tell him. "If anything, I want Amy to be. But that's not even the point. It's about change."

As the calendar turns to March and the new, green buds sprout on the apple trees, my 2010 Seed of Intention finally sticks. As soon as the word arises in my awareness, I know it is the one: blossoming. It is the energy of spring, and it is to be a year of continued opening.

Blossoming is a specific type of growth. It is not the growth pattern of vines in a forest that wind their way upward to reach the sun. It is not the growth pattern of roots that burrow down, pushing their way through soil, into the coolness, branching and anchoring. Blossoming is an unfolding, a growth that expands and opens outwardly. It is revealing. It is the growth pattern of a flower.

Flowers do not begin as flowers. The tight, compact bud forms, and all that is inside is hidden. The combination of sun, rain, earth and air feeds life. When the conditions are conducive to supporting life, the bud cannot do anything *but* blossom. This is its natural course. When nothing prevents its innate tendency, it opens. The soft petals reveal themselves. They reveal their color, shape, texture. Lastly, the center is revealed, the hub from which this beauty sprang forth.

I don't know how this year of blossoming will express, what forms it will take, but I feel it on a deep level, on an energetic and soul level. I have no doubt blossoming will occur.

I crawl out of bed. It is still cool in the morning, but the sun is shining brightly, which to me makes the day feel a little more special. It is the day to meet the booksellers. At 3 o'clock, I have an appointment scheduled with a man named Robert, the manager of Westside Books, a local bookstore chain. I wear my khaki, brushed cotton hiking pants, which can be rolled up and buckled to make capris, my dark blue, form-fitting, cotton t-shirt that I picked up at the San Francisco Yoga Journal Conference earlier in the year, and my blue Teva sandals. Apparently, I am going for the active, casual look.

I park my car and walk through the parking lot, taking several deep breaths, feeling nervous about this next step. I trot down the concrete steps, walk across a narrow street, through the double-doors at the back entrance of Westside Books, to the set of wooden steps that create a pleasant, earthy, clomping noise as I walk down them, and into the wonderful smell of books. Books, books everywhere. I can visualize my book resting on the shelves, nestled with all the others, feeling at home here.

I have been in this store a number of times before. It's the largest, most comprehensive bookstore in the small town of Sweethaven, where I live. But now, my relationship with this bookstore is shifting. I am no longer using it as a shortcut to get to the shops on Main Street or perusing books as a customer. I am here with the intention to become one of the authors whose books occupy the shelves.

Robert and I sit down at a small, wooden table with two matching wooden chairs situated in the Travel section. He is a petite man, a couple inches shorter than I, somewhere in his 40s or early 50s, dressed in business casual wear with closely-cropped gray and brown hair, kind eyes and small, wire-rimmed glasses. He looks like he is in his element.

After our friendly introductions, I proceed to tell Robert how I live in Sweethaven and wrote a book that was recently published. "I feel it may help a lot of people," I say. "I believe many will be able to relate to it in some way." He asks me what kind of book it is, and I explain that *Journey to One* is a memoir and hand him a copy. He gazes at the front cover, then turns it over and reads the back.

I ask him what he looks for in a book that he would sell in the store. "Content," Robert begins, "but also packaging. Obviously the cover has to catch someone's attention before they even pick it up to read the back." He flips through the pages then closes it again. "It was very smart to do the cover this way. The image you chose has so many levels of meaning. I would buy the book on the cover alone," he says.

"Thank you," is all I can say, taking a dry swallow. I am realizing now that he likes it and may include it here on the shelves. *Relax, breathe*, I remind myself.

He says he would like to have it in the psychology/self-help section, and also spirituality. I ask about his thoughts on displaying it in the New Nonfiction section located in the center isle of the store, where all the new books are prominently displayed. It's also the area of the store where everyone passes, serious customers and short-cutters alike. "Yes," Robert says as he nods his head, "and we have a local authors section, but I feel it deserves more exposure. I would like to set up a display on a table with one copy upright so people can see it."

"Thank you," I say again. I couldn't have asked for a more positive, first bookseller meeting experience. I feel so much gratitude... and relief. Robert lets me know they have Saturday afternoons available so that authors can do book signings. "Yes, I would be interested in that, very much," I say to him.

"Great!" he says, with a smile. "You should go to other stores. You can use my name if you like." No doubt his experience makes him a respected opinion in the area. "I suggest putting it in the same section as *Eat, Pray, Love* and *Dharma Punx*."

All in all, we talk for about 45-50 minutes. This man is so kind and genuine. He takes time to mentor me, share ideas and suggestions. I feel heard, and I feel seen. He asks for 10 copies for the store to get started, and we finalize the arrangement by speaking about terms, payment arrangements and signing the contract.

I head to my car to retrieve the copies. I clomp my way back up the wooden steps, through the double-doors, across the narrow street, up the concrete steps, and across the parking lot with the biggest smile on my face!

After this first meeting, I feel a little more confident and relaxed. Having given Robert 10 copies of my book, I decide to walk down the street a couple blocks to a smaller, local bookstore that carries a lot of

New Age and spiritual titles. While waiting at a stoplight to cross the street, I text Tony, "You'll never guess what just happened!"

He texts back, "Your CEO got fired?"

I laugh. "No, even better," I text. Then I decide texting just will not do and dial his number. I proceed to tell him about my meeting with Robert.

"That's awesome!" he exclaims. I so love and appreciate his support.

I arrive at the next bookstore and talk with one of the owners for about 5 minutes. While we speak, I glace at some of the gift items on the counter – some beaded bracelets, small figurines, and a selection of bumper stickers. The bumper sticker in front consists of a plain white background with red lettering that reads, "Just love *everyone*." I feel a warmth in my heart, and I smile. The owner agrees to take a few copies, and I sign my second contract of the day.

I consider my next steps with the Y, about possibly talking with the Board Chair, and I notice my body is shaking. I take a few moments to just tune in and experience what is happening. It is, without a doubt, fear. What do I do with this fear? What do I *choose* to do? I can choose to simply feel it and let it move through me, a wave of emotion, like any other. Unlike some emotions, like sadness or anger, fear has a tendency to restrict movement, hold a person back. I am quite familiar with fear, and I've experienced time and again how when I've allowed myself to just *feel* it, rather than try to push it down or run away from it, it tends to go away rather quickly. It was just a couple days ago that I felt fear around speaking with the booksellers, but I continued forward despite the fear. The fear soon dissipated and I experienced positive results.

Over the last few years, fear has been an indicator for me, like a big, flashing arrow pointing me in the direction I need to go. Each time I experience that nervousness over potential next steps, I know I'm on the right track for greater personal growth. I've come to welcome it. Fear can limit us from taking bold leaps, but it certainly doesn't have to. Moving forward despite the fear has allowed me to live more fully and often enjoy incredibly meaningful experiences.

There are times when I'm around John and I simply accept him for who he is, for where he is on his life path. We're all just making the journey. I know how we may have our own insecurities and how these can play out in our lives through attempts to control or overpower others.

I am reminded of a few weeks ago when John came into my office. I do not recall the reason he came in, but he made a point to say, *"I'm* at the top of the pyramid, the chart." He was referring to the organizational chart that lists all the Y job positions in pyramid form. *Actually, you're not at the top, the Board is,* I thought to myself. The organizational chart was even in the process of being updated. I'm not sure who initiated the updating, but a bubble was being added at the top, above the bubble that said "CEO," that read "Board of Directors." As John spoke his words, I heard a little boy. I felt transported in time, and I saw him at age 6 or 7, standing tall on the playground with arms akimbo, shouting to all those around him, *"I'm* king of the mountain!"

By April, I see Amy continuing to gain a greater understanding of the culture change herself. In the early months, and even years, of Activate America, it was difficult to see the full breadth of the work. By now, I notice Amy has a broader perspective about Activate America, about what the Y as a larger organization is doing, and about how John's behavior and actions are not beneficial. We speak openly about it at our weekly meeting. She shares with me how she overheard John "screaming at the top of his lungs" while talking to Ellen in her office the previous day. Ellen's office shares a wall with Amy's.

Amy also speaks about how the recent Staff Satisfaction Survey "should have been a red flag" for the Board. I chose to not complete and return the staff survey that was mailed to me. I decided to remain the silent observer. I had reviewed the complete results of the survey and saw there were comments stating John is a "power hungry leader" and "lacks the core values of the organization." Yes, it might have been a red flag except for the fact that John did not reveal to the Board the part of the survey containing negative staff comments about him. When the results were being presented to the Board, he conveniently skipped over that portion.

Amy shares with me another instance where she feels John deliberately withheld information in a delicate legal matter and lied in an attempt to cover his tracks. "How can these things be red flags for the Board if the Board doesn't know about them?" I ask her. Red flags are not always seen without someone pointing to them, particularly if the person works hard to keep the red flags under wraps. "Someone has to bring it to their attention," I say.

Later Amy shares with me how John yelled and screamed in her office, just a week after ranting in the office next door. "Normally, I don't allow it to affect me so bad, but this time it really got to me. It's affected me for days. I told my husband and he said, 'Same ol', same ol'. He's right. That's how John has been for a long time."

I can see how shaken and upset Amy is over John's behavior. I feel sad for her, and frustrated at the situation. I know the uncomfortable feeling of John's angry outbursts. I also know the discomfort and awkwardness a person feels when one walks by a closed office door and hears John yelling. What do the members think when they walk by? What do the staff think? What kind of environment is being created? It is definitely not one that builds others up or supports well-being. How long are we directors willing to put up with it? I figure the least I can do is make note of the two recent incidences of John screaming in the offices, documentation.

Through the work of Activate America, a staff interviewing process recently got underway. It is a formalized process designed to provide staff the opportunity to share open, honest, anonymous feedback regarding their work. A few leadership staff members, including myself, were chosen to be interviewers. Working in teams of 2, one person interviews, providing a warm, non-judgmental atmosphere, and the other takes detailed notes. Keeping strict anonymity, the results are then shared with the Activate America team and filed. At this time, it is still rather early in the interview process, but it is already becoming apparent that this is a necessary and beneficial step for our Y. Those interviewed to date seem relieved to be able to share their experiences, positive and negative, and express appreciation at the opportunity to be heard.

I start considering what it would be like if *all* the directors and managers had the opportunity to openly and anonymously share their experiences of work at the Y through an interview process. Currently, the senior leaders and management team, those who work closely with John, have not had that chance. I think that's where it would really get interesting. I feel our Y's need for positive change would become even more apparent.

One staff person whom I had interviewed earlier made mention of John. This person believed the sentiments she shared with us regarding him were equivalent to insubordination. "I know that's insubordination. I know it is, but it's the truth," she said. There's that word again.

The evening following that interview, I decided to look up "insubordination" in the dictionary, curious as to what it specifically stated. I blew the dust off my American Century Dictionary, circa 1995. It is the dictionary I bought when I first started college. I flipped through the yellowed pages and read the definition. "Disobedient, rebellious, noncompliance." *That's all, really?* Surely there had to be more to it.

No, of course the dictionary didn't go into detail about the myriad valid reasons *why* someone or a group of someones would desire to be disobedient, or do things differently from the mainstream. If people had not been disobedient, our country would never have been founded. We'd never have had the Civil Rights Movement, or the fight for equality in its many forms – race, gender, those with disabilities, gays. We would never evolve. We would never have forward movement without a little rebellion here and there.

I sit with Amy in our weekly meeting. We are deep in discussion. "Have you ever envisioned yourself leading this organization, seen yourself as the CEO?" I ask her. Amy's immediate response is how she can't see herself sitting around the table with all those older men. I believe she is referencing the Board meetings. She also talks about juggling responsibilities as a mom. "I have a hard time seeing myself going to Rotary meetings and making those connections, as John has done."

"You've made quite a few important connections with Kaiser and several other health-related organizations in the area. That is the direction the Y is heading," I say. "How you would be in that role might look different from how John is in that role."

"That's true," Amy replies, "and I made those connections on my own. It wasn't John. I don't know, if the position came available, maybe I'd step into that role, at least in the interim. Then maybe I would find I enjoyed it and wish to remain in it," she concludes.

My intention with this questioning is simply to help open Amy to possibility. I hope to, in some small way, nurture her growth and help Amy recognize her potential as a Y leader.

I then tell Amy how I am still feeling drawn to meet with Amanda Bennett, the Board Chair. It has been a few weeks since I first mentioned it to her. I figure enough time has passed for her to get accustomed to the idea. "It feels like the right thing to do," I say to her. I want to remain completely honest and transparent about my next step.

With concern, she asks, "Do you realize there could be some... (she searches for the word) ...consequences to all this? It may not end up well... for *you*. It may not end up looking like how you want it to."

"We're all responsible for our own actions, our own choices," I reply. I am aware of the potential costs.

I ask Amy if I have her support, not feeling I need it, but wondering if she will provide it. She is extremely careful with her answer, not saying she supports it, not saying she doesn't support it. But she says, "I feel there must be another way to somehow let Amanda know or alert her to conduct some deeper investigation, whether it's having interviews with the directors, like you mentioned, or whatever."

"How is Amanda going to have this brought to her attention without someone taking the initiative to talk with her? How else will she know?" I ask. I know Amy doesn't feel comfortable taking that step. "This seems like the only way for the Board to gain awareness of John's behavior."

I feel ready for action, ready for change. It feels time. It feels long past time.

As our meeting comes to a close, I gather my things, rise out of my chair and walk the few steps to open the door. Just as I had done hundreds of times over the last few years, I hold the heavy wooden door open and use my foot to position the doorstop in place. In previous meetings, this was the moment for the friendly, "See ya later," or similar comment, as we transitioned out of our discussion back into the tasks of serving the members, answering emails, or getting ready for the next meeting. Today is not the day for a simple, "See ya later."

"What do you think is going to happen?" Amy starts. "I mean, how do you *envision* this all turning out?"

I look at her for a few moments, searching for the vision, searching for the words. I shake my head and reply, "I don't know how this is going to end."

Chapter 9

No Turning Back

*N*ow is the time.

This step will set wheels in motion. I stand in the kitchen before leaving for work. My heart races. I dial the number to Amanda Bennett's office. Her receptionist answers and lets me know she's not currently in the office. I say I have her cell number and will just try her there. Her voicemail picks up. I leave Amanda a message stating I am interested in meeting for lunch.

A few days later, near the end of April, Amanda and I meet at a restaurant down the street from the Y. I feel a strong desire to bring my voice recorder so the conversation can be documented. However, as this is the first time I'm meeting with Amanda one on one, I figure it might be rather awkward to do so.

I have gotten to know Amanda as a Board member over the previous couple years. I recall chatting with her and her husband at length at a Y leaders' conference held at a beautiful winery in Calistoga. Over dinner and glasses of wine, we discussed the Y, philosophy, writing and a number of other topics. Amanda has a daughter just a bit younger than I. I observed Amanda and her husband to be well educated, down-to-earth and pleasant conversationalists. She's had a long history with the Y, with her daughter being involved in activities as a child, and she communicated her fondness for the organization on more than one occasion. I feel I got a good sense of who she is as a person at that event. Since the dinner, my interactions with Amanda have mostly been a simple, "Hello, how are you?" at the Board meetings or fundraising events.

For our lunch meeting, I bring my typed outline of talking points to ensure I cover everything I want to say. At the top of the outline, I have a quote by Maggie Kuhn to remind myself: "Speak your mind – even if your voice shakes."

My voice doesn't shake. The discussion proceeds very well. I inform her of my dual role with the Y. I speak about the number of exciting changes taking place in the Y world – the organizational change effort, which includes Activate America, as well as an upcoming brand revitalization and unveiling of a new Y logo, which will take place at the General Assembly in July.

I let Amanda know that I met with another Board member last October. I share with her my concerns about John, his yelling and screaming at directors, his anger issues and other matters. I let her know there are negative aspects of John's behavior that he doesn't reveal to the Board. It seems his past performance reviews were primarily based on the budget's bottom line, and may not have covered other important areas of performance.

I share how there have been numerous complaints about John over the years and how people have stated they left because of him. "I know of at least a couple other directors, maybe three, who have gone to members of the Board with complaints," I say.

"Has anyone ever gone to the Board Chair?" Amanda asks.

"Not to my knowledge, no," I reply.

I ask if she might consider digging deeper into John's behavior, to investigate, even to simply talk with Amy, as Amy has worked most closely with him. I explain to her the process of the staff interviews we have been conducting. "Maybe there could be something similar offered to the directors," I suggest, "an avenue for them to share about their experiences in a confidential manner."

"Seems like we should get a move on things fairly quickly," Amanda says. She knows she has the responsibility of conducting John's performance review. Reviews are usually conducted in June prior to the end of the fiscal year. She extends an invitation to any other manager who wishes to meet with her to share his or her experiences and perspective. I share with Amanda how those who have expressed concerns regarding John no longer have a job at the Y. I tell her there is a climate of fear, but that I will pass along her invitation.

The following day I talk briefly with Amy and let her know I met with Amanda. She does not appear surprised, but I can see she is in deep thought about what her next step is to be. I don't know if she fully grasps yet that I'm doing this for her, for all the staff, and to help move the Y forward in this organizational change effort, one step at a time.

I ask Amy if I can schedule a meeting with her and another Senior Director, Eric. I plan to extend Amanda's invitation to these two individuals first. Amy is Eric's supervisor, as well, and she asks him if he wants to get involved. Eric lets her know he is interested in joining the meeting.

The butterflies in my stomach are fluttering around like mad prior to this meeting. I walk into Amy's office. She is sitting at her desk looking very serious with writing pad in front of her and pen in hand. *Is this how it's going to be? No more smiles?* It doesn't seem to me that talking to the Board should be cause for such concern. I recall John even encouraging us to build a relationship with members of the Board. It's part of our role as directors. I work with members of the Board on a regular basis in committee meetings and during special events. I chat with them when they come in for their workout or when they attend a fundraiser dinner or attend a Key Leaders' Conference. But now it's perceived differently.

Eric sits, more relaxed than I, in one of the two chairs across from Amy's desk. I sit down in the other. My mouth is dry. I am more nervous about talking with Amy right now than I was talking with Amanda.

I can hardly find words, and the words I do find seem to come out choppy and clunky with my tongue stuck to the roof of my mouth. "Ummmm, I invited you to meet because I feel you two have good hearts and...." I hear myself beginning to ramble. I state how I met with Amanda, my reasons for doing so, and how I shared some concerns with her about John. Eric, being the excellent listener that he is, helps translate, taking my uhhs and ums and skillfully reflecting my statements, while Amy scribbles away on her pad. I find his presence to be a comfort. I feel he accurately understands my actions and helps smooth out the pathway of communication between Amy and me. He is also a witness to what is transpiring. I extend to the both of them Amanda's invitation. Eric asks if the conversation with Amanda would be confidential, and I reply yes.

"What do you hope to accomplish?" Amy asks.

"I don't know, maybe John will have a wake-up call and change his behavior," I reply. "Maybe the Board will undergo a more extensive review of him." I think about it some more. "To create positive change." Actually, I have already accomplished something. If nothing else, I have raised awareness. That is where change begins.

I continue, "None of this has been easy. Throughout this process, I've asked myself several times, 'Do I really need to do this? Do I take this next step?' I've listened to my heart for the answer, and time and time again it has said 'yes.' It's the right thing to do."

"It's the right thing for *you*," Amy says, looking at me expectantly.

"It's the right thing to do," I say again.

"For *you*," she repeats.

"Okay, I guess it's the right thing to do for *me*," I acquiesce. I'm not sure where her insistence is coming from, other than to protect herself. It sure feels like the right thing to do in general, for staff morale, for the community, for the change effort, for the Y movement.

After this meeting concludes, Eric asks if he can speak with me privately outside. We go outside and sit at the picnic bench in front of the pool windows. I don't have a lot left to say, but Eric does.

I've always enjoyed working with Eric. We have co-led workshops, and I find he brings a natural comfort and light-heartedness to the trainings. We've communicated well in our roles, and I find him to be gentle, sincere, funny and big-hearted.

Just a few days prior, Eric came into my office and said to me, "I haven't read your book yet, but even so, I can tell you are very strong."

I smiled. "We are *all* strong," I replied, "We just don't always realize it."

As I gaze ahead at the children splashing in the pool, he says, "I know why you're doing this. You're like a heroine. I've always had a lot of respect for you, but this takes it to another level. You're like a superhero!" I smile again. I don't know about superhero. "You're doing this for the greater good," he continues.

I nod and smile again, "Yes, it's for the greater good," I agree.

He proceeds to tell me how he has often thought about talking to the Board and sharing some of his experiences. He says, "I have something I keep in my back pocket, something involving John, if anything happened. That way, I can go out in a blaze of glory." As he continues to share, I understand he is referencing some financial matter, another "shady" arrangement perhaps. "But maybe what you're doing will allow me to share it earlier," he concludes. Eric thanks me for letting him be a part of it, for including him. I am reminded again why it feels like the right thing to do.

If we're lucky, we have 80-90 years on this planet. Or, we may be diagnosed with cancer next week and have 6 months to a year to live. Or we may be in a car accident tomorrow and pass from this life. How do we choose to spend our time? How do we choose to interact and communicate with others? Do we use our words to build up, or do we use them to tear down? What kind of difference can we make in the time we are given? What good can we do?

I'm reminded of some sobering words that Steve Jobs shared during a Stanford commencement speech in 2005. "Remembering that I'll be dead soon is the most important tool I've ever encountered to help me make the big choices in life. Because almost everything — all external expectations, all pride, all fear of embarrassment or failure — these things just fall away in the face of death, leaving only what is truly important. Remembering that you are going to die is the best way I know to avoid the trap of thinking you have something to lose. You are already naked. There is no reason not to follow your heart."

The following morning I call Jennifer Martin, the woman I report to at Y-USA. "I want to keep you in the loop with what is going on at my local Y," I tell her. I let her know I went to the Board with concerns about John's behavior and that I might get fired.

After listening, Jennifer says, "We support you." It feels so refreshing to hear those three simple words. "I admire you for following your conscience," she continues, "and taking steps to improve the organization for all those you work with, despite the possible consequences.

"I like telling the story of how you became an Activate America Facilitator," Jennifer continues. "It goes to show if people have a passion for this work, to make a positive change, look what can happen. If we had more people like that, willing to take those big steps, just think what kind of progress we could be making."

The YMCA General Assembly is the largest conference hosted by Y-USA for the purpose of connecting, educating and inspiring Y staff and volunteers. Attendees include senior leadership, board volunteers and emerging Y leaders. The General Assembly is an opportunity to network with colleagues from across the country, deepen one's connection to the Y cause and get a first-hand look at where the Y is headed. Professional and leadership development sessions are offered for furthering one's education and career. Past assemblies have featured prominent, nationally-recognized speakers and celebrities, in addition to speakers from the team at Y-USA. It is held every 3 years, and this year it is scheduled to be in Salt Lake City, Utah in July.

I have not yet been to a General Assembly, and I am particularly interested in attending this one. The leaders at Y-USA are encouraging all of us Activate America Facilitators to attend, as there is a special gathering planned for Ys involved with Activate America. Paul Stevens, CEO of Y-USA, and his leadership team will also be talking about the organizational changes taking place and unveiling the new Y logo, branding, and governance information. Of all the General Assemblies to attend, this one of 2010 seems to be most significant, as it highlights the work we've been doing and speaks to the transformation that is taking place across the organization.

No one at our Y had yet brought up the topic of the upcoming conference, so I talk with John about it, informing him about the significance of this one in particular. I remind him about the unveiling of the new logo and such. In addition to my involvement with Activate America, as the Director of Membership & Communications, who is responsible for communicating to the members and producing key marketing materials, it seems important and beneficial for our Y that I be there. "I worked for the Y 19 years before getting to go to a General Assembly," he begins. I'm beginning to get a sense for how this conversation is going to go. "I found it to be kind of like... a revival. You'd probably like it," he says. I've been with the Y almost 10 years, and in national staff trainings and events, there is excitement, passion, even a warm-fuzzy feeling, but I've never thought they were like an evangelical revival. Why John thinks I would like a revival, I'm not sure either. I enjoy positive people, I will say that. But John can have his perspective.

I continue to talk with him, and he says it would be nice to have some representation from our Y present at that assembly. "Yeah, okay, that's fine. We'll just deduct it from next year's budget," John concludes. I let him know I am excited and that I plan to talk with Amy about it, too, prior to sending in my registration. I mention to John that maybe she and others would like to also attend.

"John says he did not approve you going to the General Assembly," Amy says to me a couple days later, almost apologetically. There are a number of times over the years when I wish I had recorded conversations with John, and this was yet another one. For a while, I even kept my digital recorder in my desk, tempted, oh so tempted, to turn it on quietly, without his knowing, to capture his words. But I didn't.

"Well, he did say I could go, but it's kind of a moot point now, isn't it?" I reply. Now it comes down to he said, she said, and Amy is going to have to follow what John says directly to her. *We must be getting close now, for this is what happens towards the end.*

"I will be attending," Amy states matter-of-factly, along with so and so. I am glad she and others will be attending this important event, but I feel disheartened at not being able to go myself. It feels like an uncomfortable blow to the belly. The air is thick and heavy, and I feel an intense need to breathe, to have space to breathe deeply… and expand.

Shortly thereafter, I am facilitating a Membership & PE Committee meeting. As the Membership Director, I am designated to oversee this committee, and one of the Board members acts as the official representative for the committee, reporting pertinent information to the full Board of Directors. The group is also made up of other members of the management team, a second Board member, and a couple other volunteers.

Amy and I had previously discussed ways we might revitalize the work of this committee. The committee meetings seemed to have gotten in a bit of a rut and needed some energy to sustain forward momentum. I proposed a couple ideas. She liked them, and we thought we'd give it a try.

At the committee meeting, I initiate a general brainstorming session as planned and make notes on some flip chart paper. At one point I see the older gentleman, in his 80s, who is on the Board lean over to the other Board member whom I've observed to have a close working relationship with John Smith. He leans over and asks her, "Why are we doing this?"

I decide to kindly respond to his question, despite it not being directed straight to me. "It's nice from time to time to evaluate the work of the committee to ensure we are continuing to meet the needs of our members and individuals in our community."

I then see the other Board member lean back over to him and respond, "This is what happens when someone gets to be too big." She seems to be referring to me. *Did she really just say that... and within earshot of me?* Sometimes people wish others to "stay in their place." Only this *is* my place. It appears growth is not acceptable past a certain point. It gets scary for those in positions of power.

I decide to ignore her comment and carry on with the brainstorming discussion. I remind myself that this work is a marathon, not a sprint. However, it feels increasingly uncomfortable, this restriction of growth.

Amy and I meet once again for our regular weekly meeting. At the end of the meeting, she nervously tells me how she has thought a lot since we met, the 3 of us, referring to her, Eric and me. "I feel I may have been an enabler," she states.

"That's interesting you use the term 'enabler'," I reflect. There is a sense that she is like a co-dependent wife to an alcoholic husband. In some ways, the Y has mirrored the structure of a traditional, and at times dysfunctional, family. John has been the husband and man in charge. Amy has taken on the role of dutiful wife who works hard and often has to clean up after John in order to keep the household, or organization, running smoothly. Perhaps there's an aunt or uncle in the mix, a grandmother here and there, and many, many children. There are more severe levels of dysfunction in relationships for sure, whether it is in a work or home environment, but there are also healthier ways of relating. It takes humility to recognize one's enabling behavior, and I respect Amy for saying it out loud.

"It's almost like a marriage," Amy continues, echoing my thoughts. It is apparent she has been contemplating the situation and coming to some realizations. "In my 18 years here," she says, "I've probably heard the most complaints about John out of anyone!" She has heard so much, yet has not taken action to try to change it, which then perpetuates the behavior.

"I agree with your sentiments," Amy states, "but I don't necessarily agree with your approach. I just think there has to be another way." I'm open to hearing other options. I have already spoken with Amanda, though, setting the wheels in motion. There's no turning back. I can only go forward from here.

"So I want to let you know of my next steps," she says. "I will call Amanda and let her know that I will not accept her invitation to meet with her, and that I don't agree with your approach. Then I will talk with John." Amy looks nervous and fidgety. "I don't know exactly what I'm going to say, but I'll speak with him about his style and how his behavior affects morale, etc."

I feel this goes beyond "style" and extends into inappropriate behavior and questionable business practices that deserve further review by the Board. "I do not intend to tell John you spoke with Amanda. I don't intend to throw you under the bus, so to speak, but we'll see how the conversation goes," Amy concludes.

"Well, I appreciate you choosing to share your next steps. I know you don't have to, and if you end up telling him, that's fine," I say. "I wouldn't want you to try to hide anything. He's probably going to ask what's going on. You'll be coming to him to talk about his behavior, and he'll want to know where it's coming from."

Amy asks that I do not speak about my going to Amanda to any of the other managers. I respect her wishes and agree. I believe she wants to keep as few people involved as possible while we sort it all out.

Amanda and I stay in communication via email the days following our lunch meeting. I keep her informed of my talk with Amy and Eric. I also mail her a copy of a new resource put out by Y-USA called the "Leadership Competency Development Guide." She thought it might be helpful to have some general information to use in her review of John.

I think on my intention of "blossoming" for the year. If there is to be outward growth, there must be no restrictions. I myself, and the environment, must *allow* for blossoming.

Chapter 10

Jaguar in Me

*A*my enters my office, nervous and flushed. She shares with me that she talked with John. I can already tell by her behavior that she told him that I spoke with the Board, as I guessed would be the case. She proceeds to tell me how she talked to him about how his behavior affects morale. She speaks for a couple minutes then says, "There was no way around it. He asked if you had gone to the Board. I stated to him that you had spoken with Amanda."

"It feels like the conversation went pretty well. He was calm," Amy continues. "John asked me what you had said to Amanda, and I told him he should speak directly to you, to hear it from your own mouth. I told him I didn't want to be in the middle."

This is a time of a lot of reflection for me. During the evening in the quiet of my home, I take stock of my situation. There is a strong possibility I will lose my job, though it seems incredibly inappropriate that that would happen. I'm facing the possible loss of my income, career, retirement plan, health insurance... I contemplate at what standard I'm willing to live.

I weigh the costs and benefits of no longer working at the local Y. The costs are primarily financial. Perhaps it might seem the career I've worked so hard at the last few years is jeopardized as well, but perhaps not. I feel that I would still have a position with Y-USA. On paper, the contract for my role as Activate America Facilitator is between Y-USA and the Winowa County Y, though Jennifer at Y-USA says, "essentially our contract is with you." It is likely Y-USA would contract directly with me should I get fired from the local Y. But that role is currently only 25% of my time, just a few hours per week. Though it pays well for the time, at 25% it is not nearly enough to cover my current expenses. Other costs involve losing my friends, my Y family, and they would be sorely missed. Although, I remind myself, I could always visit and stay in contact.

The greatest benefit, on the other hand, would be to no longer have to work under the leadership of John Smith. I would no longer feel forced to put up with his emotional outbursts, lack of follow-through, shady arrangements, uncaring attitude, and the list goes on. Also, I would no longer have to hide myself, to downplay my strengths and restrict my light from shining for fear of making him or anyone else uncomfortable. I could be me.

Each day at the Y begins to have a new level of intensity to it, like there is pressure building, with need for an outlet. There is also a feeling in the air, one that is ripe for change. Certain staff members, people who don't usually make complaints, start coming to me privately in my office, sharing their distress over how they are being treated. A staff member, who has worked for the Y many years and has been a loyal, dedicated employee, steps in one afternoon with a distraught look on her face. I know her to be an extremely hard working, professional and patient woman. She never complained, never wanted to rock the boat, likely figuring it would do no good anyway. Sometimes, one is simply appreciative to have a job and focuses on the positives... until the discomfort gets to be too much, and/or until one discovers an avenue to potentially get some support.

She shares briefly with me a recent interaction with her supervisor. She hurries through the telling, seeming nervous, looking over her shoulder. "It's not right to treat someone that way," she says in conclusion, as she looks at me with pleading eyes. The issue is regarding a person and department over which I have no influence or authority. It's also definitely not the first complaint I've heard about that person. Similar to the situation with John, a lot of people know there's an issue with this person, but nothing changes. It strikes me as an important moment. Here is a staff person who has sat quietly by for years, putting up with negative behaviors and demeaning words. She wants to be treated better, and she is taking a step to let someone know. She is sharing her voice.

However, I feel a bit helpless. I also feel the stress of my own position at the Y teetering on the edge. I validate her experience and feelings, but it doesn't feel like that is enough. "I'm not sure there's anything I can do," I continue. I look at her with compassion. She nods in understanding, and then departs from my office.

One thing is for sure. People want something better. Staff want to be treated fairly and kindly, as they deserve to be. Those who choose to manage with a heavy hand don't seem to understand that happy employees are more productive employees. Morale seems to be on a downward spiral. I went to my supervisor. I went to the Board. What more can I do?

A couple days after my talk with Amy where she notified me that she had spoken with John, I call Amanda. I ask for her recommendation regarding next steps. She suggests that I meet with John one on one. I do not feel comfortable meeting with him, but I agree to do so, as she suggests. "I don't think it will be very... beneficial, however," I say to her, trying to find the right word.

Amanda let me know that Amy had called her, after Amy saying that she wasn't going to call. She said she and Amy talked at length, "and we talked about why it wasn't the right thing to do for *her*," referring to bringing concerns to the Board level.

"Okay, well, I'm glad we're all on the same page," I say. It sounds like Amanda assured Amy that different choices are right for different individuals.

I take my role as a change agent and organizational leader seriously. In bringing my concerns about John to the Board, I consciously took a step that I hope will set in motion the wheels of change, even if small at first. I desired to raise awareness at the Board level, and they can take it from there. Perhaps Amanda and the Board will choose to conduct a more extensive review of John's performance and behavior. I hope to make a positive difference for the staff – management and support staff alike – and work toward providing an environment that supports open, honest communication and is conducive to growth and wellness. Create a sense of urgency, they told us at Y-USA. Change begins with me.

I email John suggesting a date for us to meet. I suggest a date for the following week so that I have a few days to get my thoughts together and write up my concerns in a manner that he might be open to hearing. I doubt that I could say something like, "I am concerned about how you scream and yell at directors and have anger-management issues. I'm concerned about the rumors I've heard regarding your budgeting and financial practices. I'm concerned by the fact that so many staff have voiced complaints about you..." No, I don't think that would go over well. I need time to figure out how best to approach this delicate situation. It feels only appropriate that Amanda, or someone from the Board whom she chooses, be witness to my meeting with John, providing me a safe container in which to share my thoughts and concerns without negative repercussions.

It is a Thursday in May. I wake up an hour before my alarm is set to ring and email Amanda prior to heading to the Y. I never know what the day is going to bring, and I want to be sure she gets my note. I thank her for the time she took to talk with me yesterday and let her know I want to take all the necessary and appropriate steps in this process.

The workday starts off busy as usual; walk in the door and hit the ground running. I attend a couple meetings in the morning. I first check my email a few minutes before noon and see there is an email from John marked with high importance. In it, he states that he finds my proposed meeting date for the following week unacceptable. Of course he does. Perhaps it makes him feel anxious for me to have time to put together information. John directs me to meet with him, Amy and Darrel, the Y's contracted Human Resource specialist, at "1:00pm tomorrow." I mistakenly think tomorrow is tomorrow. However, later I see John's email was written around 7:00pm yesterday evening, so the tomorrow he refers to is actually today. At this point, it's 12:50pm and I have just 10 minutes to get ready for this important meeting.

There is not much I can do in that short time frame. I print off my recent email correspondence with John, as I have a feeling questions will come up regarding it, and I print off a copy of the local Y's Code of Ethics.

My friend and coworker, Maureen, stops into my office to ask me something. She sees what must be a strained look on my face. "What's wrong?" she asks.

"I might get fired today," I say to her.

"No," she says and laughs, thinking I'm joking. When I don't smile back, she realizes I'm serious.

I stop into the Admin office to ask Judy if she will burn me a disc with all my Activate America files on it. I still have other Ys to work with and responsibilities to carry out with Y-USA even if I'm fired from here. "I'm going to need the disc very soon," I say to her, "like in the next hour if possible."

Across the hall is the door to the conference room. Just before entering, I glance through the tall, narrow glass window in the door. I see two 6' x 3' rectangular, gray, metal tables pushed up against each other in the center of the room, creating a 6 foot gray square. Darrel sits on the left side, Amy on the right side, and John is sitting on the far side. The table seems overly large for just the 4 of us. Cold, metal, it creates such a barrier between us all. There are two black, plastic chairs on the side closest to the door, from which I get to choose as my place to sit. I place my hand on the door handle and take a deep breath.

WARRIOR SPIRIT

In that moment I notice a feeling in my body that I've felt before. It is a feeling of preparedness, despite the unknowns of the situation that is presenting itself. It is one of readiness, holding myself upright and strong, while also staying calm, focused and relaxed. There is a feeling of trust that I will know what to do, and do what needs to be done. This feeling arises automatically, familiar through years of training in martial arts. I studied and trained in martial arts before shifting my interest to yoga. The feeling of preparedness is in my bones and muscle, in my mind and spirit.

As I prepare to walk through the door, all the training comes back to me. It began simply, by signing up for a karate class at the local junior college almost a decade ago. It was something I felt I would enjoy, and I did. The instructor, or Sensei, was Mike Harvey. He was a tall, strong gentleman in his 50s with dark brown hair, graying around the temples, and a mustache. He taught a traditional style of karate, known as Shorin-Ryu, originating from Okinawa, Japan. He had a commanding presence, and at first seemed firm and gruff, reminiscent of a military colonel, not someone with whom you'd want to get into an altercation. But he didn't yell like they do in the military. Well, only on occasion. Mostly, he'd talk more softly, mumble even, and if you weren't in the front row, you often couldn't understand much at all. I made a point to always be in the front row. That's where all the interesting teachings could be learned.

As I got to know Sensei Harvey, his gruff exterior melted away to reveal a huge, kind heart which expressed through his warm smile. He had decades of training under his worn and tattered black belt. He was firm, but always fair, an excellent instructor, and tremendously skilled in the art of self-defense.

I loved the class, soaked up the teachings, gained the physical conditioning, and learned the skills quickly. I took the same class multiple times, as many as the college would allow, and then signed up as the teacher's assistant for as many times as I could do that. Semester after semester, I learned, trained, and helped teach the newer students. When Sensei Harvey decided to retire from teaching the class, I began learning from one of his Black Belt students, Sensei Hector Solis. Hector and I became close friends, and we trained together for many years at his dojo, with continued mentoring from Mike Harvey and other Black Belt teachers.

I worked my way through the various belt levels, though I felt it was never really about the belts. It was about character. It was about being authentic. It was about connecting with one's inner and outer strength. It was about strategy, using one's head and wits, and not giving up, no matter the odds. It was about honor and integrity and humility. I learned that fighting and self-defense techniques are just one layer in what it means to be a true martial artist.

The brown belt is one level prior to the black belt. It was during the test for my brown belt that things began to shift for me in my training. Just prior to the test, I felt in the best physical condition than I ever had. I had been running, increasing my endurance, and also gaining strength and flexibility. I diligently studied the katas, or movements and techniques laid out in a particular sequence, also referred to as forms, that were required for the test. I learned the interpretation of the forms, how the techniques might be applied in real-life situations. I studied the history of the art and became skilled, not only in open-hand techniques, but also in the use of a variety of traditional weapons. Finally, I prepared myself for sparring, contact fighting in a controlled manner, and grappling, how to protect and defend myself when the fight goes to the ground.

When the day of the test came, I felt ready. Another woman was also testing for her brown belt at that time, and several other students were in attendance, along with 8-10 Black Belt co-teachers. As was usual for tests, the first 40 minutes or so consisted of an intense warm-up – push-ups, jumping jacks, crunches, running and numerous other exercises. When you get to the point of exhaustion, thinking it must be time to end, you go a little more. You keep going until you are too tired to have any ounce of nervousness, perspiration is running down your face, and you have to peel the martial arts uniform, or gi, from your skin because it's drenched in so much sweat. Then the test begins.

We started with the katas, beginning with the basic forms we learned as a white belt, and continued our way through the various forms learned at the different levels. Each movement of the form was carried out with the same intensity and focus one would have in a serious, real-life situation. While holding a particular stance, it was common for one of the Black Belts to come around and test the integrity of my position, slapping legs, arms and back, making any necessary corrections in the position and making sure I was strong, and balance and focus remained intact. This was training for the real deal. If I were to ever find myself in a life-or-death situation, these skills and tools could save my life.

From the katas, we went on to do some interpretation of the forms, then onto some 1-on-1 defensive techniques with one of the Black Belts. This is where things fell apart. One of the Black Belts with whom I had not ever worked with previously was instructed to take me down to the mat where I would be required to demonstrate effective ground techniques. Very quickly, he grabbed me around my body, pinning my arms down by my sides, swept me off my feet and slammed me to the ground. In the process of the sweep, my left foot caught the mat, resulting in my foot and ankle twisting in a poor position. Then, as I was slammed to the mat, my jaw hit hard, and I felt pain radiate through my face. My jaw was hurt and my ankle was sprained. I think I may have yelped out in pain, I cannot quite recall, but the test was immediately halted.

I then found myself, rather uncontrollably, crying. I don't know why I was crying. I could deal with the pain; it wasn't that. For whatever reason, I was blubbering and simply couldn't stop. I attempted to stop it. It's not like an attacker will simply stop attacking just because a person is crying. I needed to pull it together. Really. I found it rather strange, as I had often considered myself to be strong and in control of my emotions. Even when I was a young girl and I fell off my bike, I never cried. With three older brothers, I learned how to be "tough." The neighborhood boys even made mention of how I never cried, even when I got hurt. But here I was. So much emotion was running through my body, the tears flowed and my chin quivered, and no matter how much I tried to gain composure I could not until several long minutes had passed.

Finally, Sensei Harvey came over to me as I hobbled on one leg. "You've still got one good leg and two arms, use them," he said, as he patted his chest, indicating to me to punch him. I proceeded to throw some punches to his chest area, still blubbering, until he told me to stop. I realized it was one of those moments similar to when you get bucked off a horse, you have to get back on, and I appreciated how he made me persist.

My portion of the test was then put on hold, and the other woman who was testing took a turn with the same Black Belt with whom I had just worked. Just seconds into her practice, her knee was severely injured, winding up with a torn ligament, which later required surgery and many months of painful recovery. The brown belt test had come to a premature end.

This was out of the ordinary. Both injuries were unintentional, but that particular Black Belt was reprimanded, nonetheless, and asked to leave.

We both received our brown belts that day, despite the circumstances. I continued to train, though my training began to slack off. Weeks, and even months, would go by when I wouldn't make it in to the dojo. I trained with Hector sporadically and explored some modern styles of self-defense. Sensei Harvey moved out of state, and I missed his presence, wisdom and teachings. Years passed, and my belt remained brown. I still enjoyed the martial arts training, but not as much as I had in the earlier years.

Sometimes the brown belt is referred to as the desert, where one can wander endlessly and perhaps even get lost. That's what it felt like. I lacked direction and motivation. I got to the point where I really didn't care if I ever received my black belt.

Finally, things began to shift once again. Come to think of it, the shift occurred after my second trip to Teotihuacán, Mexico, in 2006. I recall thinking as the trip neared its end how I wanted to resume my training and get my black belt, to have a sense of completion around it. Although, as the masters say, becoming a Black Belt is not the end, only the beginning.

By the time I was four years into having my brown belt, I had switched my focus to yoga, further exploring my own practice, as well as teaching. Martial arts remained a part of my life, but something new was also growing. I found some similarities in both martial arts and yoga, particularly in regard to the inner aspect – the focus, strength, awareness – but the two traditions veered away from each other in practice. Martial arts required contact fighting whereas yoga beckoned my soul to peace.

Hector sent out an email one day stating there was going to be a black belt test. I sensed something was up. I emailed him back letting him know I was not interested in testing; I didn't care about the belts; I was focusing now on yoga. He responded that that was fine, but he did need my help with evaluating and testing some of the karate students. I agreed. There was no mention of me testing, so I thought I was off the hook. However, my instinct told me to prepare, just in case. I brushed up on my forms. I contemplated how else to prepare, and it felt like I would simply know what to do.

The day of the student testing, I arrived at the dojo at 9:00am as asked. A couple experienced Black Belts were also there. I felt calm and ready, no matter what happened. The readiness had settled deep into my bones.

There was a group of several students, adults, all men, and children, girls and boys, at various belt levels and length of experience. We began with basic katas. I did each form with the group then was asked to switch out with one of the Black Belts, instructing the group and making necessary corrections. In the air was a feeling that I was being tested, whether or not I was, and I trained accordingly, with great intensity and focus. That is how I trained, period. It's always a test, even when it isn't.

After doing some of the forms, we switched to a more modern fighting style in which I had also trained for a few years and obtained the level of Phase One Instructor. There were knife-fighting techniques and various combat tactics with single and multiple attackers. Each time, the men would start engaging in the techniques, then Hector would throw me in the mix. The men who had been training in this style were good. Hector is a good teacher. One guy in particular was very big, over 6 feet and pure muscle. He looked like a body builder. He could make for an intimidating opponent, especially to a 5' 5", 130lb woman like me. But I didn't blink when Hector paired me up with him. I had no fear. I stayed present, focused and simply fought. I strategically moved and defended myself. I utilized my skill and strength, and I never gave up.

We eventually took a short break. I noticed I had a small amount of blood mixed in with the sweat on my gi. It was not my blood, though. One man had his eye poked by accident at some point during the training, and another man tore his toenail, but all in all, we were holding up well as a group.

After the break, we resumed training, sometimes working 1 on 1 and sometimes in groups. We alternated between katas and their interpretation; sparring, utilizing kicks, punches, elbows, knees, etc; working with weapons; ground fighting; locks and holds; and a variety of other techniques.

After 6 hours of intense training, I was sweaty, bruised, battered and exhausted, but continuing to stand tall. Sensei Hector took time to say a few words to the group of students and Black Belt teachers. He kindly shared how I had been training for years and how he felt I was pivotal in his own training. Turning to me, he said, "You showed great fighting spirit, which everyone saw today." He then brought out the black belt. Different from all the previous belts, this one had Japanese characters reading "Okinawa Shorin Ryu" embroidered in gold thread. Everyone clapped as I untied my four-year old brown belt with shaky, tired hands and tied on the stiff, new black belt. It was done. I took a deep breath and smiled. Of course, then there were congratulations and hugs all around. These people, too, were family.

I was only the 3rd woman in the history of this particular karate lineage to receive a black belt. In addition, I was the last person to receive a black belt in the lineage altogether. Sensei Harvey had retired from teaching new students. His teacher, Sensei Nakata, had discontinued issuing belts. Sensei Hector taught with a different approach. It felt significant that I was the "last." I hoped I would carry myself in a way that honored my teachers and training.

Sensei Harvey's school was known as Bushin Kai, which means "warrior spirit." Something deep inside me connected with that name. It denotes more than simply what is on the surface, more than just the physical. It speaks to one's inner nature.

Upon reaching this milestone, I reflected on how martial arts is more of an internal process and training than an external one. Now, moving through life as a Black Belt, I had some questions: How do I wish to express myself in the world? How can I balance strength with softness, confidence with humility? What does it mean to live with integrity and honor?

ENTER THE JAGUAR

I turn the door handle and enter the room. With only 10 minutes to prepare for this meeting, I don't necessarily have my thoughts in order. I certainly didn't have the time I needed to gather documentation and otherwise organize information about John's behavior. But I feel a sense of readiness, regardless.

"Hi Darrel," I say to the contracted Human Resource person. "Hello," I say with a look to John and Amy. Amy is the only one who says hi in return.

John begins, "How long have you been with the Y?"

During the years I was John's assistant, and even into the early years as Membership Director, I often felt nervous when talking with John. I felt small around him, even weak in a way, or at the very least subservient. When I talked with him, my voice would often be quiet, soft, mirroring the smallness I felt. But here and now I feel no hint of nervousness. Rather, I feel a confidence and strength within myself. I sit up tall, holding that strength in my body. My voice comes out strong and full as I meet him eye to eye and reply, "9 ½ years."

"Well, I've been here a long time, many, many years, and I know a lot of people," John continues.

It feels like my head was placed on the chopping block the moment I sat down.

I feel our greatest strength shines through when we walk through life with honor, integrity and love. I learned this in one sense through martial arts. I understand it on another level through the Native American teachings about Jaguar. I have learned that Jaguar is one of my totem animals in the Native tradition. Totem animals are believed to help guide a person through his or her life journey. The lessons and gifts of Jaguar center around strength, integrity and impeccability. I feel a deep connection with this incredible creature.

The jaguar is primarily located in Central and South America. It once populated Mexico and parts of the United States. It is the largest of the felines found in the western hemisphere.

The jaguar is an interesting and powerful animal. It is perhaps most recognizable by its tan or golden coat with black spots, or rosettes. It is strong, quick, adaptable and graceful. It climbs, runs and swims, finding equal comfort on both land and in the water. It also hunts in either night or day. The jaguar demonstrates mastery over varied environments.

It is also a ferocious fighter. The jaguar will strategically stalk its prey, and also rely on its brute strength. It has the strongest bite force of any member of the cat family – even stronger than lions and tigers. So powerful, it can bite through the spinal column, the bones of the skull, and pierce the shells of armored reptiles. The jaguar goes straight for the kill, and it has been known to shear the heads off of animals with a single swipe of its claws.

In Native American spiritual teachings, one of the primary roles of Jaguar is to "devour" negative aspects of human behavior. Sams and Carson state, "Jaguar teaches us the penalties of inappropriate behavior and offers the rewards of good medicine to those who stand in their personal integrity and walk through life in an impeccable manner." Essentially, the lessons of Jaguar are about connecting with our true power. That power does not come from self-serving interests, dishonesty or abuse of authority. Our true power is gained through striving to be our personal best and acting with integrity, honor and love. Those with Jaguar medicine may have the ability to take the head off of their opponents with one quick swipe, but they understand it takes even greater strength to act with compassion.

In a recent weekly meeting with Amy, we were discussing the awkward subject of John and my talking with the Board about him. I was talking about how the culture of the Y is changing, and John shows himself to be part of an older structure. The new structure that is rising is much more caring, transparent, inclusive and conscious of its actions, at least that is how I saw it. Maybe at some point, John will be able to look at himself and see that he might no longer be a good fit and move on to other things. Or, perhaps he could change and grow with the Y.

"What do you plan to do?" Amy asked me in regard to my next step.

It was a big question, but one simple answer arose, "To be as compassionate as possible."

Skipping any pleasantries, Darrel states, "So you know who I am, and we're here because you have brought up some serious allegations."

In fact, I had made no allegations. Rather, I simply talked with Amanda, raising awareness about John's behavior.

"Have you ever heard of the term 'chain of command'?" Darrel asks.

"I am familiar with the chain of command," I respond.

"Do you *believe* in the chain of command?" sounding not unlike a televangelist.

"I'm not sure what there is to believe in, I understand the chain of command," I say.

Darrel continues to ask questions, and the tone he sets seems to be purposefully intimidating. His demeanor almost appears staged, and I wonder if it is, like good cop, bad cop... only he is just the bad cop. He is emotionally charged, sounds angry, waves his arms, his facial expressions indicate disgust, and he asks a lot of leading questions. He certainly lacks the objectivity one would expect in a Human Resource executive.

John had written in the email which directed me to this meeting that Darrel and Amy would be in attendance so as to provide an "environment conducive to sharing." This is no such environment. It appears to be more of a formality so that John can say he brought in an HR person before he fires me, so it looks good on paper. I had also responded to John's email just prior to this meeting letting him know I requested the Board's presence before I would go into details about my concerns.

There is a great deal of questioning regarding if I had kept my supervisor, Amy, in the loop with my talking with the Board, which I had. I think Darrel and John are trying to see if I can be fired on the basis of insubordination.

Darrel has a copy of the last email correspondence between John and me. I had printed it out just before this meeting and so also have a copy. He references a statement of mine about assumptions. Darrel also references my offer to contact Matt Olson, our Y's Resource Director, a liaison for Y-USA and our Y.

"So you want to bring in *another* HR person?" Darrel continues with an irritated tone.

John interjects to correct him. "It's Matt Olson, he's a Y Resource Director," then he stops himself.

Darrel, continuing, "Don't you think *you* make assumptions? Don't you think it's an *assumption* that he would be willing to be part of this?"

I have had nothing but positive performance reviews through my entire Y career, and never had even a single written or verbal reprimand. It appears Darrel is grasping at straws, searching for something, *anything* with which to find fault.

"In my work with other Y's..." I begin.

Darrel interrupts, "I don't care about your work with Active uhhh... whatever it is." He is referring to Activate America, not even knowing what it is.

I continue what I started to say, "In my work with other Y's, and in talking with other individuals at Y-USA, I've heard of similar situations and I know the Resource Director has helped out."

"So you've contacted him already!" Darrel states.

"No."

Darrel angrily continues, "So you've shared information about this Y with other Y's and nationally! Who knows *how* many people you've told!"

Remaining calm, "No, I haven't shared anything about this Y with other Ys or at Y-USA. I said I've heard about Resource Directors helping Ys in similar situations. I'm simply offering an option."

"But don't you think *that's* an assumption?" Darrel asks.

I sigh, "You don't know until you ask."

Throughout the meeting, I observe Darrel to be bullying and working to intentionally create an intimidating environment. In many ways, he seems to be an extension of John himself, though scaled down considerably. Darrel was hand-picked by John a couple years earlier to provide HR support for our Y on a limited basis, and he seems loyal to John's preferred mode of operating. That MO seems to be: find a reason to get rid of those individuals who challenge the current paradigm and who bring any complaints against John, and if you can't find anything, make something up. It feels in no way to be objective or in the best interests of the Y.

The approach I take to clarify my position is to read aloud the introductory paragraph of our Y's Code of Ethics. It emphasizes how the Y's Mission and Core Values demand that the Board and employees, as stewards of the mission, uphold the public trust and act in an ethical manner in all that we do on behalf of the Y. Being a not-for-profit, public charity organization, the Y relies on the public for funding and volunteer support, which is critical to the success of the organization's mission. It is therefore critical that we operate in a manner that is "above reproach" in all aspects, including governance, fiscal management, operations, legal compliance and human resources.

I conclude the reading and look straight at John and say, "So I am stating I believe that John acts in an unethical manner, and he does not uphold the mission."

John, in his role as CEO, is the person who most represents the organization. His behavior not only affects all the staff, but the reputation and perception of the Y in the community.

"What part of the mission, specifically?" Darrel asks.

I answer directly from the Y's mission statement, "The Core Values – caring, honesty, respect, responsibility."

"Don't you feel it's the responsibility of all employees to uphold the values and act in an ethical manner?" Darrel continues to question.

"Yes," although I feel that upholding of the mission might express differently for staff at different levels of the organization.

"So you're specifically stating John doesn't do this?"

"That is correct," I reply.

Darrel says, "You are to be dismissed for about 5 minutes, and Amy will come get you."

I get dismissed for 20-25 minutes. Amy comes to get me. I return and am told by Darrel that I will get a "hearing" with the board. I am then asked to provide one specific example "right now."

"Just letting you know," Darrel says, "you *will* be getting your hearing with the board."

I contemplate the request and flip through my memory banks to determine if any specific example would be appropriate to share at this point. I hear years of staff complaints echoing in my head. I recall my own experience of John when he screamed and threw the postcard towards me. It was years ago and seems of less importance by this time. More memories of staff complaints, words spoken from managers and support staff alike, come to mind, all of which were spoken to me in confidence, with trust they wouldn't be shared.

I gaze out the windows of the conference room wondering if it's the last time I will be looking out those windows. I sit in the silence as I feel 3 pairs of eyes intent on me, waiting. I think about how many people over the years have had issue with John's angry outbursts, tantrums and lack of professionalism. I think about rumors that I've heard regarding questionable financial dealings, which people would likely take more seriously than the former issues, but those are still just rumors at this time. I hear my own supervisor's voice in my mind, Amy, who sits in this very room. I hear the conversations we've had and the information she has shared with me, all in confidence. She could share examples of her own if she chose to. Her examples are perhaps the strongest case for John deserving a more thorough review. I have the choice to voice specific examples, but it would require throwing other staff, particularly my own supervisor, under the bus. That's not my style.

Maybe it is because I went to Teotihuacán and caught a glimpse of a deeper purpose for my life. Maybe it is because of yoga and the fact that it awakened in me an incredible feeling of joy and fulfillment through embodying and teaching the practice. Maybe it is because of my martial arts training and how I'd rather take a no-nonsense approach than run around in circles and deal with the drama. Maybe it's because I feel my body needs more movement during the day and less sitting in meetings and at my desk. Maybe it is due to knowing leaders at Y-USA and witnessing how they truly walk the talk, set positive examples and are excellent role models for all the staff and Y leaders of the next generation. Maybe if I hadn't started working on Activate America or been given the responsibility and privilege of being a change agent, or asked how I might create a sense of urgency for the work... maybe, maybe, maybe. Perhaps if I didn't have these experiences, I would have been content to sit idly by, allowing things to carry out as they had long been doing, and never say a word. But I *did* have these experiences, and each of them influenced me and helped shape who I am now and the choices I make.

There is also something stirring within me. I feel full, ready for a shift. It's time. Something calls to me from the horizon, though I do not know what, and I feel compelled to answer.

After time in contemplation, it feels like my best option is to try to present patterns of behavior and trends to the Board during my "hearing." This is a long-standing and ongoing issue with John. Also, my documentation has only just begun. I have no doubt, in time, that John will "slip up" again, and I will be able to document more examples, to have more specific hard evidence. In time...

After a few moments I state, "I just don't feel it is appropriate to take a single example out of context, and I strongly feel this is an organizational issue and it needs to be addressed with the Board. I need to have the safe container of the Board in order to share more."

I am asked to leave the facility immediately after this meeting and told not to come in the next morning, Friday. I'm informed Amy will be calling me sometime late Friday morning to give me a time when I am to come in to the Y.

On my way out, I stop by Judy's desk and pick up my Activate America files on disc. It contains all my contacts for the Ys in the cohorts that I'm working with, along with the PowerPoint presentations, call notes, and the rest of the work I've been doing with Y-USA. I'm grateful to have this in my possession as I head home.

I may be fired tomorrow, not sure. Dismissals usually happen on Fridays, and it sounds like they might need the morning to get my last paycheck calculated and printed. But I shouldn't jump to conclusions.

I decide to spend the Thursday afternoon gardening, planting flowers (they are so beautiful in the spring) and smooching with Tony. Might as well make the best of it.

I spend the evening, many hours, organizing and beginning to write up my thoughts and documentation. I begin to write down notes for the Board hearing. I've been given the opportunity to take my concerns to the Board, according to the meeting this afternoon. I will just wait and see what happens tomorrow.

The following day, I get a call from Amy at 12:12pm, and she asks if we can meet at 1:30pm. I arrive at the designated time to Amy's office. As I sit down, the CFO enters, drops a manila envelope onto Amy's desk and quickly departs. Ellen then enters the room and sits down in the chair next to me with notepad and pen in hand. I'm pleased to see that documentation is finally taking place, though perhaps too little too late.

I know this is the end. Amy nervously begins, stating the information I presented was taken into consideration. It was non-specific and was shared with members of the Executive Committee this morning. "It was decided you'd be relieved of your duties immediately," she says. I knew those words were coming, but I do not expect the dreadful feeling in the pit of my stomach, nor the sudden flood of sadness and tears that overtakes me. I feel my heart breaking. I absolutely love the Y. I love the people here. It feels to be a loss, a death.

I look at Amy. She has tears running down her reddened cheeks.

"I was told yesterday at the meeting that I will get a hearing with the Board. Now that's not happening? That's not true?" I ask.

I see Amy's lips moving, as I attempt to make out her words through my emotion. "John said there was Board representation at the meeting this morning." I see my last paycheck being handed to me, with no severance, of course. I see that one of the signers of the check is the same Board member who recently remarked to me, "This is what happens when someone gets to be too big." She is on the Executive Committee; she was there. A promise of a Board hearing was made, and now that promise is broken. John does not want the Board to hear my voice. I believe as soon as he found out I had spoken with Amanda, he was on a mission to get rid of me.

I just sob, holding my face in my hands. "Do you want us to leave you alone?" Ellen asks. No, I want them to be witness to this sadness.

I look at the separation report filled out by Amy that I am to sign. In the place to note the explanation of the separation, Amy had written, "After careful consideration of the info you have brought forward and the non-specifity around this info – it is determined it will no longer work for Kristi to be employed." Specificity was misspelled, and there was a lot of white out spread across the document. I guess it took a couple tries to figure out how to word it. Under the discharge section, where it states "Dates of relevant warnings," it is blank. None of the boxes for reasons of discharge are checked, not "absenteeism" or "rule violation" or "insubordination" or "dishonesty" or "intoxication" or "negligence." None of the 12 boxes are checked, not even "other." The report is not filled out in a professional manner, nor would it hold up well if challenged in court for wrongful termination. I shake my head and sign the darn thing anyway.

I manage to get out a few words. "How many complaints do there have to be and good staff people who have to get fired, or feel forced to quit because the environment becomes so uncomfortable for them, before something is done or changed?" It seems easier to simply get rid of someone who raises concerns rather than deal with the issues.

"I don't..." I start, as the sobs deepen. "I don't even get to say goodbye." To my friends, my Y family. "I don't even get to say goodbye." That is what hurts the most. I hold my head in my hands and cry some more.

An arrangement is made for the maintenance manager to meet me on Sunday so that I can retrieve personal items from my office. He carefully watches me from a few feet away as I gather my items into a cardboard box.

After almost 10 years of dedicated service with the Winowa County YMCA, that is how it ends... and how the next phase begins.

Part III: Cocoon

Feeling fat and full as a caterpillar satisfied her.
Then one day something began to shift.
It was subtle at first, so subtle she questioned if it was even real.
"Is it just my imagination?" she asked herself.
Then it grew stronger, and stronger,
and she came to identify it as a calling, an invitation.
She was being called towards something new,
something different.
She was not sure exactly what this "different" looked like,
but she felt compelled to surrender to its pull.

She attached herself to the underside of a hefty stalk,
feeling that something big was going to happen
and she needed to hang on tight.
She waited.
Soon, her body began to undulate.
Her outer layer peeeeeeeeled away, with purpose,
and she shed her skin one last time.

Wriggle, wriggle.
Things were already different, she noticed,
her outer layer now unlike anything she'd experienced before.
It started soft, then hardened.
She felt herself start to settle and grow calm.

It is here she presently finds herself,
held securely,
suspended and enveloped in a cocoon of her own making.
What lies ahead, she does not know.
There are times when she feels fear around the
loss of that which is familiar.
She even has thoughts that she may be dying.
But these thoughts pass rather quickly.
She trusts her inherent wisdom,
holding on to a deeper knowing
that everything is transpiring exactly as it is meant to.
"I'll be alright," she tells herself.

Chapter 11

House of Geese & Frogs

*J*call Jennifer Martin at Y-USA and give her the news. I call Amanda and leave her a voicemail, as well. The next day, Amanda contacts me and says she knows how I feel about the Y, and that she is very sorry things ended this way. My contact with Amanda is to now be in writing or by leaving voicemail messages so it can be documented.

The week following my termination is extremely emotional, stress-filled and busy. I can't eat, I can't sleep, and my thoughts obsessively go over and over the events of the last few weeks. The weight in my heart feels like a lead brick. I'm confused about what my next steps are supposed to be. I don't know what is going to happen. Surely, the Board will see this termination was a gross error and do something about it.

My termination happened so quickly. Is that not a huge red flag for the Board that something is terribly wrong? I had only good performance reviews, was a key figure in the Y's operations, was well-liked and respected by both management and support staff. I had no prior warnings or reprimands. There's not even any valid reason for my termination on my separation report, which is incomplete and painted over with white out. What is going on here?

Feeling harshly booted out of the nest, I hear John Smith's words again, "It's not my job to care about the staff."

Amanda asks that I send her what information I have and to do so in a timely manner. I gather my thoughts, organize my materials, and spend hours working late into the night typing up as much information as I can. I am grateful she provides me the opportunity to share information, even though I am no longer an employee. She promises to bring to a Board committee any written information that seems pertinent to my case. She states, however, "As Board Chair, I do not have the power to change what has happened to you to date."

I get a call a couple days later from my friend, Pink, also a former employee. She has a new career and remarks that she went into the field of Human Resources partly because of her negative experiences at the Y. "You have to get an attorney, Kristi," she tells me. "I know you want to be all granola and rainbows." I laugh. "I know that's who you are, and I know how you feel about the Y. But you *have* to get an attorney." I tell her I appreciate her advice but that I don't want to get one.

"I have faith in Amanda and several other members of the Board," I say. "I *have* to trust that they will do the right thing."

Shortly after, I get a phone call from another friend, a former Y director. She says there are three others, plus herself, who are interested in filing a class action lawsuit, and she asks if I want to go that route. It doesn't feel right. Regarding these others, why now? Why not earlier? I have questions around their motives and politely decline. I trust my gut. I do find it of concern, however, that the Y seems to be teetering on the brink of a major lawsuit largely due to John's behavior, and the Board seems unaware.

Out of the first 4 days, I get a total of only 7 hours of sleep. I stay at my house during this time rather than at Tony's. I do not want to keep him awake, and I feel I need my own space during this difficult transition.

I have felt many things in my life, both positive and negative, but I have never felt stress to this extreme. I go to bed feeling exhausted and do my best to relax. There are several relaxation and stress-reduction tools that I've gained over the years through my yoga practice. However, it seems to be of little benefit right now. I focus on my breath, telling myself it is time to relax and rest, time to sleep. Within moments, my head is spinning, thoughts incessantly racing, racing, racing. I notice my brow is scrunched, a result of being in deep thought, an unsettled mind, searching the depths for clarity, understanding, meaning, and simply processing the whole experience. I make effort to relax my brow, letting the small muscles in my forehead soften. *Breathe, just breathe,* I remind myself. Seconds later, my mind goes racing off again. It's unrelenting, and my brow returns to scrunching. *Relax, soften, breathe.*

Hours goes by, caught up in the seemingly-never-ending cycle. There are moments when I feel myself drifting off... *finally* things calming down and beginning to sink towards that delicious, much-desired sleep. Maybe it's 2:00am or 3:00am, or 5:00am. Just before I touch all the way down, literally just a split second before, a word flashes into my consciousness, or a sentence, a brief thought arising from somewhere, from nowhere, and I'm jerked awake yet again. Simultaneously with the flash, my heart pounds, pounds so hard. It feels like my heart is doing flip flops in my chest, like a fish out of water. *Calm, stay calm.* So much anxiety, it shakes my body out of reach from the slumber it craves. I find myself off and running again – thoughts going a mile a minute, rehashing conversations, digging through previous experiences, planning for what and how to say what needs to be said, wondering what could possibly be going on at the Y, wondering if my dismissal means something to Y leaders, or means nothing, deciphering my next step, on and on... my mind a machine that refuses to turn off.

I'm burning more calories being awake throughout the night, and I'm unable to eat enough to compensate for it. Food doesn't seem appetizing. I might feel a little hungry, but after the first bite or two feel sick and unable to finish. After these first several days, I look into one of the full-length bedroom mirrors and see I have lost weight. I'm already a thin woman and so do not have any extra weight to lose. I turn to see the bones in my back are protruding, and my hips and ribs are more pronounced. "Wow, that's kinda intense," I say to the reflection. "I need to eat." I need to stop the weight loss and hopefully regain a few pounds.

I commit to being more aware of my eating and make sure I eat more substantial meals throughout the day, even if it feels like I have to force myself.

One evening, I feel pain, a tightness in my chest. It is, quite honestly, scary. I do some deep breathing. I'm afraid I could have a heart attack. My heart aches on many levels.

At 3:17am the next morning, lying in bed unable to rest, I feel continued pain in my chest. I flip on the light and go over to the mirror. I look at myself, from as an objective perspective as I can, to determine if I need to go to the hospital. From having taken CPR trainings several times, I am aware of the signs of a heart attack, though the signs in a woman can be different from the signs in a man. Am I pale? A little. Is my skin clammy? No, not really. I feel a tightness and pain in the left side of my neck, along my carotid artery. *That's not good.* My heart starts to beat a little quicker, feeling nervous. With being let go, I no longer have health insurance. If I go to the hospital, I'd be responsible for the bills, and now I have no income. My heart palpitates some more. I close my eyes and take slow... deep... breaths.

The tightness and discomfort in my chest continues for hours, despite my attempts to relax, and I feel compelled to write in my journal. "If my body happens to expire due to a heart attack or any other reason tonight or in the near future, which I hope it doesn't, but I feel it could, I just have one thing I wish to say: JUST LOVE *EVERYONE*." I look at the words I just wrote and chuckle. A bit melodramatic, perhaps. But in all seriousness, I feel like I could die this very night. At least I said what I wanted to say. I figure someone would read my journal at some point, probably Tony.

I contemplate for a few moments how I do feel it is possible to love humanity as a collective, despite the horrible things people do to one another. It's possible if we remember that we are all on an evolutionary journey. Individuals are simply at different places along this journey, at different levels of awareness and consciousness.

I manage to get about 5 hours of sleep later that morning. I wake up grateful to be alive and feeling I must still have things to do in this life.

Shortly after, I visit Tony at his house, and I feel the need to tell him about the physical symptoms I've been experiencing, just in case something happens. "I want you to know that I've been having pains in my chest. It sometimes feels like I'm going to have a heart attack, or maybe that I *am* having a heart attack."

Tony looks at me, "No," he says, not wanting it to be true. "Your heart is strong."

"Well, actually, what I've heard is you are more likely to die, rather than just have damage, from a heart attack if you're young, because your heart *is* so strong." But Tony brushes it aside, not wanting to think about it, perhaps. I can understand. But I also feel a little alone. I'll just take it one day at a time, one minute at a time, until I get through this. *I'll be okay. I'll be okay.*

Back at home, my eyes suddenly pop open, heart beating thunderously, and I awaken after only an hour or two of sleep. I find myself mired in another night of fitful rest and scrunched brow, unable to obtain necessary rejuvenation or relief. It's rough on the body. I crawl out of bed, flip on the light and decide to assess the woman in the mirror again. I look and see a line, a crease in my brow. "Was that there before?" I ask the empty room. *Gosh darn it!* Then I take a breath and settle into the reality of the situation. *Well, I guess it's kind of like battle scars, a marker of the road I've traveled. It is what it is. I don't regret my choices, and I respect the lines that serve as remembrances.* I decide to do some yoga in an attempt to gain a sense of nourishment.

I somehow manage to carry on with my Activate America work through Y-USA during this difficult time. I gather my strength and professionalism and have a 1 on 1 call with a Project Manager from a Y in Indiana and one from a Y in Ohio. I'm not yet contracted directly with Y-USA for the work, but I feel it's best to continue as usual and have no disruption in my work with other Y's.

Two of my friends from the local Y, Maureen and Carol, stop by one evening after they get off work with a six pack of beer and "bad-for-you" chips. BBQ flavor. Maureen, with her humorous sayings, can always put a smile on my face. I'm health conscious, but not *that* health conscious. I tear open the potato chip bag and pop the top off a beer. They put up with me still raw in my process, sleep-deprived and full of frustration and sadness. I feel their love and support and appreciate the visit.

I experience a lot of things after being let go from the Winowa County Y after almost 10 years of service. Some of these things aren't necessarily pretty, either. There's anger and, of course, sadness. There's more sadness than anger, but the anger is most definitely there. It feels like a wildcat inside of me, a jaguar. I feel my claws extend, and I could just shred him, lightening quick with both front paws, and it would be over within an instant. My hands come into a claw shape, and I strike the air, mimicking the speed and ferocity at which this jaguar could defeat its foe.

I feel the warrior energy strong. I feel the fire and fight that is present. I remember the Badger card from my wheel at the beginning of the year. I was so taken aback by this card, and now here it is. I know this aggressive energy will be alive within me through summer. So different from my usual peaceful demeanor, but I understand how it will help me stay persistent with Amanda and the Board until completion. I take a deep breath... claws retract... for now.

Late the next evening Maureen calls. "You need to eat," she says. "You need your strength to fight. Don't give up. You can't give up!" Through her words I remember why I'm doing this, going through this. I'm doing this for them. Everyone deserves better.

After hanging up the phone, I just sob and sob. It's that kind of sobbing that is felt deep in the belly. I am reminded of when children at the age of 3 or 4 are sobbing and sucking in air with lower lip quivering, a full-body reaction. That is me. *I didn't even get to say goodbye.* I go into the bathroom and sob all through the shower, my tears mixing with the streams of warm water running down my body. I sob all while brushing my teeth, and still as I flop onto my bed. It is a sadness washing over me and through me.

I feel done with it all. I want no more.

I drift off to sleep and then shortly after pop awake just like those other sleepless nights. It's a process, a mourning process, I remind myself.

As I lie awake, in between the incessant thoughts, I hear the frogs. My duplex sits at the bottom of a valley, a short distance from a creek. During the winter, the rains begin to fill the basin of the valley and a small lake forms on the property adjacent to mine. From my backyard, I can look to the other side of a wire fence, through branches of some small trees and see the lake, along with the Canadian geese that make it their nesting ground through winter and spring. It becomes quite a desirable habitat for both geese and frogs.

The geese are loud, extremely loud. During the day, I often hear them honking as they fly over the house and come to rest with a swoosh over the water. Dozens of geese gather, having found a warmer climate with no one to bother them, and plenty of food. They carry on their geese conversations with vigor. At times I find it to be obnoxious, other times I just accept it and appreciate that I am graced with sounds of nature rather than something like police sirens or jackhammers.

By day the geese, by night the frogs. The frogs number into the thousands, maybe even tens of thousands. All I know is there are a lot! A person can begin to hear these frogs from at least a half mile away, driving into the area. I am lucky (not sure if this is the right word) to be much closer. Most stay at the lake, but occasionally I find a couple in my backyard. The ones I see are cute, little, green ones.

The noise that is created when thousands of these amphibious creatures get together and produce their calls is quite impressive. The croaks and enthusiastic trills of the individual frog voice multiplied by the thousands, many with different tones, calling at different times and speeds, become amplified and echo through the night, creating a robust symphony of sound. Despite my well-insulated walls and double-paned windows, the frog song comes through loud and clear.

Needless to say, it can make it rather difficult to sleep. During this season, I've often been wearing earplugs, which brings it down to a more muffled hum. But on this night, I leave out the earplugs and listen to them in all their glory. They tell me stories about the water and the cleansing tears and the gifts they bring.

I lie in bed, feeling the presence of the countless frogs, and I am thankful for them. I realize why I am here, in this home that lies in the valley, at this time. This is where I need to be. This is the place to let go, the place supporting my healing during this transition.

As the week wraps up, I give Amanda what information I have. I hope the nature of my own abrupt termination is also cause for further review and investigation, and I state such. I drop off a manila envelope with my documents at Amanda's office.

As I return home, exhaustion settles over me. For the first time in a week, my heart is beating a little more slowly, and I feel a heaviness in my body and eyelids.

Early the next morning at 5:45am, flashes, incredible flashes of lightening shine through my bedroom window. Despite the blinds being closed, the flashes fully light up the room. Moments after, a thunderous blast rolls through the darkness, taking a good 20 seconds before it fades away. It is likely the last big storm of the season. Perhaps the worst is over. I'm looking forward to the increased light and warmth just around the bend.

"You know, I've probably taken a year off my life with the amount of stress I've experienced this last week," I share with Tony.

"But at least it's at the far end of your life, and that time period usually isn't very fun anyway," he replies. We both laugh.

We make love, and I decide to stay the night at Tony's house. Now I lie awake in his bed. I simply rest quietly, going over, yet again, in my mind the correspondence between Amanda and me, reviewing each recent interaction I've had with Amy and replaying all the events. My mind searches for some clue to how it is going to end, for some thread of hope that just action is being taken. I hope my time at the Y meant something. Hour after hour, I lie in the darkness, my body in stillness but my mind running non-stop. I listen to the sound of my beloved sleeping peacefully beside me. I hear his steady breathing, which sometimes turns into a gentle snore... until the snoring gets louder and he wakes himself up and rolls over. Then his steady breathing resumes. I find some comfort in hearing him at rest. It helps me appreciate the simple things of life.

Amanda told me a few days ago to "have faith" that she would do as promised, which was to take whichever information she deemed appropriate to a Board committee. I know she will do what she feels is best, and whatever is in her power to do, and that is all I can ask. Though it is another sleepless night, and there are undoubtedly numerous sleepless nights ahead, I have faith that all will turn out well in the big picture sense. I have so many questions and desire answers, though, for what specifically will happen at the local Y. What will the Board decide? What changes will be made, if any?

Despite a great deal of emotional upheaval and confusion following my termination, I do remain clear about this: My goal and responsibility with the Y is to create positive change. I made choices and did what I could to work towards this goal, planting seeds to help the Y grow and move forward, which, in turn, helps individuals and communities grow healthier and stronger.

In addition, I feel I stood in my integrity. I said what I wanted to say without compromising my values or throwing anyone under the bus. And despite whatever attempts were made to squelch my voice, my voice will not and cannot be squelched.

Chapter 12

Letting Go

*T*ony and I finish packing as we prepare to leave for a much-needed vacation. We're heading to Maui. It has been just 2 weeks since my departure from the Y. I know my funds will be dwindling rather quickly now, but I don't wish to cancel our pre-planned trip. I need the change of scenery. Tropical beaches, sea turtles, waterfall hikes and snuggling with my handsome, loving man are calling! Maui is one of my favorite places on the planet, and Tony has never been. I'm excited to share with him the beauty of the island.

After several hours of traveling, we get settled into our condo. It's comfortable and sweet. Slightly worn wicker furniture with glass tabletops occupies the bedroom, dining room and living room. The upholstery covering the padded seating is a Hawaiian floral print. There's tile floor throughout, except in the bedroom, convenient for cleaning up sand from beach excursions, and an A/C for Tony when he gets a little too warm. The kitchen has all the essentials, and the lanai includes a small table and two chairs overlooking the tropically-landscaped grounds. The grounds include a pool, two hot tubs, fountain, koi pond, and acres of lawn, palm trees, and tropical plants and flowers. When we look beyond the fountain, we can see the ocean.

The following day we get up early and go snorkeling at one of my favorite beaches in south Maui. It's usually rather quiet with just a few people. The first beach visit, upon taking in the view of the clear, turquoise water, brings out a spontaneous "Awe!" I revel in the warmth of the water as I walk among the gentle waves. Getting our snorkel gear and swimming out past the breakers, we find the coral reef is colorful and intact, and tropical fish and green sea turtles are abundant.

We then hit Makena, or Big Beach, a popular spot for both locals and tourists. It's over a half mile in length, a beautiful crescent of golden sand, and has deceptively strong waves that attract boogie boarders and body surfers. Adjacent to Big Beach is Little Beach. The two are separated by an outcrop of lava rock with a short, steep, winding, narrow, sandy path that requires some careful navigating. Little Beach is clothing optional and, in general, seems to attract those who go against the grain of much of society in some way or another – surfers, ganja-partakers, yogis, hippies, lesbians and gays, and all-around creative, playful folk. It provides the best opportunity to strip down to one's birthday suit and play in the warm, tropical sea and enjoy the feeling of complete and utter freedom!

After returning to the condo in the afternoon, we rest for a while, enjoy some snuggling, then decide to go out to an early dinner at a little Vietnamese restaurant in Kihei. As we walk in the door, a man with a heavy accent greets us and excitedly waves us in to sit down. The restaurant is quiet with just the two of us and one other couple at the tables. Tony and I order a couple noodle bowls, which are delicious. They are different from the noodle bowls at the Vietnamese restaurants back home. In addition to the usual ingredients – rice noodles with the option of shrimp or pork or spring rolls – there is an added sweetness to them, a hint of pineapple, reminding us we are in Hawaii.

Our waiter, who also appears to be the restaurant owner, brings us some fresh, sliced mango with our check. Tony and I devour the soft, sweet, and incredibly juicy mango with gladness. "This is the *best* mango I've ever tasted!" Tony exclaims to the man. I don't know if it is just because we are in the midst of our island adventure that it tastes so good, but it seems like the absolute best mango I have ever eaten, too. Tony raves so much about the mango that the owner comes out and hands him a plastic bag with a full, fresh mango inside. "You take home," he says with a smile, "eat!" We thank him profusely and take the mango with us.

As evening is falling, we head back towards Little Beach. We heard earlier there was going to be some kind of gathering or party this evening, and we wanted to check it out. We park the rental Jeep, taking note of the signs in the lot that warn against leaving valuables in the vehicle. This particular parking lot is known for numerous thefts. I had the unfortunate experience on a previous trip of having my purse stolen from the trunk of the rental car. I had left my backpack on the beach with the car key in it while I was out snorkeling. Someone had apparently been watching, took the key, opened the trunk and got my belongings. They were nice enough to at least leave the car. I since learned the trick of keeping my key with me in a waterproof container at all times and leaving nothing of value in the car or on the beach.

We walk the narrow path up the rocky outcrop that separates the two beaches. As we reach the top, the whole of Little Beach comes into view. The sun is making its way towards the horizon, reflecting its radiant light on the clear, blue water. There are a few dozen people on the beach and another dozen or so in the water. Some are clothed, others not. A couple boogie boarders ride the small waves onto shore. Further out, a surfer is catching some of the larger waves. A number of people are lounging in beach chairs, sipping on drinks from their coolers. Some are sunning themselves. Others are walking hand in hand.

We continue down the outcrop and walk along the sandy beach to find a good spot to settle in for the evening. Never have I been at this beach when there were so many people.

We make our way towards a circle of drummers. The drummers look like they're just getting set up, and only a couple people so far are beating out a rhythm. The drums are mostly African djembes, but there are a couple other types of drums in the mix, along with some shakers and other fun music-makers.

The evening progresses, more drummers join in, and a few people get up to dance. I ask one of the drummers if it's okay if I join them, and he says any drum without a drummer is up for grabs. I find my way to a djembe without a player. Having had several drumming lessons and playing on my own djembe at home for the last year or so, I am comfortable with the opportunity. I beat out rhythms, tuning in and finding harmony with my fellow drummers, and take in the scene around me – the beautiful sunset beginning to share with us its brilliant colors of orange, yellow and fuchsia, the sound of the waves, the warm, moist air, being in the company of all these kind people.

When it gets dark a couple fire spinners light their poi and fire staff and put on an informal show of their talents. The drummers keep an upbeat rhythm going, and the crowd, which has grown even larger over the last hour, gathers around in a circle to watch. Tony leaves for several minutes to move our Jeep, fearing that we will get locked in, since the beach closes at sunset. He misses a lot of the fire spinning, but is able to catch the last few, impressive minutes of a performance by one of the locals.

The feeling of community is what strikes me most. In this company of fire spinners, dancers, drummers, yogis and all-around free spirits, I feel free to be myself, without the presence of judgment, without censorship. I drum and I drum, and each beat, which mirrors that of our common heartbeat, feels incredibly healing.

To our surprise, we are told this gathering happens every Sunday evening, for sunset. It seems to be a way to honor the sun, to honor the end of a day and start to a new week. As darkness falls, we make the trek back through the sand, walking within the warm glow of one of the fire spinner's torches. Everybody waits patiently as we get to the bottleneck at the outcrop, taking turns, one by one, to walk down the narrow path.

We then walk the distance through the parking lot, down the short road to the street, where our Jeep is now parked. As we arrive at the Jeep, I see Tony fishing something out of the bushes in front of the Jeep. A plastic bag. *Maybe he's picking up trash*, I think. It's hard to tell in the dark. No, it's his mango. He stashed it. "They can rifle through the Jeep. Hell, they can *take* the Jeep," he says, "but don't take my mango!"

The remainder of our Maui trip includes hikes through bamboo forests, treks to hidden waterfalls, swimming and snorkeling, enjoying homemade mango-banana bread, walking along the beach and relaxing in the condo. I appreciate this time of rejuvenation that nature provides and the opportunity for the two of us to deepen our connection. On our final evening, Tony and I spontaneously decide to take a sunset dinner cruise. It feels like a nice way to end a perfect vacation.

Despite the paradisiacal surroundings, each passing day holds brief moments of thinking about my challenging, recent transition with the Y. There are times when I feel sadness and anger, but there are also moments of determination, hope and excitement. The hope and excitement lies in feeling I have played a role in leading my local Y towards positive change, even if it is just in some small way.

As Tony and I sit on the plane, with home just hours away, returning soon to the usual day-to-day life, my thoughts are directed more and more to my present situation with the Y. I eagerly await word from Amanda. Earlier she let me know that she would notify me after she meets with other members of the Board. I feel I need closure as quickly as possible. I no longer wish to bear the anxiety and heaviness in my heart. I feel the need to move forward.

Settling back home, I pick up the mail from my overly-stuffed mailbox. In the stack is an envelope from the Y. I open it, flip to the bottom of the letter and see it is signed by Amanda. I take a breath and begin to read.

"Dear Kristi..."

I read that she met with a committee of Board members on Tuesday and reviewed the material I had sent her.

"The Committee has carefully considered the material," Amanda writes, "and has determined what course of action is in the best interest of the Y and its members. The committee has determined the matter is now closed.

We acknowledge and share your sincere concern for the YMCA. We wish you good luck in all your future endeavors."

I read it and re-read it. The matter is now closed? But what *happens*?! What "course of action"? I realize it is not my place to know their decision, though I truly ache to know. What does this all *mean*? Rather than finding any sense of resolution, it just raises more questions.

Oh, I understand I must let it go. I let out a frustrated sigh. The hardest part is not knowing the outcome, not knowing what was discussed, what actions were taken, if John will indeed be reviewed more thoroughly than in past years, if other managers will be interviewed and given an opportunity to share their experiences... and so on.

It just feels like I'm waiting for something, I'm in limbo. I'm unsure of my next step. I lack a sense of direction.

The fate of the Winowa County Y rests in Amanda's and the Board's hands. My report is now strictly with YMCA of the USA. So for now, I continue to further this larger effort.

Near the summer solstice, I hold a book release party for *Journey to One* at my home. It feels nice to gather with friends and celebrate. A few days later, I have my first book signing at a large bookstore in the nearest big city, Springdale. Several copies are sold, and it's great to have an opportunity to talk with both friends and strangers about the book.

Tony joins me for about ¾ of the book signing. Though on-call for work, he comes to show his love and support. He also brings his paperback copy for me to sign. I already signed his hard cover copy a while ago. I chuckle at him but appreciate his support and willingness to make this journey with me.

One of my former coworkers and friends from the Y drops in to the event, as well. Of course, the topic of the Y comes up. She's worked for the Y for over 2 decades, a long-timer who has seen a lot.

"Are you going to sue?" she asks with a hopeful tone.

"No."

"Why not?" she continues.

"It's complicated," I say, "but at the very least, I started a paper trail. Also, I feel like I need to be moving forward right now, and it seems like a lawsuit would keep me in the past. There are other things on which I want to be focusing. Also, I still work for the Y, how would it look to sue the local Y? Besides, it's never been about the money."

"No, but this is about justice," she states.

"I'm choosing a different route," I say. "He may be able to fire me, but he can't stop change." I conclude. She nods.

I spend a great amount of the summer sitting and lying on my lounger in the backyard. It's a lot of sitting and thinking. The season is unusually cool. The fog rolls in the majority of days and doesn't burn off until mid to late afternoon, or not at all. I prefer the sun and heat. I feel I need it to recharge my batteries. With the season being cooler, I am thankful to have the free time to be outside enjoying what little sun we do get. Whenever the sun peeks through, I open the sliding glass door and make my way to the lounger to savor each and every ray of light. After some time I go inside and make a smoothie, then return to the yard, perhaps pull a weed or two, and sit in the sun some more. There is very little structure. Day after day, I soak in the sun and just sit and think.

The Y continues to preoccupy my thoughts, just as occurs when one loses someone close, such as a spouse, a parent or a child. Everything is changed. The termination continues to weigh heavy in my heart. I do not yet have the energy or motivation to figure out how to restructure my life and move forward. There is a process that needs to happen... and time still needed to heal.

As I pass through the living room on one of my breaks from sunning, there's a giant book resting on the floor. I say giant because it is 17" tall by 28 ½" wide when open. It has 256 glossy, full-color pages, and it's titled *Birds of Prey: Majestic Masters of the Sky*. Tony's sister is letting us borrow it for a time, and it's one of those perfect coffee table books.

Except instead of the coffee table, it's on the floor where I enjoy flipping through it.

It's currently open to pages 218 & 219. I have been utterly fascinated by the picture on these pages since I first opened to it a couple days ago. The photo takes up about 2/3 of the spread. The background in the photo is smooth, white snow, nothing but snow on the ground. A Great Gray Owl is swooping in with wings spread wide. Its body is covered with dense feathers, speckled brown, gray and white. Its short, yellow beak is barely visible through the feathers that protrude down the middle of its face. There are smaller, smooth feathers that radiate from around the owl's eyes. Its legs and feet, also covered in fluffy feathers, are tucked in close to its body. The large talons are curved downward. What I find most intriguing about the owl is its intent stare. The owl's round, yellow eyes with dark pupils are extremely focused. Its gaze is locked on a little, brown field mouse.

I find the picture absolutely amazing. Here we have the bird of prey at the moment of capturing its prey. The prey, at some earlier point was unbeknownst to the presence of its watcher.

Now the little, brown mouse is fleeing for its life. It has such forward movement, such momentum and motivation to give it all it's got, that it is hovering several inches above the snow. The mouse appears to be flying. Behind it are its tiny tracks. Its four little, pink feet are dangling in space, and its tail is curved down and tucked close under its belly as the mouse glides over the crisp, white terrain.

The owl is mere inches from the mouse, at most a foot. Sometimes I walk by the photo on my way from one room to the next and say, "You're never going to make it, little mouse, but good effort!" Other times, I'll pass through and say, "Keep going, little mouse, maybe there's a hole just a few inches ahead!"

For whatever reason, I liken the events in this photo to my thoughts of what will become of John Smith and Kristi Bowman. Who is the bird, and who is the mouse? What will happen?

Towards the end of June, I write a final, professional, parting email to Amy, still working to find a sense of closure, piece by piece. I let her know I appreciate her supervision and mentoring the last few years at the Y, how I feel she helped me grow professionally and personally, and how I see her as a strong person who will no doubt continue to be a leader in the growth and development of the Y. I also reiterate that I felt it was necessary to take the steps I did and to raise awareness of issues at the Board level. I wish her and the entire staff, volunteers and members all the best.

With the letter, I am able to let go of some attachment to what happens, or what doesn't happen. I am still very curious, mind you, but I work to release any expectation and just let things be.

I am reminded of a passage in the Bhagavad Gita, an ancient Indian text. "Seek refuge in the attitude of detachment and you will amass the wealth of spiritual awareness." Gandhi spoke of this detachment, too. "You must not worry whether the desired result follows from your action or not, so long as your motive is pure, your means correct... things will come right in the end..."

I receive a call from Jennifer Martin. She says Y-USA is ready to contract with me directly for the role of Activate America Facilitator. I will continue to work in the capacity of a change agent with the national Y through the end of the year, which is the term of the current contract, and with potential to start another contract in the coming year. As it's only a few hours per week, the income is considerably less than what I was getting, so I continue to explore options regarding my finances. However, it's meaningful and exciting to continue to work at this large-scale level. By contracting with me directly, it demonstrates that Y-USA values and supports my work. After being kicked out of the nest, I feel comforted in Y-USA's big hands swooping in to catch me.

A couple days later I have a phone call with my friend, Jill, who is an incredible visionary artist, teacher and shamanic guide. I studied with her for a few years after returning home from our shared spiritual journey at Teotihuacán. Phone calls with Jill are nothing short of profound. Jill is a loving and powerful guide with her head in the stars and her feet rooted deep within the earth. Through the years that I've learned from her and worked with her, she has provided countless gems of wisdom and beneficial tools that have played a huge role in helping me embody my potential as I walk my life path. Knowing her has truly been life-changing.

On this particular call, during this time of intense transition in my work, she says to me, "It's time to fully awaken. It's time to feel in your heart who and what you are, what you want, and how to present or express it out in the world. The time is now." I let the words sink into my heart. Jill continues, "There is a greater vision, even bigger than what you currently see. Allow yourself to keep aligning with the bigger vision. *Of course* it's going to be harmonious. *Of course* it's going to be balanced. That is the essence of the creation of the universe." The ache still lingers from being let go, but I let the feelings of harmony and balance begin to seep in through her words.

Who am I? What do I want? How do I wish to express in the world? I spend time meditating on these questions. I remain open to possibility. I know I'm in a time of great change. I can feel it on so many levels. I get the sense that something very special lies on the horizon, and it's just waiting for me to recognize and embrace it.

In July, the Y holds its General Assembly in Salt Lake City. Though I'm not in attendance, I get filled in on the details. The new logo is released. There is a great deal of thoughtfulness in its design. With various color schemes in the logo series, it speaks to and celebrates the diversity of the people at the Y. The logo has the overall shape of a Y, as it did previously, but it is softened around the edges and also angled forward, which removes some of the rigid, corporate feel and represents the organization's forward movement. It is fresh, current and relevant. The word "the" is included next to the Y in the logo, declaring itself to be what people have been calling it for decades, "The Y." It is a time of significant change in the organization, symbolized by this new identity. It's also an opportunity for those of us involved to make even more of a difference in supporting the health and well-being of communities across the U.S.

The Y continues to preoccupy the large majority of my thoughts. In the midst of thinking about the Y, worries come up, too, about how I'm going to pay the rent and take care of my needs. Accompanying the worry is the feeling of fear in my belly, the fear of possibly having to go without, the fear of not knowing if everything will be okay. When there are significant life changes to navigate, it's easy to worry.

Just as I'm experiencing this worry, Bob Marley comes onto my iTunes random mix singing, "Baby, don't wor-ry... 'bout a thing... 'cause every little thing's... gonna be alright..." Out of more than 2000 songs in my iTunes library that could have played in this moment, that is the one that did. Thank you, universe.

I take stock of what money I have in the bank. I also have a retirement account, some of which could be cashed out if absolutely necessary. I also know I will be receiving a check in the mail soon for the contract work with Y-USA. My electricity is on. I have food in the fridge. It's not like I'm destitute. In this moment, everything *is* alright.

It feels necessary to release fear around my finances. The "what am I going to do?" question keeps cropping up, heavily laden with anxiety. I must let go of the worry. Fear can immobilize or weigh a person down. It feels to be weighing me down. Fear also clouds vision, making it difficult to see the positive things that are possible. I decide to consider the question, "What am I going to do?" in a different way. Rather than have the question come from a place of fear, I change the tone and ask it simply from a place of strategy, anticipated action. Doing so feels less stressful and more beneficial. I must trust in my own skills and abilities as I move forward in my work, as well as trust that I am walking my path.

In early August I fly to Chicago for an Activate America Facilitators' meeting. As usual, I feel a sense of belonging with those at the national office. The national headquarters is different this visit. The offices recently moved to a different floor of the building. Jennifer gives all of us facilitators a tour of the new place. The space has been designed and decorated to reflect the new image of the Y. Everybody is giddy with excitement. The walls are primarily white with splashes of vibrant colors. The logo, in its various color combinations, is prominently displayed. Workspaces include social areas with a small table and comfortable chairs. In one room, I see a jigsaw puzzle in progress, and a small toy monkey that some playful person brought in, sitting in one of the chairs. Down one of the hallways are images of children in Y programs around the world, and the 119 countries are listed where the Y provides services. Positive messaging is displayed tastefully throughout the facility, such as "Making a difference," "Dedicated to community," "Learn grow thrive," and one of my favorites, "Push for positive change."

Also, each of the corner rooms, usually designated as corner offices for top executives in a corporation, has instead been designed as social spaces, where people can gather and chat, and everyone can enjoy the high-rise view of the city. I find it so interesting and encouraging how humility is built into the very design. It is apparent how the Y strives to carry out business with great awareness and for the good of the whole. After all, it is *together* that we can create the most positive change.

At one point in the tour we pass by a timeline of the Y from its founding. I notice how since 1891 the logo, which has continued to evolve over the decades, includes the triangle that represents spirit, mind and body. Now, many fitness facilities and wellness programs across the country and around the world promote this integration of spirit, mind and body. Here the Y has been focusing on it well over 100 years.

The final two dates on the timeline are 2004 and 2010. I read the entries. In 2004 "Activate America was launched as the YMCA's response to our nation's growing lifestyle health crisis. Through this ambitious effort, Ys are redefining themselves and engaging their communities across the country to better support Americans of all ages who are struggling to achieve and maintain well-being of spirit, mind and body." For 2010, "Y-USA launched a new visual system as part of a national brand revitalization strategy. The refreshed logo is designed to reflect the vibrancy and diversity of the Y movement." I am reminded again just how cool the Y is.

As we come together for our 2-day facilitators' meeting and catch up with our hellos, Jennifer Martin says I can share whatever I feel comfortable sharing regarding the transition of my job. I let the group know I was "let go" from my local Y and leave it at that. Those at Y-USA who need to know more, such as Jennifer and Aaron Rothenberg, Vice President of Health Strategy & Innovation, already were provided the necessary details.

Later in the evening, we go out to dinner as a group. One of the other facilitators asks me if I have read that article in the Harvard Business Review, "the one on leading change?" I recall it and how it starts off talking about the "high-stake risks you face when you try to lead an organization through difficult but necessary change."

"Yes, I remember it," I reply.

"Sounds like that's what happened to you," she continues.

"Yes, and it sure doesn't feel very good," I say.

"No, it doesn't."

It is somewhat comforting, though, that I'm not the only one to whom this has happened. Articles are written about it. Actually, I'm not even the only one in our small group of 21 facilitators. Another one of the facilitators also recently got fired from her local Y. It is an inherent risk of the work we are doing. However, we are working for the parent company, and Y-USA supports our change efforts. Getting let go hasn't dampened my spirits. I'm still passionate about the work, and it is apparent that everyone else in Chicago on the Activate America team is, too.

For fun, Jennifer Martin initiates a brief talent show for all the facilitators. I love the idea of talent shows, for I believe we *all* possess talents. We *all* have a tremendous amount of creative potential. Often, it's just a matter of getting past our own fear and unleashing it!

For my time of sharing, I have a few copies of my book, and I also lead a movement activity for those in the group who wish to participate. Before I left for the trip, I made several pairs of training poi, objects that you hold in each hand and spin around in various configurations. After having considerable training with practice poi, a person might move up to spinning fire. It's an invigorating experience to spin fire, but not something you want to do on the 15th floor of an office building. A large, heavy rubber ball stuffed inside a bright red or purple thigh-high stocking makes great practice poi. I don my black and red extreme-flare-leg pants, turn on some music and provide instructions for a few simple movements with the poi. It's good exercise, increases coordination and is simply a lot of fun. With all the laughter, I can tell everyone enjoys it. I enjoy seeing and hearing the talents of the other facilitators, as well.

Throughout this Chicago trip, in various capacities, I am able to simply be me. I never feel I have to shrink down or be in fear of shining my light. It is quite different from how it was at the local Y. I appreciate the supportive atmosphere at Y-USA. Encouraging creativity and building each other up not only helps us learn, grow and thrive as individuals, it strengthens us as a team, and it ripples out to benefit the organization and greater community.

I'm later invited to a special 1-day meeting. The meeting is an information gathering session for those involved in health strategy and innovation, as well as discussion about how the Y is expanding and moving forward as a leader in disease prevention, particularly diabetes and cancer.

As I arrive in Chicago, it, like any large city, is hustling and bustling. As I have done a half-dozen times before, I walk along the sidewalk in the heart of the downtown business district making my way toward the Y headquarters. The scene is replete with cars speeding by, horns honking, construction projects, and business men and women crowding the walkways, consulting and communicating through their iPads and smart phones. There's an assortment of high-rise office buildings with walls of glistening glass. It is all abuzz, just like a hive, worker bees busy, busy, busy.

I notice there is no nature around, not even a single pigeon that I can see. Walking hastily to the next block, crossing the street carefully so as not to get run over by a kamikaze taxi, I wonder if I am the only one around who is feeling disconnected from natural life in this setting. Perhaps there are others, too. Maybe it's recognized or maybe it's simply on an unconscious level, evidenced only by a feeling of overwork and stress or depression. I realize with each passing year I appreciate more and more my home environment, the quiet place on the outskirts of town, surrounded by nature. I suppose if I were to be amidst the hustle and bustle on a daily basis, I, too, would grow accustomed to it. I'm grateful I am not, however. It helps keep life real for me. It keeps me feeling connected to our planet, the beautiful blue-green globe beneath the asphalt and concrete.

I slip through the revolving doors of 101 N. Wacker Drive and take the elevator to the 15th floor. The culture of the Y is familiar, and I find some respite in the warm, welcoming atmosphere of Y-USA.

In attendance are Activate America facilitators, physicians, consultants, and numerous YMCA professionals, all involved in leading the movement to create healthier communities. Aaron Rothenberg takes a few moments to speak directly to those who are Activate America facilitators. He states how each of us has demonstrated the "highest level of professionalism." He continues, "This level of work provides a big boost to your careers, even if you choose to have a future with a company or agency other than the Y." I am told that Activate America is also helping Y-USA identify the Y leaders of tomorrow, or today, as the case may be. One of the facilitators in our group has recently become the CEO at a Y on the west coast. "As positions open up, Activate America-aligned professionals are being moved in," Aaron shares. It is part of the culture change.

The following day, I fly to LA to attend the Advanced Relationship Building Institute, which is the follow-up to the Listen First Institute and focuses on supporting change. I awaken the following day not feeling rested, for the noisy neighbors and hotel bed didn't lend for a peaceful night's sleep. After spilling half of my breakfast on my pants and getting yelled at by a taxi driver for no discernable reason, I feel more than ready to go home. As soon as the training is complete, that is just what I do. The 2-day whirlwind trip helps remind me of the challenges many people face on a daily basis to find some peace of mind, or a place in nature, or a sanctuary in which to retreat from all the busy-ness, busi-ness of life and be able to connect with the quiet space and wisdom within.

I have learned so much from the Y, but I feel there is still more that I can learn, and also a lot more that I can do. What lies in store for me? My work is shifting significantly and the future is not yet clear. I think about my last phone call with Jill, about there being a bigger vision than what I currently see and aligning to it.

As the cool, gray summer lives out its final few weeks, a shift occurs. It feels time to fully, wholly and completely LET GO. From the days following my dismissal, there have been many things that have strained and pulled on me. The past few months, there were times when I was able to let go of certain aspects of the difficult Winowa County Y experience. I felt some sense of release after writing Amy the parting letter. I later wrote a letter to Amanda, and then Aaron Rothenberg, finding some more release. But despite this and other actions, something has remained this entire time. I have continued to be attached... to something. The attachment has felt strong and heavy, too, fastened with steel chains – cumbersome, clanky, a burden.

With further self-exploration, I finally recognize the attachment. That "something" is *wanting to know*. It is *wanting to know* if the actions I took made a difference, *wanting to know* if anything changed for the better. I don't need specifics, I just *want to know.*

It is a true test of letting go of attachment for me. There's nothing wrong, per se, with *wanting* to know. I believe it's natural to wish for something positive to result from my actions, as my intention was that something positive would arise from them. However, there is no value in waiting to hear for word of change at the local Y. Each time I put thought into *wanting to know* what is going on, my energy feels pulled in that direction, and I have a difficult time moving forward while dragging those heavy chains. By fully letting go, by detaching, I attain freedom. Perhaps this is what the Bhagavad Gita is referring to when it talks about amassing the "wealth of spiritual awareness" by adopting an attitude of detachment. This freedom.

In truth, it's not about results. It's about choices and actions. Sometimes in life you take a leap of faith. The leap is not about getting from one side to the other. It's simply about taking the leap... and trusting.

It's about doing what I feel is right and important and compassionate, no matter the personal consequences. It's about helping and supporting others – coworkers, friends, communities, YMCAs. It's about being part of a team and working for something bigger than myself.

I feel the benefits of leading change far outweigh the risks. Yes, there are losses, some pretty big ones. But being an integral part of this special process with the Y is giving me so much more than I ever initially anticipated. I get to be part of an amazing and beautiful, large-scale movement that is making a positive impact on the well-being of individuals and communities all across the country.

This experience has also taught me about being myself, wholly, completely, without shrinking. I feel I must respect and honor my own potential and desire for continued growth. I must allow room for blossoming. I realize this year, 2010, is the year when the blossoming *begins*. I have a feeling the blossoming will continue for a few years more.

So rather than hang onto the desire that I will hear of change, of *wanting to know*, I detach. I let go, once and for all. As I do, something beautiful occurs. I feel satisfied with my part in it all, and I begin to simply enjoy my time, my flexibility. I get to go for nature walks when I choose, and have a work schedule that I choose. With chains cut, I get to use all of my energy, directing it forward to my future and into what I wish to create next. I get to align with the greater vision. I feel lighter and brighter... and absolutely free.

Chapter 13

Dreaming

My eyes slowly blink open. I hear Tony rustling around downstairs. Sometime during the night he had gotten up and put a makeshift bed together downstairs where it was cooler and where he could more easily sprawl out. I shout from the upstairs bedroom, "Are you awake?"

"I'm awake," he responds.

"Are you ready to go camping?" I ask. This morning we're going to head northeast for a few hours to Plumas County to camp for 4 nights near Lake Almanor. I'm looking forward to spending time with just the dirt, trees, the water and my lover. Tony will get to fish, and I'll get to relax and explore. The truck is all packed, and we just have a couple final things to add before we hit the road.

"Yes, I'm ready to go camping!" he says with excitement. The next thing I hear is the sound of his footsteps rushing up the stairs. He tops the stairs with a blanket and pillow in his arms. I smile at his youthful innocence.

"The question is," Tony starts, "are *you* ready to go camping?" He bounces into bed and gently tickles me as we both giggle.

I feel I can take things too seriously at times, and I find Tony's playfulness to be balancing and refreshing. He helps bring out my own playful nature that sometimes gets forgotten in the carrying out of day-to-day adult responsibilities.

A couple weeks after returning from our camping trip, Tony and I build a fort in his living room. It's the kind of fort you make when you're a kid with blankets draped over the furniture. Our construction of the fort starts off simply, pulling the two couches parallel to one another, tossing a couple blankets between them, and weighing down the corners of the blankets with whatever is nearby – backpack, Scrabble game, folded beach towel. Tony then ties a heavy string across the room as support for the center of the fort to take out the sag, "crucial for the integrity of the structure," he says with a smile. Now it looks like an old-style tent.

During the next couple of days, the fort evolves and becomes more of a tent cabin structure. Tony raises the roof, which I find symbolic of allowing for greater growth. The walls get moved a little further apart, and the whole fort is fortified with rope. Finally, a wooden staff is positioned at the center of the door for optimum support and easy access. It's pretty awesome, really.

Tony and I snuggle inside and christen the space, as it were. Something about this little bout of lovemaking seems different. We go to a deeper level. We both seem more open – emotionally, spiritually. There are times when I feel in complete bliss, off in another dimension. Then I return to earth, and we check in with our eyes, seeing each other without any barriers that would prohibit such deep connection. We check in, exchange a couple words, a smile, and then, as if carried by waves, get swept away and immersed in a sea of pure love, joy and passion.

I believe this state, this experience, comes as a culmination of our relationship being loving, playful and in balance. It is the everyday, kind and respectful interactions that help strengthen the connection between us. "Kristi, I'm making some tea, would you like some?" It's keeping each other in mind and treating each other with the consideration of close friends. It's remembering to say "please" and "thank you." It is being present with one another, making eye contact, and communicating openly and honestly, even when things might feel a little uncomfortable or challenging. It is encouraging each other's creativity and having fun together. My experience is that it is all these things that add up and contribute to greater happiness and satisfaction in a relationship.

Shortly after, we lead our first hike together as a couple. I've been leading hikes solo for over 2 years, first through the Y, then on my own, feeling the desire to continue this service to the community. It's a new experience to have a co-leader. There are about a dozen hikers this morning. There is an extra element of fun on the hike today, as one woman, a long-time friend of Tony's, brings temporary tattoos of various animals. Before we start our trek, each of us pick out a tattoo and apply it to our arms or hands. Tony chooses a gorilla face tattoo for the underside of his forearm. I choose a small, blue dragon and affix it to the underside of my wrist.

After the hike is complete, Tony and I treat the group to some hot cocoa using our camping stove propped on the tailgate of his pickup to heat water. As we sip our cocoa and share stories, I think about how much I enjoy witnessing Tony as he begins to step into a leadership role. It seems natural for him, and he lends a unique perspective and boisterousness to the activities. Everyone seems to enjoy the hike, the opportunity to be in nature, the treats and each other's company.

Still feeling energized later that evening, Tony asks if I want to go for a walk. I agree, so we drive towards town and park at a walking/bike path. We've walked this path often, and Tony tells stories of when he was a child walking the very same path. Except it wasn't a paved trail then, but a dirt path alongside a set of railroad tracks. He shares experiences about getting into mischief as a young boy with his friends.

As we saunter along, hand in hand, a young woman rides by on her bike. "She has tats, too," Tony says, noting the plentiful tattoos covering both her arms, "like me!" He turns his forearm over to reveal the gorilla face, and we both laugh.

One Sunday morning in the heart of autumn, I feel a little on the cranky side, for no reason in particular. We go to yoga, and it's a beautiful class with friends and playful discussion about items on our "bucket list." I always enjoy teaching, and no matter how I feel prior, by the time class is over, I feel invigorated and on top of the world. This is one of the amazing gifts of yoga.

Following class, Tony and I go out for breakfast at a local restaurant, a family-owned breakfast joint chock full of charm. Charm in the old, country way, not necessarily the chic type of charm you might find at a local bed and breakfast. The food isn't really that great, but it's the kind of place that reminds me of my grandmother and that simple, "down-home" feel of her generation. The walls are covered in photographs of the owner's family, revealing brief moments in time over the course of several decades. In the restaurant, there are also two, life-size cowboy statues, not something you see every day. One is at the entrance with one hand reaching out as if to shake hands and say, "Howdy pardner!" and the other is near the cash register with both pistols drawn.

On the wall next to the booth where we sit are several pictures of a woman and her horse. There are some pictures of her hugging a foal just a few days old. The young woman in the photo is now the middle-aged waitress — a little heavier and a few more lines in her face — pouring Tony's cup of decaf. As he asks her if he can please have some honey, another waitress, Mildred, arrives with honey bear in hand and says, "Here's your honey, Tony." She knows him by name and anticipates his wishes from serving Tony his breakfast for years.

I find Mildred both fascinating and admirable. She has to be in her 80s with a pronounced hunch in her back, which keeps her head looking at a significant downward angle the majority of the time, until she, with effort, chooses to raise her head. Mildred goes scurrying around sharp as a tack and quick-witted in her black orthotics. She often kindheartedly gives Tony a hard time, like the time we came into the restaurant with my friend, Maureen, and she told Tony it wasn't fair to have *two* women on his arm.

After breakfast we get on our bicycles and ride to Diego Park, stopping to climb and sit in a tree. We ride through a nearby neighborhood, taking a few minutes to visit with a couple of Tony's long-time friends, parents of one of his boyhood buddies. We then continue our bike ride onto the paved trail that follows the creek, past the high school and into town to Whole Foods for an Island Breeze smoothie.

Tony chats with a gentleman outside the store as we sip on our tropical delights. The subject is Tony's bike. His bicycle is one of the most effective conversation starters I've seen. On our ride so far today, 6 or 7 people have commented on it and been intrigued by its uniqueness. It's not uncommon to see several heads turn and look at it on any given day.

It's a recumbent bicycle, which is already a little out of the norm, but it is also a recumbent that sits up taller than most. Tony likes to tell people, "It's like sitting on the couch with your feet on the coffee table."

The weekly farmers' market is still going strong across the street, so we decide to stroll on over and enjoy the live music and peruse the booths. The market hosts a wide selection of fresh, organic veggies and fruits, in addition to woven baskets, clothing, and other gift items. There's usually a diverse group of people of all ages – locals, as well as visitors from nearby towns and tourists from around the Bay Area passing through on their way to the coast. We run into my former African drum teacher and friend and say hi, and also chat with a couple other market-goers.

We then make our way back to the bike path, continuing our leisurely pace, enjoying the view, the friendly conversations throughout the day, and the 80 degree weather in November. We decide to make one more stop at the park to climb another tree before circling back home.

Despite the cranky beginnings, it turns out to be a special day, and one of my favorites spent with Tony. It has been almost a year since Tony and I have been "dating," or been partnered. It is apparent to me what kind of person he is through his interactions with others. He is kind and approachable and nonjudgmental towards everyone. He is my small-town friend and lover with an open mind, open heart and strong spirit. It's a joy to share these everyday life moments with him.

On Thanksgiving Day 2010, Tony and I celebrate our 1 year anniversary, or 1 year of sharing the journey together. He wakes up to find a wrapped gift sitting on the chair next to the bed that I sneakily placed there after he fell asleep. Crawling out of bed in the buff, he says excitedly, "You got me a gift?" He begins to try to guess what it is. "It's a…… one of those things to put under my laptop; it's for my computer," he begins.

I give him a quizzical look. "Just open it," I say.

"It's some sort of organizer…" he continues.

"Just open it!" I say again, laughing. He tears at the paper. "Wait!" I interrupt him, "Did you get the card?" He digs around and finds the card mixed in with the bed covers. He reads it, smiles, then resumes tearing at the paper.

While he opens the gift, I am reminded of the Medicine Wheel that spontaneously came about those many months ago. The animal card I drew that was linked with the season of autumn was Beaver, the builder. I feel it. I have been building. Tony and I both, actually, have been building the foundation for a lasting relationship.

"It's a photo album!" he guesses, just as he is about to uncover it. We look through the album together, snapshots in time of the places we've visited, the fun activities we have shared, and the time spent with family and friends over the past year.

"This way when we're old and gray, we can look back and see when we were young and beautiful," I say with a grin.

"When we're old and beautiful, we can look back and see when we were young and beautiful," Tony rephrases.

Yes, absolutely.

I have a dream early one morning that feels significant: *In the dream I'm in an unfamiliar place that seems like a business or government building. It has a spacious interior with tile or cement floor and double-doors. It reminds me of the type of building you'd find at a school. The dream begins as I open one of the doors to the outside. There are a ½ dozen or so*

concrete steps and a railing, then a sidewalk and street at the bottom of the steps. I open the door and see a mountain lion on the sidewalk.

I quickly close the door most of the way, surprised to see the lion. It's a female, and she seems out of place in this environment. As I peek through the small crack in the door, I see her simply standing there looking at me. Her right side is facing me, like she was just walking down the sidewalk.

I take my hand, reach it through, and slap it on the outside of the door a couple times, creating noise that I hope will send the cat on its way. But the mountain lion continues to be still.

"Hey, get!" I say. Still she remains with her intent stare. There is a sense that she is waiting. What is she waiting for? I wonder. The dream fades.

I crawl out of bed and look up Mountain Lion in *Medicine Cards*. I read that Mountain Lion is about leadership. I get the sense that in the dream Mountain Lion wanted me to come out and follow her. She was waiting for *me*, a message about assuming the role of leadership. In Native teachings, Mountain Lion is not about the type of leadership that involves controlling or exerting power over others or being demanding. Rather, as Sams and Carson state, "It is the ability to lead without insisting that others follow" and is about balancing power, intention, strength and grace. They continue, "The first responsibility of leadership is to tell the truth. Know it and live it, and your example will filter down to the tiniest cub in the pride." Lead by example.

I realize that how I live my life is the best way to teach. Or how *we* live our lives, you and me, for we all are potential leaders in our own ways, whether through parenting or work. One of the greatest things we can do is set a positive example.

On December 4, 2010, I host an event at my home, led by my friend, Jill. The event is called Sacred Dreaming 2011, and it is an opportunity to look towards the coming year and explore what we might receive, but even more so, contribute, in relation to a larger, collective vision.

When Jill arrives in the early afternoon, we exchange hugs and hellos. I show her around my place, taking her out to the backyard, then through the house. We spend a considerable amount of time in the 2nd bedroom that I use as my energy room and creative space.

After several minutes, Tony and I take Jill to a nearby waterfall, one tucked away on private property on which he received permission to visit. We enjoy time hiking near the waterfall and taking in the beautiful scenery. Jill and I gather some fresh water to take with us for the event later.

As evening falls, people begin to arrive. Some participants have traveled considerable distances from around the Bay Area. There are 10 of us total, including Jill and me. We chat, munch on snacks and sip on hot apple cider. For the evening, I will juggle the roles of hostess and also participant in the sacred ceremony.

Following introductions, Jill plays the Native flute, says a few words and initiates our special time together. We then move to the energy room, which has various cushions and pillows to allow for comfortable sitting or lying.

Jill has a variety of items that she brought, and each of us is given something to hold while we are guided through a visualization, or shamanic journey. I am handed the feather of a red-tailed hawk. Hawk represents the "messenger" in the Native tradition.

Once everyone receives his or her item to hold, Jill picks up the water that we retrieved from the waterfall, dips her finger in it and begins to go around the circle one by one. She touches the water to an individual's forehead and identifies the person by his or her spirit name. After 4 or 5 other participants, she approaches me, dips her finger to the water, touches my forehead and says, "Granddaughter White Eagle."

Immediately I feel a sense of recognition, and also an incredible amount of responsibility. Eagle represents Spirit. Eagle medicine is known as the power of the Great Spirit, the connection to the Divine. The feathers of an eagle are considered to be the most sacred of healing tools by Native people. The color white denotes a purity and clarity in this divine connection. I let the name touch my heart, but I tell myself to not think too much about it at this moment, not wishing to feel overwhelmed by the responsibility.

Once Jill finishes going around the circle we settle in for the shamanic journey. For those who may not have experienced a shamanic journey before, it is just like story time in kindergarten, all cozy and relaxed, but it has depth that can lead to powerful personal insights. Jill uses guided visualization, sparking the imagination and creative potential within each participant. It's a way for each of us to connect with our inner wisdom.

During the journey, Jill invites us to visualize a symbol, which we will have an opportunity to draw later in the dining area where we have set up a craft table. I am interrupted in the visualizing of this symbol by the sudden smell of something burning. I dash out of the room fearing the kitchen may be ablaze. I find the apple cider has boiled down to black, charred, sludgy remains, billowing smoke throughout the kitchen and dining area. I open the sliding glass door and quickly place the pot outside.

Because of the interruption and due to busily attending to other hostess duties, I do not complete the guided visualization or draw a symbol. The other participants gather around the dining table or use space on the floor to create their symbols using paper and colored pencils. Still desiring to participate in the process, I decide I will create a symbol in the coming days.

Following that portion of the event, the group gathers once again in the living room to wrap up our time together. We have a brief writing exercise and then share what we wish to contribute to 2011. I express that my contribution is to support growth and positive transformation, and I state that I feel this may extend well beyond 2011. It's a special evening, and the Sacred Dreaming ceremony seems to be enjoyed by all.

The few days following the event, I continue to feel the effects of the dreaming that Jill initiated and facilitated. I continue to feel like I'm in a visioning process. At night, I do not sleep consistently. I lie awake for hours, feeling the dream that is my life, the dream that is life, unfolding, and feeling tremendous creative energy. I surrender to this flow, allowing my body to rest while my mind is busy with creative thought. Even during the hours I sleep, the time feels more like meditating or journeying. It is from such a deep journey within that there is an emergence of something incredible.

In the early morning hours of December 9th, when all is still dark and silent, I awake with a start. At this very moment, I feel like I have just emerged from some place of depth, and I have come through 3 doorways, one right after the other, as I made my ascent to this waking state. It was very quick – bam! bam! bam! – each door quickly slamming shut as soon as I passed through it. My eyes opened and I awakened immediately upon passing through the 3rd door. I blink, finding no differentiation between eyes closed and eyes open. Against the absolute darkness that fills the room, an image of a butterfly is emblazoned in my mind. It is simply there, clear as can be, accompanying me from the sleeping realm to wakefulness.

Everything about the butterfly is important to remember, I hear my inner voice of wisdom say. I continue to picture the image in detail – the butterfly's shape, colors, markings, and the feelings invoked in me as I gaze at it. The image is a symbol, one that offers guidance to me on this part of my personal journey, and also speaks to the transformative potential within each of us.

Chapter 14

Butterfly Creation

Everything in your life is there as a vehicle for your transformation. Use it.
— Ram Dass

*L*ater that day I set out to recreate the image of the butterfly. I gather my colored pencils, still left on the dining room table from the Sacred Dreaming event, and a piece of 14" x 17" Bristol board — a very heavy, white paper that provides a nice, large surface for just such a creative project. I bring the items to my energy room and splay them out on the floor. Out of the 108 colors in my collection, I pick up the azure pencil, the blue-green that most closely reflects the color I saw in my dream. My first few attempts result in misshapen figures only slightly resembling wings. They look like the drawings of a young child.

I've never felt I was gifted with any special drawing abilities. There are individuals who, with ease, can pick up a pencil and within moments sketch out a fantastic image. I am not one of them. *How am I going to create this butterfly?* I wonder. But I persist, as Butterfly herself inspires me to continue.

The primary teaching or gift that the butterfly provides is about transformation. There are few things more spectacular, in my mind, as the changes that take place through the four stages of a butterfly's life. It begins as an egg, laid by the female on a leaf or other plant material. Upon hatching, it moves into the larva, or caterpillar, stage. The primary activity of the caterpillar is eating, a *lot* of eating. It can grow 100 times its size in this stage. As it grows, it splits and sheds its skin about 4 or 5 times. When the caterpillar is full grown, it stops eating, hangs itself from the underside of a leaf or twig, sheds its caterpillar skin one final time and enters the third, or pupa, stage. Technically, for the butterfly, it is known as the chrysalis, and for moths, it is referred to as the cocoon. However, the word cocoon has a special appeal to me, and it is sometimes used regarding the butterfly as well.

The cocoon is where the magic happens. Hidden away in its enclosure, the caterpillar literally digests itself, releasing enzymes to dissolve all of its tissues. If you were to cut open a cocoon (I'm not saying I encourage this, by any means) at just the right time, a liquid, soupy mess would ooze out. Everything that once made up the caterpillar no longer exists. Well, almost everything. There are certain, highly organized groups of cells, known as imaginal discs, that survive the digestive process. When a caterpillar is still developing inside its egg, it grows an imaginal disc for each of the adult body parts it will need as a mature butterfly – discs for its eyes, for its wings, its legs and so on. For many species, these imaginal discs remain dormant throughout the caterpillar's life, only to be activated in this cocoon stage. Once a caterpillar has disintegrated all of its tissues except the imaginal discs, these discs use the protein-rich soup all around them to fuel the rapid cell division required to form the wings, antennae, legs and other features of the adult butterfly body.

How amazing is this process! "Imaginal" is of the same root as imagine, image and imagination. Though the butterfly in form does not yet exist, within the caterpillar lies the *potential* for the butterfly. It is as if these cells hold an image of what *can* be, just as our mind, our imagination, holds the potential for the creation of something altogether new and beautiful.

The fourth stage is that of the butterfly. Having completed its metamorphosis, it breaks out of its chrysalis and is now a very different creature from the caterpillar. The caterpillar has a few tiny eyes, stubby legs and is long and plump. It stays close to the ground and makes its way along very slowly. The butterfly has a lean body, separated into a head, thorax and abdomen. It has an exoskeleton, two antennae, long legs, compound eyes, and a long straw-like structure through which it drinks up nectar, known as a proboscis. The proboscis doesn't have any taste sensors. Interestingly, the taste receptacles are on the butterfly's front feet. Its sense of taste is 200 times stronger than that of humans. Butterflies taste flowers simply by walking upon them. The most apparent feature of the butterfly, though, is its wings, so delicate and colorful. These wings enable flight.

From an egg, to a caterpillar, to goo, to a butterfly. The transformation is remarkable.

It is hard to see a butterfly and not smile. They flitter and flutter about, dancing in the air and flashing their beautiful colors. They seem to spread sweetness and joy wherever they go.

Eventually, through repeated efforts with colored pencil in hand, an image appears on the paper that looks close to the shape of the wings of the butterfly in my mental image. I hold it up and gaze at it with some small degree of satisfaction. I decide, from this stage in her development, I will continue to work on her tomorrow.

As I return the next day and sit down in front of the drawing, I feel something important is happening through this endeavor. It extends beyond the specific task of creating this butterfly. It is linked to the creative process itself.

We all possess creative ability. It is in our very nature. Many of us have a tendency, though, to think only people who can paint a masterpiece or play in a symphony or design a house, or can draw a complex picture within a few short minutes, are artists, or are creative. Creativity comes in many forms, limited only by our beliefs.

In my work with Y-USA, I was talking a couple weeks ago with one of the Activate America Project Managers at a Y. I was encouraging her to gather her team and explore some creative ways to implement some of the suggested environmental changes. "We're not very creative," she said. I've heard this same sentiment come out of the mouths of several individuals in a wide array of situations, from top executives to yoga students to friends and family. So I challenged her a bit. "I think everyone has creative ability," I said. After talking further and helping her look at creativity in a different way, she expressed that she felt creative in her gardening and the way she had done the landscaping at her home. "Yes!" I exclaimed. It was a starting point, a door opening to a new perspective.

I've learned that overcoming our own limiting beliefs is often the hardest step. Once we shift our perception around creativity and around what is possible, we've overcome a huge obstacle and just cleared a pathway to being more creative.

With this understanding of the creative process, I begin to think about the next step in creating my butterfly. I don't know how I'm going to get to the end result, but I will find a way.

Similarly, we don't always know how we're going to get from point A to point B regarding some life situation, but if we're persistent and stay open-minded and trust that with a little ingenuity and creativity, we can do it, we will. That is, if we do not judge ourselves and instead allow for experimentation and a variety of approaches in the creative process. It's also important to allow for "failures," also known as learning opportunities. This, too, might be considered art. It is how we become the artists of our lives.

With some simple outlines completed on the paper, I go to my laptop and begin to browse through Google images for butterflies that might resemble the one from my dream. I do not find any that match, but I am drawn to 3 specific images. A couple are clip art images and one is a photo of a tattoo on the low back of a woman. The tattoo design is closest to what I'm looking for, but I utilize some elements from each of the 3 butterfly images for my drawing, and I include new elements to reflect the unique image that wants to be expressed. At the conclusion of this phase of the process, surrounded by a number of incomplete attempts, I have a half of a butterfly, the body and one wing, drawn on the Bristol board.

Over the course of the next few days, I continue to work in earnest on the butterfly. There are several occasions in the creative process where I feel I just do not know how to proceed. I come up to obstacles in the road. Each time, I decide to just sit with it, and allow time for the answer to come. Moving through the unknown can be challenging, and perhaps downright uncomfortable, but it is possible to take one small step at a time, even in the dark. If we choose to keep moving forward, feeling our way along, the solutions eventually show themselves.

The butterfly gradually unfolds. In a burst of insight as the single-winged pencil drawing lies before me, I rummage through my art supplies and find a piece of tracing paper. I copy the half butterfly onto the tracing paper with a regular #2 pencil. I then fold the tracing paper in half and draw the other wing, lifting the paper and drawing, lifting and drawing, until the full 2-winged butterfly comes into view. I then use the butterfly image on the tracing paper to duplicate it on regular paper and use the colored pencils to fill it in with color – blue-green and lavender, different shades. I smile as I gaze at her sweetness and feel filled with creative inspiration.

The next thing I wish to do is recreate the butterfly yet again with acrylic paints. I decide to make a photocopy of the colored pencil drawing so I'm not painting on the shiny pencil lead and to preserve each of these layers, each of these phases of metamorphosis. I paint directly onto the photocopy, and sweet Butterfly is born. It just so happens that I complete the butterfly painting on Christmas Day. The whole process has felt incredible. The butterfly emerged from the dreamtime with lessons to teach, not only me, but all of us, about the process of creation and the beauty of transformation.

A new year brings further change. In March of 2011, a significant shift occurs. *Now it's time to move*, the intuitive voice within says clearly. It's time to move in with Tony. Up to this point, it hasn't felt right to make that transition, but now it couldn't feel more natural. Up to now I needed my own space. I needed time to mourn the loss of the Y... and, of course, the butterfly needed to be born. Tony and I discuss it and both feel excited about this step. Though there are a number of details to work out, we conclude that all will be well. After all, we love each other, and we intend to do our best to be flexible, relax and go with the flow.

After yoga class one Sunday morning, I spend the rest of the day at Tony's place doing some cleaning and organizing of kitchen storage, bathroom storage and visualizing possibilities for the space. It has many elements of the typical bachelor pad, but there is potential for it to feel like home. My mind starts to go a mile a minute as I glance around each room, strategizing how the space might best be used and imagining decoration, arrangement, and use of color on the walls.

Tony has lived at the location for over 5 years. I've essentially been living here the last several months, out of an overnight bag. So my moving in is primarily a matter of moving my furniture and belongings. I know we will create a warm, comfortable space together. I adore him. I know whatever challenges arise, we will navigate our way through them with gentleness, respect, caring and no small amount of playfulness.

It is the ides of March and my 35th birthday. It's a rainy day birthday and one of the final days of being at my own home. It has been raining all day without let up. I gaze out the sliding glass door, past the lawn, beyond the wire fence and trees, to the widening pond in the open field. A wild goose flies in every now and then.

This home has provided a place for releasing and cleansing. The frogs croaked and sang their song, supporting healing. The tears flowed just like the rain and washed away the heartache. I was allowed to bathe in my sadness and at the same time not be drowned by it. It flowed through me and out, out to this land, where it was received so graciously.

Releasing allows space for new things, a new home with my dearest love. This birthday, I give myself the gift of a deepening partnership. I smile as I imagine the possibilities that this new chapter may bring.

Through the previous two winter months, which has felt like a time of hibernation and self-reflection, it became even more apparent to me just how special Butterfly is and how intricately involved she will be in the creation of a second book. Yes, I will begin to write again.

As we work out some of the details of the upcoming move, Tony and I come to the agreement that I will use the room at the top of the stairs for my writing and creative projects. It feels important that I have space to call my own, particularly as I write *A Butterfly Life*.

The layout of the house is very interesting, in both a physical way and energetically. The further I move along in my personal development, I feel myself attuning to the energetic nature of things more and more. I've stopped questioning it, or trying to figure it all out with my logical mind. I just go with it, and it seems to lend a depth and richness to my day-to-day experience.

The front door of the home enters at ground level into the living room. Adjacent to the living room is a nook that can be used as a small dining area or office space. From the living room, you walk up four white, mosaic, tile steps to the kitchen. There's a back door from the kitchen that goes to a patio and the backside of the property. Turn left, go up one step, and that takes you to the bathroom. If you don't continue towards the bathroom, turn left again and walk up 8 carpeted steps to the bedroom and another nook, or office space. At first it seems this is the furthest part of the house, there's nothing else to it. Turn left, and left again, and open a narrow door that appears like it might simply be to a closet. You find, yes, a closet space, but also 5 slatted, carpeted stairs leading further upward to a 9' x 10' room. Moving from ground level to the top, through all those left turns, creates the sensation of spiraling upward. It is a counterclockwise motion, the direction of opening.

I am reminded of the chakras from the yogic tradition. The chakras offer a way to look at ourselves and support our well-being on a different level. There are many ways to look at the human body – the skeletal structure, the muscles and tendons and ligaments, the many organs, each of the various systems, such as the nervous system, the digestive system, the limbic system, circulatory system, and so on. We can look at the surface level of ourselves, the skin, hair and facial features. We can view the body at the cellular level or the atomic level. There are also ways, less physical, that we connect with the body. When we say, "That person has a good heart," we are not referring to the physical muscle that pumps blood throughout the body. It's something completely intangible, yet we know immediately to what we are referring. There are also our thoughts and emotions. There is so much amazing complexity to being human.

The chakras might be considered yet another aspect. Each of the 7 main chakras is considered to be an area of focused energy, or an energetic wheel of sorts, aligned vertically along the center of the body. Each chakra is associated with various qualities, as well as a color. They are often illustrated as lotus flowers with different colors and number of petals. There is much that can be learned about the chakra system. Those who are interested can explore it further. Here I'm keeping it simple and brief.

Just as one desires to maintain a state of equilibrium in other systems of the body, it is believed that when the chakra system is in balance, we experience greater health and well-being. The physical, mental, emotional and energetic systems influence each other as well. Greater balance can be achieved through a variety of ways. I primarily work with the chakra system through yoga movement and meditation. I find that yoga serves to support wellness on all levels.

The first chakra, the root, is often depicted as red and is located at the base of the spine and extends downward, connecting us to the planet, like roots. It is associated with the qualities of stability, safety, and having our fundamental needs met.

The second chakra, orange in color, lies at the womb or navel area. It has to do with reproduction, sexuality and creativity in general. The third, yellow, is at the solar plexus. It is our power center and is associated with strength, self-esteem, and our work or career. The fourth chakra, green, is at the heart and is linked to love, compassion, our relationship with self and others. The fifth, blue, lies at the throat, our communication center.

The sixth, violet, is located between the brow, often referred to as the "third eye" center, and is connected with intuition, inner wisdom and visioning. The seventh is at the crown of the head and opens upward towards the sky. It is often depicted as pure white light or encompassing the entire spectrum of colors. It is linked with our spirituality, or sense of the big picture, or simply something larger than oneself, such as the immense universe.

The ground floor of the house feels to be at the level of the first chakra. It is a firm foundation, stable, resting right on the land. Walking up the stairs feels like moving up through the chakras, through higher levels of awareness. The room at the very top feels like the 7th chakra.

After getting everything moved from my old place to this new shared space with Tony, I begin work on the room up top. Tony had been using it as a large walk-in closet and for storage. Now it is empty and ready to be transformed. I proceed to paint the walls. One wall is a gentle lavender, the other three are painted "morning crisp," a pale greenish-blue, with a darker, forest green trim. I give the ceiling and area around the skylight a fresh coat of white, and Tony and I work together to mount natural wood base boards. Another piece of natural wood trim with a sweet leaf pattern is mounted above the large window that overlooks the backyard.

I get a large, vanilla shag rug that covers most of the floor. It's very plush with carpet fibers about 2 inches tall. I love the feeling of running my fingers through it. The rug is very comfortable for sitting, lying and awaiting inspiration.

After a few weeks, it is complete. The room exudes a unique playfulness, as well as a place for quiet contemplation and meditation. Here is where I will create, where I will write. Feeling content, I lie on my back on the soft rug looking around the room and enjoying a moment's rest. Then I notice something. Oh! I'm surprised I didn't see it before. The colors of the room are almost identical to the colors of the butterfly. How perfect. So I dub it The Butterfly Room.

In the spring, another significant transition takes place on the home front. Tony has been having some pain in his back and neck the last few months, which is directly related to his work. It is his body's way of telling him it's time for a change. At the end of April, he leaves his job that he'd had for seven years.

Mixed feelings arise at this time. As a yoga teacher and wellness specialist, I support Tony's need to heal and have the time to increase awareness around his body and ways of moving. I also sense that he has to leave in order to express more of his potential. As his girlfriend who just moved in with him a couple weeks ago, a lot of fear and frustration come up regarding the circumstances. He says he has no plans to return to work until he feels ready, which doesn't seem like anytime soon. My mind starts going a mile a minute. *What do you* mean *you're not working? You have to! With neither of us working full time, how are we going to survive? Don't you know you have* me *to think about now, too?* It's so easy to fall into worry and fear. My patience and trust is tested. Truly.

But under the voice of fear is a stronger, clearer voice. I've heard it before, many times. As I've listened to it, it has led me to the most amazing of experiences. It offers guidance. It is intuitive and wise and authentic. It seems to work at a higher level of consciousness. Some may call it Spirit. I know it simply as the inner voice of knowing. *Everything is going to be alright,* it says. *It is time for you both to experience a transformation. This is what needs to happen. You are supported. You are loved. It will be alright.*

My work has shifted. Tony's work has shifted. The home environment, our relationship... a metamorphosis has occurred. What was old is no longer. What is new is now forming. Before us lies nothing but opportunity, potential, to create what we imagine.

Chapter 15

The Red Blazer Incident

ony and I navigate through his job transition. After some time, Tony picks up some temporary, part time work that doesn't put so much strain on his body. My contract with YMCA of the USA finally comes to a close. I have the opportunity to pursue full-time work with Y-USA in Chicago, or pursue an Executive Director role at another Y, both of which would carry a great amount of responsibility, along with a nice income and benefits, but would also require relocating. Though I am fond of the Y, I have a feeling that my life's work extends beyond its walls. Tony and I choose to instead start a small community organization known as the Center for Sacred Movement, which focuses on providing yoga and outdoor activities to support greater health and well-being for individuals in our local area. With this endeavor in its early stages, I decide to also take on part time work as an Administrative Director at a local non-profit for a limited time. The non-profit is in the midst of an organizational transition of its own, and I'm happy to lend experience and expertise to help the transition take place in a smooth manner. I work with the Board of Trustees, and I find the environment very supportive. The hours are perfect, as well, to continue writing my book and managing the center.

During this time period of Tony's healing and establishing healthy habits, we live on a shoestring budget. Though both of us are making considerably less income than we had been, we never seem to go without. We always have money to pay the rent and money to go to dinner when we want, or out to the movies. We still shop at our local markets and pick up our organic fruits and veggies. We do yoga, walk on the beach, and do a lot of hiking, things we enjoy. He shows me secret trails and his favorite swimming spots along the river. We support one another, and our love and appreciation for each other deepens. It feels like we are a couple of high school sweethearts thoroughly enjoying summer break! I was concerned about meeting our needs when Tony initially let me know he was quitting his job, but now life feels truly abundant. I'm proud of him for taking the time he has needed and am reminded how each of us has our own personal process. When that process is supported, and not judged, positive things result – growth and transformation happen.

Days pass in a gentle way. I work on *A Butterfly Life*. I have time to take breaks in the afternoon to get some sun, garden or enjoy a nature walk. All in all, there is a comfortable flow to life.

Then life takes a detour. It's an important detour, one that I feel deserves to be shared in detail.

In late 2011, I find out my niece, Maddie, is in jail in Placer County. Her life is anything *but* comfortable at the moment. I look up the address and information online and write her a letter. She writes back and says she agreed to a sentence of 2 years, 8 months for some drug related charges.

Maddie and I grew up together. My sister, who is 12 years older than I, got pregnant with her when she was only 16. My mother watched Maddie during the week while my sister finished high school, and this continued after graduation when my sister worked. She and her younger brother, Rick, stayed at our house several days a week for a few years. Maddie was hyperactive, always on the go, and was deemed a troublemaker. Neither my sister nor her second husband seemed equipped to appropriately handle her behavioral issues, and their corporal punishment tactics seemed to only make things worse. I was greatly affected by how Maddie was treated. I voiced my concerns and wrote a lengthy letter pleading my case, but I was only 13 or 14 years old. Who was going to listen to me? I saw her frequently up until she was around 9 years old, when my sister and her family decided to move to Arkansas.

I write 2-3 times while Maddie is in Placer County. Sometimes weeks or several months go by in between responses, either it takes her a while to respond, or it takes me that length of time. She will spend her 30th birthday in jail, but will be released a few months later.

As adults, Maddie and I have stayed in touch only occasionally over the years. She always seems to have a lot of drama in her life. Part of the drama may be due to her high-spirited personality. But it's also not surprising, considering her past.

While living in Arkansas, things apparently got more difficult in the household, and my sister presented Maddie, at the age of 11 or 12, with the option to go live with her biological father. This same man raped my sister years prior. Maddie chose to go, feeling uncomfortable in her current environment and, of course, not knowing the history. It ended up being a case of jumping out of the frying pan and into the fire. He horrifically abused Maddie sexually and psychologically every day during the 6 years she lived with him. She tried to reach out to get help. Early on, she told her step mom, who mentioned it to my sister. Neither of them believed her. How could such an atrocity be true? It must be Maddie just making up stories.

She tried to run away twice, but both times, he tracked her down. In addition to the abuse, he introduced Maddie to drugs, including methamphetamine. By the time she was 16 years old, she was not only using, but making meth and dealing. Her father left his second wife, choosing to have a sexual relationship with his daughter instead. Things got worse from there. He forced her to make pornographic videos and would hang himself in the bathroom until he blacked out. He would make Maddie get him down from hanging as soon as he went unconscious. It was a sick and twisted message telling Maddie if she ever told anyone, her father would be taken away, gone, and then she would have no one.

At 17 years old, someone close to her father's side of the family realized she was being sexually abused and notified someone to get Maddie help. The abuse finally stopped. Maddie went back to live with my sister, now with severe emotional difficulties from years of trauma, and issues with drug and alcohol abuse. Things didn't go smoothly, to say the least. It was at this time that I initially heard about the abuse she experienced. At first, my sister still didn't know how much of what Maddie said to believe. During this same time I was remembering and realizing the abuse I, too, had experience from this man.

When Maddie was about 22 years old, I attended one of the days during her trial where she testified against her father. I looked around the courtroom and saw that no one else from the family was there to support her – not her mother or grandmother, not her husband, no one. It had been 5 years since she had escaped the abuse. Her father was facing a maximum sentence of close to 300 years in prison. The trial lasted 7 days. When I saw her up on the stand and heard her testimony, I knew it had to be one of the most difficult things for a person to do. She answered the attorney's questions, telling details of the molestation, while the perpetrator, her own father, sat there in the courtroom. She was clear and somehow, someway, seemed to take it all in stride. At that moment I recognized an incredible strength in Maddie. Many victims of abuse choose to not pursue legal justice, for it is so extremely difficult mentally and emotionally.

Her case was followed by the local newspaper. Maddie's testimony resulted in her father going to prison for the remainder of his life, sentenced to 76 years without possibility of parole. The judge stated Maddie's stepmother should have also been on trial, as it was apparent she knew about the abuse and failed to protect the children. Maddie not only obtained justice for herself, but justice for all the other women and girls whom this man raped and abused, which have been numerous, and also protection for the countless women and girls that he would undoubtedly have abused in the future. This legal step was powerful, too, because it was there in the courtroom that Maddie was finally heard. She was *believed*, and people took steps to help her.

Most of the years progressed with very little communication between Maddie and me. I was caught up in the details of my own life, and she was off living hers.

Through hearsay from my nephew, Rick, she was to go into a transitional housing program after her release from Placer County. Much of the info I got about Maddie through the years came from hearsay. I had not been in contact with my sister, Maddie's mom, or my own mother in years. Rick would sometimes fill me in after talking with his mom. I had to stay mindful, though, of the perspectives and filters through which my family, particularly my mother and sister, viewed Maddie. She's always been "a problem."

The real problem, though, is much more complex and far-reaching. There has been so much abuse and abandonment and neglect throughout Maddie's life. Yes, there have been behavioral issues, and later psychological issues, but many in the family system have played a role, as has lack of education on the part of the caregivers, and religion and societal norms. Yet the problem is perceived by many to lie solely with Maddie. It's very complex, indeed.

After her release at the end of 2012, I hear that she doesn't stay long in the transitional home, which is a clean and sober house. Shortly after, my sister and her husband refuse to provide any more assistance to her.

So Maddie bounces around from place to place, staying at people's houses for a day or two and in a homeless shelter on occasion. I receive a few phone calls from Maddie during this time. Each time she calls, it is from a new phone number, for her previous phone has been lost or broken.

Her life seems so completely different from mine. I have never spent a day in jail. I don't have experience with addiction. I have made different choices in regard to the friends I keep, and my actions. I'm not sure how much I should get involved. I know boundaries are important, and I feel a bit guarded. Plus, I am not even sure how to help, other than listen.

Rick calls me one day. He says he let Maddie know that if there is anyone in the family who could help, it is me. "Aunt Kristi's like a therapist," he said to her. Well, I'm not a licensed therapist, but I understand what he means. I offer life coaching, and my educational background is in psychology with an emphasis in counseling and clinical work. I also had 5 ½ years of my own therapy, which proved to be life-changing and lifesaving.

So that is what I do – I listen. I listen without judgment. Maddie shares a little about what is going on in her life, and she is honest. She tells me about being attacked and "pistol-whipped" a couple years back, resulting in a brain injury that now gives her seizures. She tells me how she stayed sober for a little while after she got out of being locked up but then went back to using. On one of our calls, I let her know that I will research some of the resources in Winowa County to see if there is something available to help her. She appreciates the gesture.

With nowhere to live after leaving the transitional housing, Maddie ends up staying with her girlfriend in the Sacramento area, who happens to also be her previous cellmate. In addition, this woman is abusive, an alcoholic, addict and drug dealer with gang ties. Can Maddie be in any worse of a situation?

I get repeated phone calls from Maddie one day in early 2013, with the 3rd voicemail message stating, "Auntie, please call me. *This is important.*" There is urgency in her voice, a call for help. I know the situation needs immediate attention. I call her back. "I can't stay here," she says. "I have a broken nose. This place is roach-infested. It doesn't get much worse than waking up on the sidewalk in your own urine. Are there any resources there?"

I decide to drive to Roseville to pick her up and bring her to Winowa County to try to hook her up with resources for housing and income. I have no idea what to expect. I envision her with just the clothes on her back, her face all bashed up, run down, worn out. I get together a backpack, throw in some snacks, some paper and pen in case she needs to write down a phone number or address or something, and a sweatshirt, so she'll at least have that. My plan is to pick her up and find her a shelter for the night and then work on helping her get some solid ground under her feet so she can start to rebuild her life.

She meets me in downtown Roseville. Her straight, brunette hair reaches to the middle of her back. She's dressed in nice jeans, 2 snugly-fitting layered tank tops, one white and the outer one red, silver hoop earrings and dimple piercings. Her familiar dark brown eyes are hidden behind large, dark sunglasses, and she's wheeling a suitcase behind her, the size that fits in the overhead compartment of an airplane. She looks better than I anticipated. In fact, she's strikingly beautiful, as she always has been. She's like a younger version of Demi Moore, but with attitude.

She gets in the car, and I give her a quick hug. It's clear she's feeling a little nervous and ready to leave this place.

During the drive, Maddie talks about feeling suicidal and how she has made previous attempts on her life. Over the years she's made about a half dozen attempts. She tells me how about 3 years ago, she took over 200 pills. She had done some research for how to make this particular time successful. In the process of taking the pills, she vomited some of them back up. She said she rinsed them off and swallowed them down a second time. The determination to die doesn't get much stronger than that. When the pills started taking effect, Maddie said she fell to the floor and was unable to move. She saw and felt bugs come and swarm her body, then she saw a tunnel and a white light, and she figured she was on her way out. An ambulance was called by a family member who found out what happened, and Maddie was taken to a hospital. CPR was unsuccessful. The doctor had to bring out the paddles to get her heart started again. When she finally regained consciousness, the doctor said, "Welcome back."

"Fuck!" was her immediate response. She didn't want to be here.

Just a few weeks prior to me picking her up from Roseville, she attempted suicide by OD'ing with pills again. With this incident, she couldn't move or lift her head off the pillow for several days. This time she refused to go to a hospital. Acquaintances, or fellow addicts, cared for her until she regained function. By all accounts, that should have killed her, too. But Maddie is like a cat with nine lives.

She says the doctors will now only give her prescriptions in 2-week quantities so she cannot overdose on them. She's acutely suicidal even presently. Maddie is in an extremely difficult situation. She has no money, no job, nowhere to live, no social or family support, she's been in and out of psychiatric hospitals, has a long history of drug abuse, a criminal history... the list goes on. It's understandable how the desire to just end it all can be so strong.

I remember with great clarity when I, too, felt hopeless, all seemed dark, and I looked at everything in my surroundings as a weapon for self destruction. I don't think much now about the depression I experienced earlier in life. Years have gone by without a thought. But here is someone who is reminding me of it, and mirroring it in so many ways.

"There is light at the end of the tunnel," I assure her. She seems relieved to hear those words.

Maddie talks about how she feels her girlfriend loved her and says she loved her girlfriend in return. She's been in abusive relationships as an adult, in many ways continuing the abusive familial relationships she had as a child and teenager. Given her history I understand why she would feel this abusive relationship is somehow love. I just hope she has the opportunity to experience what love *truly* is.

Many things come up in our conversation, including mention of the abuse from her father. It doesn't matter how many years have passed. She has not yet fully healed from these atrocities. It is like a festering wound that was never properly cleaned and dressed. It lies just under the surface and continues to have influence on her actions, world view, thoughts and feelings.

She is 30 years old now. There seems to be significance in that. On a deep level, I feel a shift is occurring for her. It feels time. It's Maddie's time. I say to her, "I want you to be able to look back over your life and be able to say, 'My childhood pretty much sucked. My 20s sucked. But my 30s, my 30s... they started off a bit rough, but then they were *awesome*.'"

Making our way out of the valley, driving west towards the coast to a new environment, something comes to me that I feel drawn to share with Maddie. She started riding horses when she was 5, or perhaps even younger. It was an enjoyable activity that she and her mom shared. I feel her strong connection with horses even now. "You're like a wild mustang," I say to her. "Your spirit is like a wild mustang, and people have been trying to break and corral you all your life. And you're just meant..." simultaneously Maddie and I complete the sentence, "to roam free." I feel I understand her fairly well, and I'm willing to listen and work towards understanding her even more.

I notice on the drive how Maddie is hypersensitive to her surroundings, taking in all the details. We pass the place where I teach yoga. She is in mid-sentence as we pass by, so it's not until a few blocks away that I tell her I teach yoga right back there on the hill.

"Oh, that place that had 'Yoga & Pilates' written on the windows?"

"Yes, that's the one. You're very observant," I reply. It seems more than just observant, though. It's that hyper-vigilance indicative of PTSD. She's had severe and extensive sexual trauma, has been living on the street, she's had her head smashed by the butt of a gun, and no telling what all. She's in survival mode.

The day is nearing the end, so I decide it is probably best for her to just stay the night at our place, and we'll figure out the temporary housing tomorrow. When we arrive, Maddie leaves her suitcase near the front door next to our shoes.

"Well, she's in better shape than I expected," I say to Tony. "She has a few clothes, and a suitcase."

That evening, we engage in idle chit chat, and she offers to help make dinner. Despite all that has transpired in her life the last many years, she reveals herself to be polite and respectful. It's an emotional evening for her, and she sheds a few tears. "You're seeing me at the lowest point in my life," she says. I'm just glad I can be here when she needs it most.

Despite this lowest point, she continues to hold her head up, which speaks to her tenacity and strength.

I invite her to make herself at home. I let her know she can take a shower, do laundry and whatever else she needs to do.

Maddie takes the opportunity to call her oldest daughter, Hope, with whom she's had only occasional contact for much of her life. Hope will soon be a teenager and is being raised by other family members. I'm glad they're able to talk during this pause amidst the chaos. Maddie also has two other daughters of whom she lost custody a few years ago. These two are being raised by their father.

Since it is just for the one night, rather than set up a camping bed for Maddie, she and I decide to share the queen bed upstairs while Tony sleeps in a bed downstairs. I could sleep with Tony, but for some reason, I choose to stay close to Maddie. I feel a feminine, maternal energy arising in me, protective and nurturing.

Prior to crawling into bed, Maddie opens her bag of medications, and there are several bottles. Some I recognize as antidepressants, some she identifies as being for her seizures, and there's valium and a few other odds and ends. She pops a few in her mouth. "Isn't that crazy," she says, as we both look at the spread of pill bottles. "But I need it all." I figure that may not be the case, but it is what it is right now.

Maddie seems to sleep okay, but I don't sleep well. I lie awake for a long time in the dark, just witnessing her sleep. She's very quiet. There are two or three occasions, though, when she shuffles under the covers and lets out a small, fearful squeak. No doubt, she is trying to get away from whatever is haunting her in her dreams. At one point, she sits up, facing the head of the bed. I open my eyes, just barely making out her shape. She flips her long hair over to the other side. I ask gently, "What, what's going on?"

I don't know if she is awake, just getting her bearings, or asleep. She lies back down, wraps both of her arms around my left arm, lays her head on my shoulder for a minute or two, then scoots over to her side of the bed. When I tell her about it the next morning, she says she doesn't remember doing it. "Have you ever been diagnosed with PTSD?" I ask. Yes, she says.

"One of my pills keeps me from remembering my dreams and helps me sleep," she states.

I can sense there is so much fear. There has been so much running in her life. There's also a lot of sadness and anger, no doubt, that hasn't had the chance to be appropriately expressed. "Sometimes sadness and anger can be like a poison that eats away at a person," I say to her at one point. "It needs to have a safe place to be released." I open my mouth wide and demonstrate a quiet version of a really big, angry scream.

"So I probably shouldn't do that in front of a mental hospital," she says. We both chuckle.

Whether it's from my earlier training to be a psychotherapist, from my experience with Native shamanic energy work, or just from natural instinct as her aunt, I can see the healing that needs to take place for her to feel better and be able to make more conscious decisions. I see her potential.

Maddie is very intelligent, and she shows some understanding of herself and her own process. She recognizes that her thoughts are not who she is. I also observe her to be in a place of acceptance. She keeps her wit about her as well. There is, of course, still a tremendous amount of growth and understanding to be gained.

On my way to work the next morning, I show her the downtown area of Springdale, the bus transit mall, the library where she can access the internet, and then I drop her off at the homeless resource center. She has her backpack full of snacks, and the plan is for her to look into the housing situation and then hang out until I get off work when we will go run a few errands.

I pick her up in the afternoon, and we head to the store to get her a temporary cell phone. She shares about her day and says she walked around downtown and then spent some time in a grassy area where there were some trees. She says she couldn't help staring up into one of the trees, imagining how she could hang herself from it. "I hate feeling this way," she says. I understand.

After the cell phone situation is taken care of, we get some food. Maddie just nibbles a bite or two. Then we head over to a small shelter for women and children tucked away in a residential neighborhood. After a few phone calls and running into a few dead ends, Maddie got in contact with this place. It's a house that has been transformed into a shelter.

We both walk through the house and check out the room where she will sleep for the night. As we pass by the kitchen, an old woman with crooked, yellow teeth, wearing baggy, colorful, mismatched clothes and a flowery hat, asks Maddie, "You want something to eat? We just ate, but I'll wrap something up for you if you want." It's nice that they have dinner, too. Maddie, with her beauty, style and polite manners, thanks her but declines, stating her stomach is nervous, and she doesn't feel much like eating. "I understand," the flowery woman says.

In the room where Maddie is to sleep, there are two sets of bunk beds and an additional twin bed. There's a young, hippie-ish woman about Maddie's age in the separate twin. One bunk bed looks empty. The other has a 40-something woman seated on the top bunk rummaging through a cloth bag. Maddie's bed is the one underneath her. It seems like pretty close quarters but clean. It's not a space I would want to stay if I didn't have to. As if reading my mind, Maddie says, "It's not that bad. I've stayed in a lot worse."

It strikes me again how Maddie seems to find acceptance with her situation. Through yesterday and today, she has had no expectation from me. There has been no pleading. It seems she has not wanted to impose herself in any way. She not once has asked if she can stay with me longer. Instead, there is simply gratitude. She has thanked me several times, and Tony, too, for what we have provided.

I feel a tug to want to help further, but I also understand the importance of boundaries in the situation. For both of us, there is an unspoken agreement that this is how things are to be right now. Maddie and I are both getting to know each other – again. Trust has to develop.

Maddie thanks me again, and we part ways. "You have my number, right?" I ask, wanting to be sure. We'll stay in touch by phone. I'm glad she is in the area, for now we can spend a little more time together and work towards getting her more stabilized with a living arrangement and healthier environment. But it will undoubtedly take some time.

There are necessary boundaries, and there is trust that must develop further, but in less than 24 hours with Maddie, we shared years through stories. A deep connection was made. It is clear we have a lot of love for each other. We are family, after all.

The following day, I am a little surprised to call Maddie and hear she is no longer in Springdale but is instead in a small town about 40 minutes east. A couple days later, she is 45 minutes further away, a couple days after that, she's way up in Humboldt County. She is on the move and still in survival mode, looking for places to stay, looking for friends willing to take her in for a night or two, and hoping to find something more permanent.

We talk on the phone and text regularly. "I didn't expect you to leave the area so soon. I was hoping you'd stick around," I say to her. She doesn't have transportation, but is relying on others to get her from one place to another, seeming to go where the wind takes her.

Amidst the unfolding situation with Maddie, my brother unexpectedly dies in early March. There is a family gathering on March 9th at my mother's house. I decide to attend and make the 3-hour drive to her house in Red Bluff. Tony accompanies me, a chance to "meet the family." There are a number of family members in attendance, including some aunts, uncles, cousins, nieces and nephews whom I have not seen in many, many years, and, of course, my mother and siblings. I haven't seen my mother in several years, along with my sister and brother closest in age to me. There is one brother with whom I've been in contact the last year or two. Unlike my mom, sister and other brother, he's not a Jehovah's Witness. He reminds me of my father – quiet, loving and accepting. With the family members who are Witnesses there is an ever-present awkwardness and emotional separation. Disapproval and disappointment hang in the air. There are some family members with whom I will likely never be close, and it's neither good nor bad, but just how it is. I'm glad to be in attendance to honor my brother's passing, and I get to introduce Tony to a few folks.

The night of the spring equinox, I have a dream that I recall in great detail. Prior to this I didn't have any memorable dreams in many, many months. This one truly stands out. It is as follows:

I walk into a living room full of people. Just inside, I encounter a girl about 3 years old, and her mom is near the door. The little girl is standing on top of a table and playing with a rope or piece of chord around her neck. Her mother isn't paying any attention to her. Her mom is only a few feet away, but she has her back to the girl talking to other people. I make a mental note to keep an eye on the girl, for all she has to do is step off the table and she could end up hanging herself.

I proceed to make my way around the room, weaving my way through the crowd. A door to another room opens and I see carcasses from family members who have passed away – my grandmother, my brother and a few others I don't recognize. The carcasses are at different stages of decomposition. I experience no fear or disgust; I just observe the scene. Then I notice a couple carcasses are walking or floating through the crowd of people. They are somewhat ethereal or ghost-like and somewhat fleshy and material. No one else seems to notice them.

I then decide to make my way back towards the front door where the little girl and her mother are located. I arrive to find just what I had predicted, the little girl dangling in the air at the end of her rope. Her mom is oblivious to the situation, still facing away, talking to others.

I quickly wrap my arms around the girl's legs and lift her weight, stopping the hanging. I then call to her mother to help get the noose, which is now a necklace, off her neck. She comes over and helps me unfasten the clasp and remove the necklace. The little girl is now fine. Dream ends.

The very next day, I get a call from Maddie. She is sitting in a friend's car crying and sharing with me how she just wants to die. "It's too hard... nothing helps." Her voice is weak. She sounds defeated. "I don't want to be here anymore. All I can imagine is driving this car off a cliff."

"I'm sorry it's so hard right now," I say. "Have you been using?"

"No. Well, just alcohol. It would be easier if I was using. It helps numb it," Maddie says. "It seems like no one cares whether I live or die."

In the pause after she speaks these words, I put myself in her shoes for a few moments, seeing the world through her eyes. Things are bleak, very bleak. If things don't change for her, she will likely end up dead at a young age or spend the rest of her life locked up. She is down so deep, it seems almost impossible to crawl out. Where to even begin? Also, it does seem as if no one cares. Members of my family, our family, have given up on her. Perhaps it is through lack of understanding *how* to help. Or, the intensity of Maddie's life is perhaps too overwhelming for them. Or, they have just closed off their hearts, or had been unable or unwilling to open their hearts in the first place, dismissing her as a lost cause.

Maddie is unique and special and has been judged and, in my opinion, largely misunderstood for most of her life. Maddie and I have different personalities, and clearly we have made different choices in life. I don't know what it's like to live on the streets, or be incarcerated, but I do know what it's like to feel like no one cares.

"I care," I respond.

"I just want to die..." Maddie is several hours away. As I hold the phone to my ear, I ask myself, *What can I do, what can I say right now to help?* I feel the words come...

"Can you think of an alternative?" I ask her. "What do you need to help you feel better?"

There's a pause. "To be near you. To be honest, I miss you," Maddie replies.

I feel it, too, the pull drawing us closer together. "I will look at more resources in this area," I assure her. Then I hear words spoken by my own therapist so many years ago now coming out of my mouth, "It sounds like perhaps that it's not necessarily that you want to die, but you just want to feel better, you want the pain to end."

"There is so much pain," she says.

"Despite everything you've been through," I continue, "all the suicide attempts, *everything*, you're still alive. There must be a small part of you that wants to live."

Maddie is quiet. Finally, after some time, "A very small part," she says. I can hear the weariness in her voice. She is at the end of her rope.

I close my eyes and envision that I can see into Maddie's very soul. "In all that darkness, there is a tiny spark of light," I say.

She must be here for a reason. She has certainly tried her best to end it all.

"It'd be nice if you were closer, so we can work on getting you the support you need," I tell her.

"So if I make my way back through Springdale, should I call you?" she asks.

"Yes." She says she will work on finding a ride.

I prepare to set up a bed for her in an alcove off to the right of the bedroom at the top of the second set of stairs. It feels cozy and secure there.

Up until only a week ago, a cumbersome desk occupied the space. On a whim one morning, Tony said he was moving his bed upstairs. We often sleep in different beds, mine upstairs, his downstairs. It seems to work best given our different sleep schedules and the fact that I rustle around a lot upstairs when I get to writing. We both seem to sleep more soundly this way.

However, I've wanted Tony to move his bed upstairs for the last year and a half. It has been a frequent topic of conversation. His bed takes up the middle of the living room, making it challenging for me to feel serene in the environment, not to mention a bit awkward to have dinner guests.

So on this whim, he began dismantling his desk, screw by screw, piece by piece, clearing the space. I was getting excited about having a living room again. Then, once the space upstairs was all clear, he changed his mind and decided to leave his bed downstairs, much to my dismay... at first.

Until now when I realize he cleared the space for Maddie. He may not have done it consciously, but instead on a deeper level, clearing the space in support of this young woman's much-needed recovery. When there is synchronicity and alignment such as this, it's a reminder for me that it's the direction in which to keep moving.

I gather a Thai massage mat that I have and place it in the alcove. It's a perfect fit. On top of the Thai mat, I place a thin, air-filled camping mattress, followed by a soft, fluffy blanket, sheet, comforter folded back, and pillow. I test out the comfort level of the bed by rolling around on it a few times. Feeling satisfied, I smooth out the blankets and sit back and wait.

With each passing moment, I feel the maternal energy growing stronger within me. It is a new experience. Sure, I've always loved and cared about my nieces and nephews. But this is something altogether different – an incredible force that feels very grounded, and at the same time lighting up my womb and opening my heart wider than ever before. It is the energy that can be as gentle as a kiss on a newborn's forehead or as ferocious as a mother bear protecting her cub.

This is her time. This is her chance to heal and have a fresh start.

Maddie and I text message a few times the remainder of that evening and into the next day. She's unable to find a ride right away. I text her that night letting her know I found a booklet that has all the resources in the area for homeless people, including housing assistance, meals and various other county programs. Just prior to turning into bed, I text her, "That tiny spark of life in you will grow stronger. Sending you lots of love." She texts back a thank you, a good night and an I love you.

I feel an urgency in the need to support Maddie during this time and to stay in close contact with her. The following afternoon I send her some texts. Several hours pass, and I still do not receive a response. I write, "Hey M, things going alright today?" Nothing. The following day, I try checking in with her again, asking if she can just send me a quick text so I know she's okay. Still nothing. Starting to feel worried, the following day, I call and leave her 3 messages on her voicemail. It's not like her to not respond.

Scenarios are beginning to play out in my mind. Did she finally just get too overwhelmed, give in and kill herself, or attempt to kill herself? Is she just out of cell phone range? Is she in trouble? Did she hook up with some unsavory characters? Is she in jail?

"She's probably just partying it up somewhere," Tony says. He doesn't yet know her as well as I do. No, I can feel in my gut something is wrong. The worst of it is, I have no way of knowing what has happened until I hear from her again... *if* I hear from her again. I decide if I don't hear from her in another day, I will start calling the local hospitals and police stations.

I remember a passage by Jamie Sams and John Carson that is written in the first few pages of *Medicine Cards*. They mention how Native children know that if they are lost, to call on the medicine of their parents for assistance. The parents can feel the pull of the child's need, and sometimes will be able to see psychically through the eyes of their child and determine where he or she is.

I can feel that pull from Maddie. I close my eyes and try to see where Maddie is. I cannot determine where she is, though. I only see darkness... and the tiniest spark of light.

The following day, in the late morning, my phone rings. My heart skips a beat. I don't recognize the number. I hit the button to receive the call. "Hello?" Immediately a recording begins. It's a collect call from (Maddie's voice says) "Maddie." There is reference to a detention facility. "Do you accept the charges?" the machine voice continues.

As my mouth is forming the word yes, the Verizon voice cuts in and says my account does not allow the transaction and abruptly hangs up.

"What?!" I say to my phone, as I stare at it in disbelief. Well, at least I know where she is located and that she is alive.

It's not until the following morning that I receive a second call from her. This time the automated machine starts talking, I hear Maddie say "Maddie," then I hear instructions asking if I want to add money onto the account. I start going through the process of pushing numbers, and it's sending me in circles. It's early and I'm not yet fully awake. After a few moments, I'm not even sure if Maddie is on the line anymore, and I hang up. Ugh, what did I just do? I think how I wish I could have gone back and finished the process of putting money on the account.

I realize how it may look from Maddie's perspective. That's twice I've hung up on her. What if she thinks I don't want to talk with her? That I'm upset with her? That I've just kicked her to the curb like others have done? I hope she can feel I care and that I do want to talk with her. I hope she tries again.

I tell Tony about my mistake in hanging up the second time. "You have to get hold of her," he says. "Otherwise, she's all alone in the world." The words hang in the air, and we both momentarily transport ourselves to the feeling of emptiness, hopelessness, and in that place where it seems no one cares. Then we pull ourselves back out.

"I know! I know..."

The phone rings again later that evening. By this time, I have figured out the phone system and deposited money into the account. "Do you accept the call from..." the recording begins. Maddie's voice comes on, but rather than hearing "Maddie," I hear a rushed, "Aunt Kristi, I need to speak with you." I press zero to accept, being extra careful to not hang up, as the hang up button is right next to the zero on the touchpad.

As soon as the call connects, we both say hello and I immediately start in a hurried fashion, "I'm glad you called again. I didn't want to hang up," and then Maddie quickly shares about what happened and what the attorney said. She was picked up due to a bench warrant, which gets issued when one does not show up to a scheduled court date, and landed herself in jail in Contra Costa County.

Both of us know time is limited on the call and speak the essentials. I let her know I have a bed set up where she can stay for a few days until she gets housing. "I'm still here, and I want to support you through this process," I say. So much needs to be said in such a short time, and we get it all out. The hurried energy dissipates, and we both know everything is going to be alright. My heart is still open. There is still love in the world.

At this point, I imagine some of you readers might begin to question my involvement with helping Maddie. We've all heard from friends or family members, or even have experienced personally, situations where a person tried to help an addict or felon and ended up getting burned. There is a tendency to not want to get involved, and oftentimes encouragement from others to not do so. However, the maternal energy and the path of my soul are leading me forward. I respect boundaries, and I strive to balance it with the wisdom from my heart.

This is how it begins. I hear these words from somewhere deep within, perhaps the voice of Spirit, or of Love itself.

For several days I pass by that bed in the alcove. The energy is much different from before. I can feel Maddie's presence. I can feel it will be a time of healing for her. There are times I feel drawn to play my Native flute or sing. Songs spontaneously emerge. They are old songs, not really of words but chants or sounds emerging from the time of the indigenous ones. There are times I feel called to dance, a medicine dance. There is an important and powerful shift taking place, and it gives cause for celebration! There is a special energy working here, and I simply flow with it, feeling the love. I hear the words, *the healing has already begun.*

I visit her one day while she is in jail in Richmond. It's the first time I've ever visited someone in jail. I show my ID at the desk and sign in. The man behind the bulletproof glass instructs me to head over to the metal detector. There is another deputy at the detector sternly telling the visitors ahead of me to remove their jewelry and shoes. I do so before I get up there so as not to receive her wrath. Once through, we are told to line up single file so we can be escorted to the visiting area. Just outside the visiting room, we are scolded about not remaining in single file and are told to line up against the cinderblock wall to wait for the door to be opened. Instructions are shouted out to us, specifics on how to behave during the visit. *Who's the prisoner here?* Once inside the visiting area, which is a large open room, I see Maddie seated on the other side of a wall of Plexiglas. One could reach around the side of the Plexiglas to touch the other person, but that, of course, is not allowed. I figure this visiting area is for inmates who are low security risk. Maddie fills me in on the latest legal information. It sounds like she won't have to be here long, thankfully.

April 12, 2013, Maddie calls me at home in the evening. I spent much of the day keeping busy, feeling anxious to hear from her and hoping to soon be picking her up. She reports that she spent the whole day in court, and the judge decided to not release her of her own recognizance. A new court date was set for April 30th.

She sounds exhausted and disappointed. With expectation of a place to stay and the chance to begin rebuilding, she had hopes to be released this week. She starts to cry. "I don't want to be here any longer." Her voice is soft. I can barely hear her. She is defeated and deflated.

"It's only a couple weeks," I assure her. I share a few more encouraging words. I want her to feel happy and enjoy life. It won't necessarily be easy to rebuild her life, but it will no doubt be better than how things are for her right now. "I believe in you," I say. "I trust that you will achieve wonderful things in your life. I love you very much. Try to stay positive." I let her know we will work together as a team, taking it one step at a time.

That night I have a dream, another one of those dreams that feels especially important.

A dark brown horse, a Quarter Horse, is tied with a rope to a pole. Nobody else is around. The setting is a city street. The horse is tied to a tall, metal street lamp.

I see her repeatedly pulling and screeching, trying her best to get away. The sound is haunting. It is obvious the horse is not accustomed to being tied. She is wild. Sometimes the horse jerks her head around, causing the rope to press deeply on her neck. Other times the rope gets wound around her front leg and she pulls and injures her leg and almost falls down. She makes a strong, determined effort to release herself. She fights, though she is exhausted. This continues for several minutes.

I awake with questions about the bail process and end up bailing out Maddie, cutting the rope so that she may be free. I pick her up from Richmond this very day and make the return drive home.

She gets settled in, and we spend the weekend talking and doing some yard work. She proceeds to wash my car as a thank you for picking her up.

Tony just got hired full time at a new job and is out of town at a work-related training. He is feeling good in his body, stronger and healthier. Prior to getting the job, we sat down and clarified what he desired in his work and he wrote down his intentions. He is excited to start this next phase.

So it's just us girls at home catching up some more and making plans to move forward. On Monday, as I rouse myself from sleep, I emerge with insights about Maddie and her healing process. I jot down some notes and draw an illustration that includes stages of healing in pyramid form. We get up, have breakfast, then sit down to chat. I share my thoughts with her, and she listens intently, making eye contact and sharing her thoughts, as well. I talk about how I feel I can support her in some short-term and long-term goals, as well as how I can facilitate her healing. I offer a suggestion for her to list all the traumas she has experienced, not in great detail, just a simple list. I feel it can help me gain a greater understanding of her needs, and also help Maddie begin the process of releasing those experiences. As our discussion feels complete, I ask her if I can give her a hug, and we exchange a heartfelt squeeze.

We head out the door to complete some errands, stopping at a few places where she picks up a job application. She also calls a couple horse ranches in the area inquiring if they need any help.

As we go through our day, I listen as Maddie shares stories. In a way she reminds me of my grandmother. She has a strong personality and is an animated storyteller. She seems comfortable talking with me and expresses how it is nice to not have to lie or hide anything with me, because she can tell I don't cast judgment. She shares stories about her childhood abuse. It is apparent she feels a deep sense of abandonment by the parental figures.

Maddie also shares a story of how she managed to get herself out of a situation where she was nearly raped and killed two years earlier. This is the incident that resulted in her brain injury. When she was in the thick of her addiction, staying in the ghetto, she went to buy drugs from a dealer. This guy had a pistol tucked in the front of his jeans and was higher than a kite. Things went bad and he made an attempt to rape her. She quickly struggled to free herself and turned over to her hands and knees to make a run for it. At this time, he hit her over the head twice with the butt of his pistol. He then stuck a needle, with a syringe full of some kind of drug, into her neck. It's likely he was trying to kill her and make it look like an overdose.

She tells the story in great detail, with all the sights, sounds and smells, what people said, their gestures. It is quite a feat that she made it out of the situation alive. With blood gushing from her head, running into her eyes, she took advantage of a moment when the man had turned away, and ran and jumped out his second-story window. She took his car, which had the keys in it, and called the police to meet her in a nearby parking lot. As the drugs were taking effect, she pulled into the lot with the cop cars waiting, fell out of the car and then everything went black.

It is that situation that landed her the extended jail time. There were drugs in the car, drugs in her body. She never received the proper medical care for her head injury. She also refused to take it to trial and testify, not wanting to see the man's face again, and instead chose to do the time. "I put myself in that situation to begin with," she says in conclusion.

I take in all this information. I have a greater understanding regarding her PTSD symptoms and how they are not just from her youth but from the more recent attack and living on the streets. I am reminded how people mistreat and abuse one another. I am reminded there are ghettos and hard-core drug dealers. I realize how people get lost in those environments, are off the radar, long forgotten by family and friends. Or the family and friends are in the ghettos, too, having lived in that type of environment their whole lives and not knowing a different life. The cycle continues generation after generation.

Throughout the day and into the evening, Maddie turns to me for answers, as if I have come to a place of greater knowledge, holding the answer to all life's questions. Sometimes it is a question about our family. Sometimes just simple things like, "Have you figured out why you're only supposed to get on a horse on the left side?" I chuckle.

"I think it's because they're trained like that. People train them to be mounted on the left, so that's what they're used to," I reply. She seems satisfied with whatever wisdom I can impart.

Even though only 6 years separate us, and our interaction might sometimes appear more sister-like on the outside, she always references me as Aunt Kristi and treats me with the level of respect that comes with that familial role. And I feel to be her aunt, not her sister or friend. As I interact with Maddie, I feel and embody the mother and teacher.

The following day, Tuesday, is Maddie's 31st birthday. On my way to work, I drop her off at the county Social Services building so she can fill out the necessary paperwork to start receiving some money for food. We keep in contact throughout the day, and she lets me know she figured out the bus system enough to take the bus from Springdale to Sweethaven and walked around town. I pick her up after work and drive her to one of my favorite coffee/tea shops, then to one of my favorite vintage clothing stores where we browse through the racks. I enjoy showing her around town. She loves the clothing store and asks for a job application. In the evening, we soak in the hot tub for a while and share more stories. Things seem to be going well.

"I should have gotten you a cake," I say, feeling like I dropped the ball a bit. Then I remember I have a Reese's peanut butter cup in the cupboard. I put a single pink birthday candle in it, light it and sing her a quick happy birthday tune. I laugh. She laughs, too, but I see she is also touched by the gesture, even though it is just a silly, simple thing.

"That's so sweet," she says and snaps a couple pictures of it with her phone.

We talk about things changing for her in her 30s, things being more positive. She refers back to the suggestion I gave a couple days ago about listing her traumas. "When you said that, it felt right. I might do that," she says.

Wednesday morning I get ready for work, and Maddie gets ready for her day. The plan is for her to do some weed-eating around the property, then ride the bike down to the park and spend the afternoon hanging out around town until I get home from work. It's the first I've left her at the house alone. "I'm entrusting you to hold down the fort," I say to her.

"No worries," she says. "I'll check in with you when I'm getting ready to go on the bike ride." We text several times just after noon. She says she will be going on the bike ride in a few minutes.

I call her again a little after 3pm, just as I am getting off work. She answers, and it sounds like she is outside. "Are you out riding around?" I ask.

"Yeah, I'm out riding around," she replies.

"Are you at the park?" The call gets lost. I try calling again. It goes to voicemail. Bad signal, I figure. Cell phones. As I get into town at 3:30, I text her that I will be home soon.

I pull into the driveway at 3:40pm. Barreling down the driveway straight towards me is a red Blazer with Maddie behind the wheel. It takes me a couple seconds to realize the vehicle is our landlord's and what she has done. My heart sinks. I partially pull off to the side of the driveway out of instinct, and Maddie pulls off the other side to get around me, driving like a bat out of hell. She gets to the intersection to the paved road in a few feet, screeches around the corner without pause, and I hear the sound of the engine rev as she speeds off into the distance.

I pick up my phone and get her voicemail. "What the hell, Maddie?! Call me!" Figuring it's a slim chance she will call me, and knowing I need to act fast, I dial the police. I file a "reckless driving" report. The 911 operator lets me know I cannot report a stolen vehicle, as the vehicle is not mine. The registered owner of the vehicle must report it, and she is in Mexico, where she and her husband live several months out of the year. They are the owners of the property on which we live, our landlords, and our friends.

I pull up to the house and see tiny bits of broken, tinted glass scattered everywhere. The garage door is closed, but it is apparent the glass is originating from inside the garage where the Blazer had been parked. I feel so angry and sad. It is uncomfortable to pick up the phone to call the landlord's son who lives a couple hours south to tell him what happened, but it must be done. I get hold of him right away, thankfully, and give him the news. He creates a conference call as he dials his mom in Mexico. I tell her what happened, apologizing profusely. He then dials the police, adding the operator to the call.

While I wait for the police to arrive, I quickly go room to room in my house looking for missing items. My laptop and camera are still present. Everything seems to be in place. I feel somewhat relieved. My laptop has my manuscript on it. I would have been in such despair if that had gone missing. I see Maddie's stuff is gone, along with some clothes I was letting her borrow.

I call Tony, as he is still out of town at his work training, and break the news to him. He is furious.

The next couple of hours are spent talking to the police, filling out the report, and being interrupted by numerous calls from both the landlord's son and Tony checking in to get the status, then Tony's sister asking if I needed help. It's no small task to juggle it all. In process, the officer gets a call stating they have retrieved the vehicle still in the county on Hwy 101 about 15 miles south. Thank goodness. Through my description, they positively ID her. Maddie is in custody.

What could she possibly have been thinking?! I'm very confused by her behavior. *Did she think she'd get away with it?* The betrayal of trust feels heartbreaking.

A CHP officer drives me to the vehicle, so I can drive it back to the house rather than it getting impounded and having to pay hundreds of dollars for storage fees. The back window had been completely shattered, likely accidentally while getting it out of the garage. There is glass everywhere inside the Blazer.

Later that evening, I get a call from an officer down at the station. They found some jewelry in Maddie's possession. He gives me a description to pass along to the landlord to see if it belongs to her. Things just keep getting worse. Now it becomes apparent she had entered the landlord's house on the property and taken some jewelry.

That night, I am just beside myself. I just sit and cry. I cry over the whole situation. For the life of me, I cannot understand why she would make such poor choices. She had an opportunity for a better life, yet she ran back into the fire. It seems there are some pretty severe emotional and psychological issues.

I spend 2 days cleaning up the glass from the garage, driveway and vehicle, and getting all the stuff out of the Blazer. It looks like things had been thrown into the vehicle with great haste. I see my bag of nail polishes scattered, along with clothes, shoes, Maddie's makeup, medication, some paperwork, her cell phone, and jewelry, all tossed haphazardly in the back of the Blazer. I find a large open bottle of Brandi tucked behind the front passenger seat. I recognize the bottle as one that had been in our pots and pans cabinet for I don't know how many years. Neither Tony nor I drank any of it. It was a gift to Tony from someone years ago. The alcohol provides a small clue as to what happened, but much remains unknown. It feels like I am cleaning up the aftermath of a hurricane – Hurricane Maddie.

Tony returns home for the weekend. He is still angry. Like me, he has never had anyone betray his trust like that. The weekend is rough. The energy is very heavy. Both of us try to make some sense of Maddie's behavior, but no answers come.

We continue to walk through our place, the landlord's house and the outside property. Like detectives, we begin to piece things together a little more. She had removed the screen on the back window of the garage and crawled in that way. She had used a key that we had in our home to enter the landlord's house. Inside there she got the keys to the Blazer and took some jewelry, most of which were simple bangle bracelets and not of much value. Some more valuable jewelry had been left behind. It seemed like a child playing in her mother's jewelry chest. She also had used some ingenuity to remove the battery from Tony's work pickup, apparently for use in the Blazer. From what the neighbors reported, she had gone onto their property and asked them for a jump, as the Blazer wouldn't start. One of the neighbors said he helped, and he apologized for "being an accomplice." As we come across new evidence of things Maddie had done, each one feels like a fresh stab wound.

It is a very difficult situation, but things could have been worse. The landlords have some silver and a lot of wonderful artwork that he created over the course of a lifetime, none of which was touched. Thankfully, the vehicle was retrieved, along with the other items. The landlord's trust in us is likely compromised. Tony and I are responsible for caring for the property while they are away, and I had left my niece at the house unsupervised. Hopefully we will have a chance to rebuild the trust.

One morning as I'm making my bed, I notice a small heart, about the size of a nickel, drawn in pen ink at the corner of one of my blankets. I stare at it for a long while. I question how long it has been there. I know it must have been left by Maddie. There is a little girl here, still needing to heal.

It is clear Maddie cannot be trusted. I have doubts that she can even trust herself at this time. There are so many unanswered questions. I know if she is to ever get out of the vicious cycle that includes incarceration, addiction, life-threatening situations, abusive relationships and suicidal depression, it is going to take a *lot* of work on her part. For starters, it seems she needs to be in a residential drug and alcohol treatment facility for an extended period of time. She seems so far down, I don't know how she is going to be able to get out. I have a lot of compassion for Maddie, but her situation is so severe. I'm not sure what's going to happen. It's been 5 days since I've seen her. I haven't heard from her. I don't know what I'd say if I did.

On April 25th, I feel drawn to visit Maddie. It's been 8 days since the incident, and I feel like some of the heaviness has lifted. It's a visiting day at the Winowa County jail. I hope to get some answers. I don't know what sort of state she'll be in or what to expect.

I notice the security is more lax than it was in Richmond. No one is standing at the metal detector barking orders. There is no escort to the visiting area, only instructions from the person behind the desk: "Go to the elevator, press M, turn left. She's in A mod." I get off the elevator, turn left and walk down the hall towards three individual booths designated for the A module. As I get close I see Maddie sitting inside one of them, the tears are already falling. I open the door to the small, closet-sized visiting booth, and sit down in the plastic chair on my side of the Plexiglas barrier. There is complete separation. The Plexiglas starts at the chest-high stainless steel shelf, reaches wall to wall and continues up to the ceiling. There is a door behind her that leads back to the cells. Large cinderblocks make up the walls. Here we are back to this.

She just cries, and I start crying. We sit for several moments crying, until I say hello. "I am so sorry," she says through her tears and quaking chin. "I am so, so sorry." Maddie looks uncomfortable in her own skin, the remorse and sadness weighing heavy on her. "I don't remember what happened," she continues. She tells me how she has been in suicide watch for the last 8 days, only just getting to a regular cell last night.

"I only know what the police told me," she says. "I don't remember the vehicle. They were asking me if I knew what color it was, I didn't know. I remember doing some yard work. I got into your brandy, I'm sorry. I remember taking 2 shots then going back later and pouring one of those carrot juice glasses up to the friggin' top. I remember reading some of your book, and something happened. It brought up some stuff, and something in my brain switched. The next thing I remember is waking up Thursday in suicide watch with just a green blanket."

I knew she had started reading *Journey to One*. I did not suggest that she do so. It's pretty intense in the first part, and it's close to home for Maddie. It's not just close to home, it *is* home. I can see how it could be a big trigger and bring up feelings she's not able to digest just yet.

"They said I did a hit and run. I was so worried it was you. I was so worried I had hurt you. I love you so much. Out of all my family, you mean so much to me. I love you." Maddie continues, "I keep something with me at all times... just in case. A cord, a piece of string, that I snuck from the laundry. I keep it just in case it all becomes too much, and I have to check out."

I explain to her more of what she had done. I do so compassionately, but I want her to have those memories back. She doesn't remember going into the landlord's house, or taking the Blazer, or passing me, or driving fast and recklessly. "You saw me like that?" she asks and pulls the neckline of her jail-issued, navy blue sweatshirt up over her eyes, feeling so much shame and sadness, wanting to just find a place to hide. She says the cops told her she was weaving in and out of traffic on the freeway. She says later they told her the hit and run charge was because she had walked away from the vehicle. She has a number of charges against her, including grand theft auto, burglary, DUI and resisting arrest. She is being presented with 5 years. It seems like her life is a nightmare.

Maddie has a very heavy heart and shows a lot of remorse. She blacked out, and it was as if someone else had taken over that afternoon. "Something in my brain is broken," she says through more sobs.

"It's not broken," I say. "In some cases with people who have experienced severe trauma, it's like pieces of yourself get partitioned off, compartmentalized, as a way to cope with the trauma, a protective mechanism. I don't know if that is part of what's going on with you," I continue, "but it's a possibility. At the very least, some kind of dissociation is involved. You've been through a lot in life, that is for sure."

Maddie says blacking out is new for her. "Now I know what people mean when they say they are a 'black out drunk.' I'm an addict and an alcoholic," she says. I nod. She mentioned it to me before, but now I truly get it.

This incident is a huge wake-up call for both of us to now be able to see the severity of Maddie's issues, addiction and distress. "I see how much I really do need help," she states, as she continues to wipe away tears. "I can put on a good front and make it seem like everything's okay, but there's so much in my head. I don't want it in there anymore. I want it out."

"I'm going to continue to support you on your journey," I say to her. "You don't have to go it alone."

"Thank you. Sometimes I can feel you," Maddie says to me, touching her heart with her fingertips and glancing off to the distance. "There are times I can just feel you."

"I feel you too, Maddie. We have a deep connection." We are family, of course, but it feels like I am working with her on a deep level, a soul healing. I get the feeling it is going to be the most intensive healing work I've done to date, and perhaps will ever do.

"Don't kill yourself," I say, thinking of her string. "Hold onto hope. Hold onto love. Know that I am here to support you. We'll get through it together."

I share with her an image that comes to mind in regards to the red Blazer incident. "I see a 3-year-old Maddie running full speed right toward the edge of a cliff. I had to call the police. I had to reach out and snatch you up before you went tumbling off the edge. I'm so glad the police caught you before you got out of the county. I needed to snatch you up and keep you close." Though I would not wish jail time on her, I cannot help but feel this is where she needs to be right now. Here she is contained. I know where she is. She has a roof over her head and 3 meals a day. I'll be able to visit with her 1-2 times per week, and we can get to work.

There's a tap on the door behind her, just one quick click, made by metal on metal, maybe a key. I almost didn't hear it. "They're telling me time is up," Maddie says. We stand. She places both of her hands against the Plexiglas, eyes still wet with tears and pain and deep sadness in her face. "I love you so much," she says again. I put my hands up on the glass to meet hers. It's going to be a long time before there will be no barrier, but the heart connection cannot be separated by mere Plexiglas. We exchange I love yous, and I promise to see her again soon.

The healing has already begun.

For a time, prior to reconnecting with Maddie, my days felt blissfully content – teaching yoga, going for walks, watching the deer graze from the kitchen window, writing and spending time with my love. I live in a peaceful, progressive town with sweet farmers' markets, beautiful parks, and a diverse, accepting community. For the most part, life was filled with blue skies and sunshine, and everything else transpiring on the planet seemed distant and of little consequence.

What an abrupt arousal from my peaceful existence. Oddly enough, I feel this is a good thing. Maddie helped remind me of the suffering that goes on in the world, in my own family, the pain, the need for help. It's not about turning away so that my little slice of paradise doesn't get interrupted. Instead, it's an opportunity for me to be a guide, to help someone else navigate through the dark, heavy stuff of life and come to experience their own joy and contentment.

I drop a letter into the mail for Maddie that includes lots of love and encouragement and also information about boundaries, letting her know she will not be allowed back at our place until trust can be restored. Along with the letter, I include some photos of when Maddie was younger, information from the Native spiritual tradition about the power of Horse, the Pyramid of Healing illustration that I drew earlier for her and some other things I thought she might find of benefit.

Four days following the visit in jail, I get a call from Maddie. I had already set up the phone system so there would be an avenue for open communication. "I got rid of it," she says.

"What?" I ask.

"You know, what I told you about." I think back on our conversation and cannot recall.

"What I told you I was keeping with me. I threw it away," she continues.

"Oh!" I say, recalling now the cord, the noose, she had been keeping with her at all times. "That's wonderful." It's a big step for her.

We talk about visitation and a few other odds and ends. She has some life and energy in her voice, sounding hopeful and stronger.

In the coming weeks, she meets with a counselor who says she qualifies for referral to a drug and alcohol treatment facility. I write a letter for her hearing with the judge. Maddie talks with her public defender and reviews the details of her case. By this time some of the charges have been dropped, and it seems likely that she will be sentenced to one year, which is about 6 months served, and then be transferred to a treatment facility for a 6-month program. I feel relieved, for this is much better than 5 years. If she doesn't go into treatment, though, it is required that she will be in jail for 2 years.

After a little trial and error, I learn the ins and outs of visitation at the Winowa County jail. I must arrive early, since there are only 3 booths per module, and it is first come, first served. I learn what not to wear to keep from setting off the metal detector, and which deputies in the lobby are kind and which ones never smile and treat people rudely for no apparent reason other than they themselves seem unhappy. I begin to see a few of the same faces in the crowd of visitors, other regulars like me.

As Maddie and I have our frequent visits, I start to see changes in her attitude. She begins to surround herself with positive images. She tells me how she has been cutting out pictures of beaches and hearts, lots of hearts, from magazines and placing them around her bunk. She begins to imagine herself making different choices, like drinking iced tea. She plans to sign up for an introductory drug counseling program that is offered through the jail. It's an innovative program that includes non-violent communication, NA & AA meetings, meditation, art therapy class, fish bowl exercises, job skills, tools for relapse prevention, stress management and more. "This place seems to have more emphasis on rehabilitation," she remarks in comparison to other detention facilities. There's a reason I wanted her to be able to stay in this county. I feel she has a chance here. With her history of incarceration, it's apparent how jail has not been a deterrent; she simply adapted to the environment. Punishment has been ineffective. She needs treatment. Now things are aligning to provide her the resources and support she needs.

"You're stepping into a new phase of your life," I say to her one evening, "and I have a feeling this next phase is going to look a lot different than the last one, much more positive."

"I feel it, too," she replies.

At times I get glimpses of a younger Maddie, along with the addict part of her, who hasn't yet gained the coping skills and strategies to fully manage her emotions or stressful situations. "You're my grounding point," she says to me. "Everyone in here can see it. All I have to do is hear your voice on the phone or visit with you, and I feel better, more grounded." I'm happy I can support her in feeling more stable during such a tumultuous time.

There is a great deal of work around helping shift her perception around things, a type of reprogramming, in a sense. We all experience certain "programming" to a degree, from our upbringing and society, but with addicts it can be even more extreme. For example, an addict who has had a number of run-ins with law enforcement may develop an "us versus them" mentality. There's sometimes a belief that all cops are "bad" and "out to get me," and a lack of understanding of how the addict is responsible for her actions. Cops are people, and there are those who may not act honestly and professionally, but there are also those who strive to carry out their job in a fair and understanding way.

Maddie is open to learning, and in fact wants to learn as much as she can. I work to help raise her awareness about her thought processes and addictive behaviors so she can begin to gain control of her addiction rather than let her addiction control her.

The following months are a roller coaster ride of emotion, and each step of the journey of recovery is not without its challenges. I experience many sleepless nights. Obstacles arise, that oftentimes seem insurmountable, leaving Maddie and I both questioning what the heck to do.

For example, in June Maddie is sentenced, and it is indeed a term of just a few months, then referral to a residential treatment facility. After about 5 months in jail, a bed opens up at the facility. That morning in early September is an exciting day. It's a day that marks a transition to the next step of her recovery and growth. Maddie gets packed up and is in process of getting released through booking. Twenty minutes before she is to leave, a bench warrant pops up from Yolo County. She must be transported now to the jail in Yolo County and await her hearing with the judge to deal with a case from a few years back for which she is currently on probation. There's a lot of "clean-up" to do in this process. Maddie has been in the criminal justice system in multiple counties for quite a while.

It feels like a devastating blow. Maddie tells me later that she cried all night long, cried about everything that has happened. Perhaps the purging is necessary. I feel sad and a heaviness, too. Maddie recovers fairly quickly, though. Sometimes there are detours along the road to recovery, but you keep putting one foot in front of the other. Giving up is not an option, and it's important to stay positive.

She remains in Yolo County for a little over a month. I make the long drive and visit her a couple times, as well as attend the hearing and advocate on her behalf with the judge. It's a very different environment. The detention facility is smaller, more rustic and everyone wears those striped jumpsuits like you see on those old TV shows. There are no stress management classes or job skills training. It seems to be simply a place to detain people. Thankfully the judge decides to allow her to continue forward with the plan for treatment in our county.

Transported back to Winowa County, she again must wait for a bed to open up at the treatment facility. On November 7th, she finally gets her chance and is transported to rehab. I drop off some clothes and toiletries for her. For the first time in 7 months I'm able to visit with her for a few minutes without Plexiglas between us, and I give her a hug. I think the last hug she received was the one I gave her just prior to her arrest. It makes me think how hugs may have been few and far between for Maddie over the years. I do not recall her mother or any other family member showing her affection. Much of the physical contact she received was in the form of spankings. Love. We need more love.

Things seem to go fairly well. It's a challenging situation for Maddie to be in a house with close to 40 other women who are also addicts and/or alcoholics. There's a lot of drama. It feels chaotic at times, as I get a sense for the place through attending a few of the family sessions offered on Saturdays. But this is where she is for now.

On Thanksgiving Day, I prepare a salad and am just about to take it over to the treatment facility. Family members have been invited to bring a dish and share dinner with the clients. I'm excited to be able to spend a holiday with Maddie, as I haven't done so in the past, and this is such an important time for her. Following the dinner there, I plan to share a Thanksgiving meal with Tony and his family.

Maddie calls me as I'm driving to the facility with my salad. She's crying. "I've been kicked out," she says. What?! My stomach does a flip flop. Oh, no. This treatment program was her opportunity. Now what? I pick her up at the drug store down the street. I can't believe they would kick someone out on Thanksgiving and just put an addict out on the street. She could have gotten some alcohol to drown out some of that pain, but she didn't. I arrive to find her deeply saddened and at a loss as to what to do, but sober. In jail Maddie made a commitment to stay clean and sober, and passed up opportunities to use drugs multiple times from people who had smuggled them into jail. It's amazing how many drugs circulate in there, despite efforts to keep them out.

Both the counselor Maddie met with while in jail and I feel the dismissal is unjustified. (I later find out a few other young women have been kicked out seemingly without just cause. Turns out, a few months later, the director of the program is fired.) But back to jail Maddie goes. The rollercoaster ride continues. Giving up is not an option.

I resume my visits. I secure my spot, pick up the visitor's tag and wait outside on one of the benches until it's time to line up to go through the metal detector.

I see a homeless man that I've noticed on every occasion that I've been here. He seems to live on one of the cement benches outside the jail entrance under a covered walkway. At first I found it peculiar that he would choose such a place to set up camp. He's a 60-something year old black man, about 6 feet tall, big boned, and has a brace on his right leg below the knee. He's always wearing khaki green shorts and a heavy, two-tone gray coat, no matter the temperature, whether it's 60 degrees or 90. On his bench he has a small, blue ice chest, a reusable grocery bag and a small radio among his few belongings. Sometimes I've heard him singing along with the radio. A few times, I've heard him have full-on conversations with someone only he can see. I listened intently to one such conversation, and he told a story of being in jail. So this place is familiar to him.

I'd smile and say hi when I passed by him. He'd smile and say hi back. I observed several regular visitors engage him in conversation, and he seemed to enjoy the company. He appears quite friendly.

It's encouraging to see how we, as a community, can be accepting of our differences. I'm intrigued how, in this place where sheriff's deputies are constant features, and attorneys, and visitors from all walks of life frequent the grounds, this man is allowed to have a place to stay and sleep. I would think in a county complex with so much law enforcement, he would be instructed to leave. But he is here day after day. Everyone needs some place.

As visiting time nears, I go back inside and line up against the cinderblock wall in the lobby. I like to be near the front of the line so as not to be delayed by newcomers getting buzzed for wearing belts or jewelry or buckles on their shoes.

As we visit in the booth at A mod, I empathize with Maddie that it is a challenge and very frustrating to be back in jail. I encourage her to look forward and gently remind her what she is capable of accomplishing. We talk about the different experiences she has been through, from childhood through adulthood: surviving horrific and long-term abuse, living on the streets, miraculously making it through her own concerted efforts to end her life, the depths of addiction, years of being in jail, etc. It certainly is more than most of us have ever experienced. Through the Plexiglas I watch her turn her head off to the side and gaze off somewhere far beyond these cinderblock walls. "If I can do all that, I wonder what will happen if I direct all that energy?" she inquires. She turns back to me. "I wonder what I'll do?" she asks and smiles.

"Whatever it is," I reply, "it'll be remarkable."

She nods, still pondering the possibilities. "Yeah!"

Maddie works with her attorney, and through no small effort on her part, gets referred by the judge to an outpatient treatment program, which neither of us knew about at first, known as Drug Court. The Drug Court treatment model began in 1989 in Florida and is now available in all 50 states, though it is not yet available in all counties. It is designed for individuals who have committed non-violent drug and alcohol related offenses. Locally, it is a collaborative effort between the Winowa County court system and a local, non-profit, drug and alcohol treatment center. The minimum term is one year.

In January 2014, Maddie is released from jail and begins this program. The program includes weekly classes, almost daily drug testing, one-on-one weekly sessions with a drug counselor, mental health services, numerous AA/NA meetings per week, and weekly or biweekly court appearances where she checks in with the judge. Failure to comply with the requirements, and even minor infractions, such as showing up to class one minute late, results in jail time for a period of 3 days or more. It is a challenging program, but provides more freedom and less drama than a residential program. With this structure, I am also able to work with Maddie closely and continue to provide her the support she needs.

During the first year of the program, Maddie's stress level is extremely high. There is a scramble to find permanent housing and the need to find work. She experiences numerous health issues, including difficult to treat seizures which necessitate multiple trips to the emergency room. On one occasion, she ends up in the ICU on a ventilator, and it takes several days for her to recover. I advocate on her behalf throughout the year with numerous doctors and nurses to ensure she gets the proper care. I feel for all those who do not have an advocate.

Without letup, obstacles arise around every corner. A tremendous amount of diligence, trust and surrender is involved. With time, a solution always presents itself and things continue to move forward. It never ceases to amaze me how things align, one after the other, in support of her healing and recovery.

Maddie works hard, and I work hard. Together, we work to rebuild her life one step at a time. Eventually, things stabilize for Maddie and get easier. There are fewer obstacles and more opportunities.

Transformation happens. She meets a man, Kevin, who is kind and loving, and Maddie begins to learn what it is like to be in a healthy romantic relationship. After 1 year, 9 months, she graduates from Drug Court. In addition to Tony and me, there are several others in Maddie's corner at the graduation ceremony – Kevin, who is now her husband, and his parents, Maddie's sister-in-law with her two children, and several friends who encourage and support Maddie in her continuing recovery. As she stands at the podium, giving her speech and sharing her story, I feel so proud. My eyes well up with tears. We did it. She did it.

At the time of writing, Maddie has been clean and sober for over 3 years. The cases she had in the other counties have been closed. Maddie's charges in Winowa County were expunged upon her graduation from Drug Court. Spending time in jail is a thing of the past. Her health is managed with only one medication. She hasn't had a seizure in over a year. She's living with her husband in a house a couple miles from me and works at a job she enjoys. Maddie is taking steps towards rebuilding and strengthening her relationship with her 3 daughters. Of course, it's not the end. Recovery is a continuing journey. But she is experiencing something that she's never experienced before – happiness.

Part IV: Butterfly

After some time passes,
and much change takes place,
she feels herself wanting to stretch beyond her current boundary.
It feels complete.
She has come to an understanding of how
transformation happens
and why each stage is necessary.
She understands the meaning...
and yet still marvels at the mystery of life.

She falls into moments of dreaming and imagining.
"What will be revealed? What will unfold?" she asks.
She receives answers, not so much as pictures in her mind
but as a feeling throughout her whole being.
Down to the cellular level,
there is a sense of greater opening,
a sense of unbounded opportunity and possibility.

A whisper on the wind tells her it's time.
She feels ready.
Wriggle... wriggle, wriggle.
She hears the sound of something tearing, releasing,
and then feels herself tumbling out.
She tumbles until her legs happen to catch onto a
small twig beneath her.

Out of instinct, she grasps.
Her wings are moist, wrinkled and heavy.
She slowly, carefully, walks herself upright.
The sun shines its warmth
and begins to dry her wings.

Chapter 16 – Key #1

Power of Words

If nothing ever changed, there'd be no butterflies.

J shared teachings and tools with Maddie to support her in her healing and recovery. I have shared many of these same tools with coaching clients, students, and with individuals and couples in workshops and other settings.

I feel a strong desire to share these teachings with as many people as possible, for I know from personal experience, and from working with others, that they can and do transform lives. They can help you enjoy more happiness and fulfillment, better health, and live your potential. So in this fourth stage of the book I offer 4 Keys. I hope you find these practical tips and tools of value in your relationships, health, work and personal development.

These tools are actually quite simple. That doesn't necessarily mean they are easy, however. Learning new communication skills or providing our bodies more physical activity takes a certain level of dedication and practice. I have broken down the concepts into manageable steps. As you begin to explore them, you might feel the simplicity become apparent as they help us reconnect with a more natural, and perhaps more authentic, state of being. They can help us to stop struggling against ourselves and instead surrender to a gentle current that will carry us to a place of greater health and happiness in life. These tools have been used to positively transform even the most challenging of situations, and you can use them to transform your life, a little or a lot.

Let's get started with communication. Communication has an incredible amount of influence in our relationships and how we view ourselves. I will first cover specific communication strategies that fall under the category of Listen First. Then we'll explore the internal chatter, how we talk to ourselves, and the power of words.

LISTEN FIRST

First, some background information. I'm borrowing the term "Listen First" from the Y. It is the name given to the communication and relationship building strategy which I was so heavily involved with at both the local Y level and while working with YMCA of the USA on the Activate America endeavor. Though I first gained familiarity with the term "Listen First" from the Y, the techniques have their roots in counseling psychology and motivational interviewing. I have adapted and broadened the original application of Listen First for the purposes of this chapter.

Using the skills daily in my work at the Y, it wasn't long before Listen First overflowed into my personal life. I saw the tremendous value of using these skills in various settings. I began using them with friends, with my significant other, with my yoga students, with the check-out clerk at the supermarket. I credit Listen First with helping me establish a relationship with the love of my life, Tony. It was my deliberate use of the skills that allowed me to gain more understanding about this man, see his many beautiful facets, and appreciate his unique perspective.

I continue to use the skills today, and I will use them tomorrow. They now simply feel part of how I communicate. I find Listen First to be helpful in how I relate with others and life-enriching.

The following concepts and skills can apply to all forms of relationships, such as a relationship with a romantic partner or spouse, a friend, coworker, child or parent. As we explore these, for simplicity's sake, you may want to first **focus on just one specific individual** in your life with whom you'd like to enjoy a more satisfying connection.

LISTEN FIRST: Key Concepts

- **We appreciate feeling heard.** Being heard, or feeling understood, is an essential aspect of a happy relationship. You might think of an example when you didn't feel heard or understood. What feelings arose for you? Perhaps you felt anger, frustration, sadness, stymied, like you'd hit a roadblock, or deflated, feeling as if your opinion or perspective didn't matter. What happened in the conversation? Did you shut down? Did it turn into an argument? Likely, most of us have felt the stress and weight of being in an argument with someone we care about. Perhaps we talk over each other, end up saying things we wish we didn't, feelings get hurt, anger flares up, or we shut down, and nothing ever seems to get resolved. In short, nothing about it feels very good. Many arguments arise as a result of one or both individuals not feeling adequately heard.

- **It's about *how* we relate.** As the adage goes, it's not what you say, but how you say it. How we relate has a big effect on how people feel and choices they make. That's not to say we are *responsible* for another person's feelings, but we do not exist in a vacuum. What we do and say ripples out and has an impact on others. Putting effort into how we relate lends to others feeling more supported, comfortable, cared about, loved, understood, and minimizes arguments and conflict.

- **Genuineness.** The strategies involved in Listen First come from a place of respect, caring, compassion, and a genuine interest in getting to know a person. We usually *want* to present ourselves in a caring, respectful manner, (after all, that is how we often see ourselves), but sometimes we just don't know *how*. We may have a communication style that mirrors that of our parents, for better or worse. We are taught the skills of driving safely so as to avoid accidents, but many of us are not taught the communication skills that are useful for avoiding conflict and misunderstanding. For Listen First to be effective, it has to come from the heart. This genuineness is helpful, too, when we first begin to practice the techniques. Sometimes it can feel awkward as we verbally stumble our way through the process. It may take time for the skills to feel natural and sound sincere. We can be more patient with ourselves and others when we remember the intention behind the effort, which is to create a stronger connection.

- **Non-judgmental attitude.** This key concept is closely related to genuineness. It requires each of us to set aside any notion that we are better than the other person, for whatever reason, be it income level, sexual orientation, race, gender, nationality, age, education, religion, political affiliation, title or role, life circumstances, or anything else that we humans use to create a sense of separation. It comes back to the heart, opening our hearts so that we are able to listen without judgment. It is also about letting go of believing that we know everything, that we're "right." Instead, we respect and actively seek each individual's perspective.

- **Develops trust.** The approach of Listen First is collaborative; it creates a sense of partnership, and there is a balance of power. As I speak, and you reflect to me what I have said and the feelings behind the words, it tells me you care about me and what I have to say. Trust builds, and I feel encouraged to share more. The skills of Listen First further the flow of open, honest communication, and that is crucial for enjoying a stronger, more meaningful connection.

- **Patience and practice.** It's a process. Like learning any new skill, it takes repetition and patience. It's a verbal dance, where over time the partners gain techniques so as not to step on each other's toes and learn to read each other more effectively and move about the dance floor of life with greater ease. Remember, patience and lots of practice.

LISTEN FIRST – The Skills

Each of the skills offered in Listen First might be thought of as a tool to add to our toolbox, or a color to add to our palette. The introduction of these skills does not propose that our current way of communicating is "right" or "wrong." Listen First may simply be new or different for some of us. It can provide an alternative. We are free to use the skills as we wish to build connections and add beauty to how we relate.

It is said that people don't care what we know until they know that we care. Listening in an empathetic manner is a wonderful way to show that we care.

Empathy is our capacity to identify with another. It does not necessarily mean we have the same view, but we can understand and be open to another perspective. Having greater empathy is correlated with better performance and satisfaction in many professions, including medicine, law enforcement, human services, sales and financial consulting. In addition, communicating with empathy and compassion creates stronger, more fulfilling personal relationships. Empathy requires a genuine interest in others and a sincere desire to expand our perspectives and learning. Listen First is an avenue for increasing our ability to demonstrate empathy through the use of 4 helpful skills.

1 - Reflections (mirroring)

Reflections are the most important part of Listen First. They are the most powerful and effective for strengthening relationships.

What it is: A reflection is a statement that expresses the meaning of what was just heard. Sometimes referred to as mirroring, a reflection restates what the person says in a little different way.

What it does: Use of reflections demonstrates caring and communicates understanding.

Some typical reflections might be:

- It sounds like you're dissatisfied with...
- It sounds like you are feeling...
- So you are saying that you feel conflicted about...
- So you are saying that you'd like things to change in regard to your...

Statements like these might at first seem rather corny or feel unnatural. It's just a starting point, a frame of reference. With time and practice, we can refine the skills so they feel and sound more natural and sincere. Remember the intention behind the effort. The goal is to create a better connection and enjoy more satisfying relationships. Our efforts to be a more effective and empathetic listener is usually appreciated and well-received by others, despite any awkward moments.

As we become more familiar with the use of reflections, we can drop the "It sounds like" or "So you are saying" part of the reflection and simply state:

- You're feeling excited about...
- You're struggling with...
- It's been difficult for you...
- You're ready to...

Example 1: Nicholas walks in the front door to his home. Emma, his girlfriend, recently got home, too, and asks how his day was. Nicholas begins to explain, "I can't believe Scotty didn't just come to me first and ask if I could complete the report. Instead, he goes to my boss and tells him I haven't finished it. If I had known they needed it today, I would have had it ready. So now I look like I'm not doing my job."

Emma reflects, "It sounds like you are feeling frustrated at work and wish things had been communicated with you differently."

There could have been many different responses. Emma could have replied, "Oh, well you won't believe what happened to *me* today," trying to one-up Nicholas. Or, she could have responded, "Maybe you should have just done the report earlier," criticizing his approach, or "I'm sure everything will be fine. Hey, let's go get something to eat," attempting to reassure Nicholas and divert his attention. There are many, many ways we can respond. The value in the reflection that Emma provided is it conveys empathy. It acknowledges his feelings and mirrors his experience. Emma's reflection allows Nicholas to feel heard and understood, and he is more likely to communicate further with her. It deepens their connection.

Example 2: Cesar and Rachel are in the break room at their place of employment. "I'm feeling really run down lately," Rachel says. "Maybe I've been taking on too many hours, I don't know... but I like having the extra income. I think I'm just tired of not getting the recognition that I feel I deserve."

Cesar reflects, "You seem conflicted about your schedule, and are feeling unappreciated."

Rachel continues, "Yes, maybe not conflicted so much as just confused about what to do. Overall, I like my job and the hours. I guess I'd just like to get a thank you every now and then. I don't know how to approach that with my supervisor or even if it's worth bringing up."

A common response (we might recognize this from our own personal experience) is to want to jump in and "fix" the situation. "Feeling run down? Maybe you should try to get more sleep." Or, "Who's not appreciating you? I'll have a talk with them." Always, there are a number of possible responses.

In this example, Cesar's reflection and empathy allowed Rachel to confirm that she did feel unappreciated and clarified her sense of confusion. One of the many benefits of reflections is, as others reflect for us, it very often helps us come to a better understanding of what we want to convey, or help clarify our own feelings. In this way, we may then find our own solutions. It can be enough, though, to simply feel heard. Rachel likely recognizes Cesar as a good listener and caring coworker.

Example 3: Diane and her 15 year old daughter, Caroline. Diane is listening as her daughter begins, "Missy invited a bunch of us to have dinner at her family's restaurant to celebrate the end of finals. I really want to go, but she invited Shannon *Miller*, of all people. Missy is my best friend, I don't know why she would go and invite Shannon. She knows how I feel about her."

"You're struggling with going or not," Diane says.

"Yes," replies Caroline. "I wanna go, I just don't know if I can be around Shannon right now," she continues.

Reflections don't have to be lengthy. They simply need to show you're listening in an empathetic way.

Something to note, a reflection is a statement. In other words, it's not a question. In the English language, our voice goes down at the end when providing a reflection, not up in a questioning tone. "You're struggling with this?" and "You're struggling with this" can have a very different feeling and meaning. The first one sounds like the person is in disbelief that you are struggling with such a thing and feels a little condescending. The one that is the statement compassionately reflects that you are struggling with the situation.

Reflections become more effective and sound more natural with practice. You might set yourself a specific goal, such as "I'm going to use reflections today with my co-worker, Joan." Or, "I will make a conscious effort to use reflections with my husband at dinner." Starting small is helpful, and you can always build on it. With repetition, it can become an incredibly beneficial habit in how we communicate.

Reflections can also be used to acknowledge how a person is feeling through his or her body language. We can tell by a person's body language if she is frustrated or sad, or if he is feeling nervous or excited about something. "You seem frustrated," is an example. Much of non-verbal communication is instinctual and relatively easy to read. It's often a matter of simply recognizing it and verbally responding in an empathetic manner.

When you practice reflections, take notice of how the speaker responds, how the conversation goes. Does the speaker share more? Does the conversation turn into a familiar argument or is it a more pleasant interaction? Experiencing the positive benefits of using reflections is a powerful incentive for continuing to use them.

2 - Open Questions

A second skill of Listen First is the use of open questions.

What it is: An open question is open-ended. In other words, it is not something that can be answered with a "yes" or "no" or any single word or short phrase, such as in the case of a closed question.

For instance, a closed question might be something like, "What is your favorite color?" or "Did you enjoy the movie?" An example of an open question is, "How was your experience in class?" or "What options have you considered?"

What it does: An open question encourages elaboration and the sharing of ideas, wishes or plans.

Of course, there is nothing wrong with closed questions. We use them frequently and they serve a purpose. Many of us rarely use open questions, however, and there is much value in adding more of them into our communication. With a little effort, we can often turn a closed question into an open one. Open questions demonstrate that we are interested in what the person has to say, and they provide us more material to help us become better listeners.

Let's further the conversation from the above example of Cesar and Rachel. Cesar reflects, "You seem conflicted about your schedule, and are feeling unappreciated."

Rachel responds, "Yes, maybe not conflicted so much as just confused about what to do. Overall, I like my job and the hours. I guess I'd just like to get a thank you every now and then. I don't know how to approach that with my supervisor or even if it's worth bringing up."

Cesar then asks an open question, "What might be some benefits of bringing it up to your boss?" We can see how this question invites Rachel to share in more discussion and ponder possibilities.

Example: Let's take a new example, incorporating the use of both reflections and open questions. Brian and LaShawn are seated near each other on the subway. LaShawn excitedly starts talking to Brian, "I get to spend the whole weekend with my kids. It's the first weekend in months that I haven't had to work.

"I can see you're looking forward to it," Brian responds.

"Yes, I think we'll spend some time at the park, maybe get some BBQ. Before we go out and do anything fun, though, my youngest two boys will need to clean their room. It's like pulling teeth to get them to do it. It drives me crazy sometimes."

"Sounds like a chore for you and them," Brian reflects. "What has worked in the past when you've asked them to clean their room?"

There are often multiple opportunities in a conversation to use reflections. Adding an open question or two can enrich the communication that much more.

For open questions, you might again set a goal for yourself, "I'm going to ask more open questions at work this week."

3 - Affirmations

Another important skill of Listen First is the use of affirmations.

What it is: An affirmation is a supportive comment, a few encouraging words.

Affirmations may express appreciation for a person's effort. They are more effective when they are genuine and they focus on things that are important to the speaker. Affirmations usually feel really good to receive.

What it does: An affirmation builds collaboration, strengthens relationships and shows you care.

Affirmations are a bit different from compliments. A compliment might be, "I like your shirt." Though kind, that simply states what I think about your shirt. Affirmations are a little more personal. They keep the focus on the other person. "James, you really put a lot of care into how you dress" is an example.

In one sense, affirmations are quite simple. However, they can also be challenging. It takes careful listening to know what to affirm.

More examples:
- "You worked hard on that project, and it shows."
- "You're an attentive and supportive mom."
- "That's so creative how you rearranged the furniture."
- "Wow, you stayed strong and determined despite those obstacles."
- "It's admirable how you maintain a positive attitude and keep a cool head even when things get hectic around you."

We don't have to worry about being perfect in using affirmations or any of the Listen First skills. It's an ongoing practice. There is always room for growth when it comes to communication. The intention can also say a lot. When we strive to use the skills in a genuine and supportive manner, it generally has positive results.

As we put into practice these first 3 skills, our conversations with others continue to unfold – sharing, **reflecting**, sharing some more,

reflecting, sharing and clarifying, **reflecting, asking open questions,** sharing, **reflecting**. Then the roles may switch and the original speaker listens, and the original listener speaks and shares – back and forth, the dance. Over time, relationships transform and grow more meaningful.

4 - Sharing Information Sensitively

It is worthwhile to spend considerable time (weeks or months) regularly practicing the above three skills of Listen First before venturing into this fourth one. One may choose to focus on just reflections for a few weeks, and then focus on open questions for a couple weeks, and so on. Many of us are in the habit of sharing what we know or think more so than listening. We love to give advice. We're at the ready to jump in and give our two cents whether it's asked for or not. **The value is in the listening**. That's why I list this skill last. Once we feel we have a good grasp of the previous 3 skills, particularly reflections, and feel comfortable in our use of them, we can explore how to share information, and be more effective in doing so. Remember, in our Listen First communication, the goal is to maintain a listening framework. It is generally *after* we have demonstrated that we have listened to the other person and that we care about his or her situation that the other person can best hear what we might have to say.

In addition, the majority of the time, the person speaking comes to his or her own decisions about an issue, aided simply through our listening and reflecting, asking open questions and affirming. When we have our experience mirrored back to us, it can give us new perspective and insight. The conclusions we reach on our own have more sticking power than advice from others.

There are occasions, though, when we have information to share, such as advice, and the other person wants information from us at the appropriate time. This is especially true if we're parents or in a profession in which others seek our support or expertise. Here is where the how comes in, *how* we give suggestions or share ideas is critical. We can share in a sensitive way. Here are a few helpful tips.

I. A collaborative approach. With both youth and adults, a collaborative approach can be beneficial. That means, I'm not presuming to be an expert on your life. I don't know all your life experiences or perspectives. I don't know how it feels to be in your body and I don't know all the thoughts that pass through your mind. In the approach of Listen First, you are the best expert on you. That can be a hard one for some of us to swallow, as we may sometimes think we know best in regard to others, too. Each of us is a unique individual with options and choices before us. Rather than the advice-giver assuming the role of expert, the two work together as a team.

I've observed parents who skillfully redirect children or teenagers through collaborative means. A person's potential naturally blossoms in a nurturing, supportive environment. With a collaborative approach, the interactions are less likely to turn into power struggles, there tends to be less conflict, and the parent-child relationship continues to grow stronger.

I experienced the value of this collaborative approach in my communication with my niece, Maddie. When I would try to assume the I-am-your-aunt-so-I-can-tell-you-what-to-do role, I usually hit a roadblock. For instance, when I would say something like, "You need to do that paper," it was much less effective than, "Have you identified a time when you'll be able to finish your paper?" In the first example, I'm essentially trying to control her behavior. In the second example, I'm not taking away her autonomy. She knows her responsibility, and is more likely to take ownership over the task when I provide a caring, respectful, collaborative approach.

If we think about it, not many of us like being told what to do. I know I don't like being told what to do. When someone jumps into advice-giving or tries to be controlling, I find myself thinking the person doesn't even know me, dismissing what he or she has to say or immediately getting resistant. Remembering this, putting ourselves in the other person's shoes for a moment can help us find the words to share information in a more sensitive and collaborative way.

II. Ask permission. Another way to share information is to ask permission before providing advice. For example, "It seems like you're feeling stuck. I have a suggestion that worked for a friend in a similar situation, do you mind if I share it?" Or, "Are you up for exploring a couple of ideas?"

Similar to asking permission is offering the option to disregard your advice. "One thing that I've found helpful, and this may or may not apply to you, is…" Or another example, "What you do with this information is completely up to you…"

Although suggestions are sometimes helpful, the temptation is to provide unsolicited and strong advice. Very often, that approach falls flat. When we ask permission before giving advice or preface it with permission to disagree, it prepares the person to receive the information. When you've been given the okay to share your suggestions, he or she is more likely to take them into consideration.

III. Provide a small menu of options. Perhaps an individual has opened the door to receive your advice. People can be overwhelmed by information they didn't expect, so another helpful strategy is to give only a small amount of relevant information. It's easy to get excited when we have the opportunity to share, but it's best to not share *everything* we know about the subject. The intention is not to force-feed, but to offer bite-sized chunks. It allows the person to digest the information more easily.

We might also offer a range of options when sharing information. Someone may be open to our advice about a situation, and we can share a few things that are of varying intensity.

Example: One of my students comes to me after yoga class and says she and her husband want to eat healthier dinners, but it has been difficult since they both work and have little time for meal preparation. She says they often end up eating quick, frozen dinners or stop by and pick up fast food. "You want to eat a healthy dinner, but it's been hard to find the time," I reflect. She nods her head. I ask an open question, "What have you and your husband tried?" As the conversation continues, I use reflections and ask more open questions. Through our discussion, I realize I have some information that she may find beneficial. "There are a few things that couples in your situation sometimes find helpful," I begin, "is it okay if I share them?" asking permission.

"Yes, I'd be happy to hear some ideas," she says.

"One thing is to possibly stop by the grocery store and pick up something like a roast chicken and fixings for a quick salad. Or a crock pot can also be useful. If you have time in the morning, you can throw the ingredients in the crock pot, and dinner is ready when you come home. Others have taken advantage of a healthy meal home delivery service." Without overwhelming her with a lot of information, I provide a range of options. Some options are simple. Some are more involved and costly.

It's always nice to follow up the suggestions with another open question, "Do any of these suggestions sound like it could work?"

"There are quite a few healthier food options that are pre-made at the grocery store. It wouldn't take any longer to pick that up than it does to go through the fast food drive-thru," the student replies.

"So stopping at the grocery store sounds like one possibility," I reflect.

One of the suggestions offered might be appealing to my student, or she may go home and begin brainstorming with her husband to find something altogether different that works well for both of them. When the person has a hand in generating the solution, such as by choosing from a menu of options, it is more likely he or she will own the idea and put it into practice.

We've covered the main points of Listen First. I cannot say enough how powerful and beneficial it is to **simply listen**. We all want to feel heard and know that someone cares. Listening leads to respectful, caring and more loving relationships, where there is less frustration and more enjoyment. Listening gets easier with practice and time, and I hope you experience for yourself how it's well worth the effort.

POWER OF WORDS

Eckhart Tolle, the wonderful teacher that he is, popularized and reminded us of the power of now. What has also become apparent is the incredible power of words.

We've seen how words can be powerful through our use of the 4 skills found in Listen First. Using reflections in an empathetic way can change the course of a conversation, like veering away from conflict to enjoy a more caring, respectful encounter. Something as simple as asking permission prior to giving advice creates an environment in which a person is more likely to be receptive, rather than resistant, to hearing our words. There's greater collaboration, which lends itself to stronger, more meaningful relationships.

There is also remarkable power in the words that are not spoken, those that remain in our mind as thoughts, our internal chatter. Let's ponder that a moment. Our thoughts are made up of words. When we are infants, prior to learning language, our thoughts are of a different quality, likely more sensory based. But from early childhood through adulthood and for the remainder of our lives, words play a huge role in our thoughts. We can also visualize, and so have images come to mind. We can imagine how a feather feels against our skin or the smell of an apple pie cooking. Connecting with these sensory experiences might also be considered part of our thought process. For simplicity's sake, I'm going to summarize that our thoughts are made up of words, for it seems that no matter what else our mind is preoccupied with, coursing through those neural networks is a steady stream of words.

These words sometimes well up emotions, sometimes they captivate us. They can go round and round in circles processing intense experiences. They can be used in planning for an important event. They can be used to get ourselves motivated. Words are very useful, and they have a powerful effect.

In our exploration of communication, it is essential that we look inside ourselves. Within each of us is a beautiful gem. For some of us, that gem may stay hidden indefinitely. For others of us, with some personal work, that gem will get to see the light of day. All of us have the potential to unearth that inner beauty. **The more we can work on ourselves, the smoother and more enjoyable our connections with others will be.**

Each of us might consider how much we've dug through our own layers of mucky muck. Through making a diligent effort, we can identify and begin discarding habitual ways of doing things – habitual ways of thinking and interacting with others – which have kept us from experiencing happiness. What is this mucky muck? Things such as:

- Blame
- Insecurity
- Anger and resentment
- Being judgmental
- Fear/doubt
- Hate
- Pain
- Inflated ego
- Holding onto victimhood

Perhaps you can think of a couple more items to add to the list. The mucky muck gets built up over the years, perhaps due to others around us modeling those particular thought processes and behaviors, as well as mere life experiences.

We might note how several of these things can arise when we are not in the now, when we're focusing on something in the past or thinking of what could happen in the future. We may hold blame and anger over a situation that happened long ago. Or we may experience fear in taking a bold step, worrying what others may think of us if we do not succeed.

One thing we all know but sometimes forget is how **words carry energy**. For instance, if I say to you, "You did a great job," it feels very different from, "That was really stupid of you." The first one carries the energy of encouragement. The second one has an energy that is condescending and hurtful. When we feel hurt, we're sometimes told we need to just grow some thicker skin. On the contrary, each of us must take responsibility for the words and energy we put out to others. The second sentence reveals that I need to work on myself more, to get over my anger or pain or resentment, or whatever it might be that is holding me down, and now trying to push you down. I need to take a moment and think before I speak, and see if this is really the energy I want to share. It is the same with our internal dialog. The words that make up our thoughts carry energy.

Everything is connected – words, thoughts, emotions, our energy level. Oftentimes, we get swept up in the day to day thoughts and activities of life. Maybe something stressful happened at work. Our mind is preoccupied with it, and we feel tired and drained. Or maybe we get a new puppy, and we feel excited and begin to think about what we need to do to puppy-proof the house. Thoughts and feelings are constantly flowing and interacting.

Because of this interconnectedness, **we can influence how we feel through our words**. The more we begin to observe our words, the more we can use them to better our lives.

This act of observing helps bring an unconscious thought pattern into conscious awareness. Here we can decide if it is unhelpful or helpful, if we want to discard it or keep it. We can see if it has been dragging us down, limiting us, or if it has been supporting us.

There are various thoughts that might pass through our mind that put ourselves or others down in some way. Let's take a look at a few.

- "I'm not smart enough to do that."
- "Look how that person is dressed, I can't believe she'd even go out of the house."
- "I can't do anything right."
- "What will he think of me?"
- "Those people are just lazy."

- "I hate people who seem to have it all."

- "I don't deserve it."

- "It's not my fault, my dad raised me this way."

- "Nothing good ever happens to me."

- Any thought that we are somehow better than another person.

As you read through the above examples, you might have gotten a sense how such thoughts or beliefs cause us to lose energy. Like having a slow leak in an inner tube, they deflate us. When I think to myself, "I'm not smart enough to do that," I'm limiting myself, limiting possibility. When I think I'm not smart, I feel down, depressed. I feel a heaviness in my body.

Many thoughts come from a place of judgment, victimization or fear. "I can't do anything right," reinforces a view of myself as a victim. It implies there's something wrong with me, and it keeps me down. There is a judgmental attitude in thinking I'm better than the guy driving the beat-up Datsun, or the woman who struggles with addiction. We sometimes think poorly of others, which can be an unconscious attempt to make ourselves feel better. Very often, we simply get into a habitual way of thinking and do not question *why* we think that way.

Having a good counselor or coach can help with working through unconscious thought patterns and behaviors that diminish our potential and lead us to feeling dissatisfied. This book is not intended to provide *all* the tools that we may need on our journeys. Rather, it introduces a few concepts that can be helpful.

A key to enjoying greater health and happiness is to bring the unconscious into the conscious. It can start simply, by bringing awareness to our internal dialog. **We can start identifying whether the words that make up our thoughts tear down or build up.** This makes room for change, something different. We begin to notice the messages we tell ourselves, and then we can create new, positive messages to replace the old. We must treat *ourselves* with care, respect and compassion before we can effectively extend these things to others.

Here are some examples of messages that might be used to replace ones that tear down.

Old Messaging	New Messaging
"I'm not smart enough to do that."	"I'm going to give it my best effort."
"Look how that person is dressed, I can't believe she'd even go out of the house."	"That person is dressed in an interesting way."
"I can't do anything right."	"Sometimes I make mistakes. It's part of learning."
"What will they think of me?"	"I will not limit myself based on fear of what others may think."
"Those people are just lazy."	"I don't fully know what their situation is. I'll focus on my own actions."
"I hate people who seem to have it all."	"I wonder if there are ways to have more of what I enjoy."
"I don't deserve it."	"I deserve to be loved, to be happy, to be safe…"
"It's not my fault, my dad raised me this way."	"I see unhelpful patterns from my father in me."
"Nothing good ever happens to me."	"I am open to receiving more good things in my life."
Any thought that we are somehow better than another person.	Thoughts that we are all equal individuals at different places along the road but making the journey together.

Rather than deflate us, these words feed us, give us more air, more life. (At the very least, the new messages are neutral – without judgment or victimization – which retains our energy.) They are more closely tuned into who we are beneath the layers, our authentic gem selves. As we start noticing our thought patterns, we can usually find areas that could use a little reprogramming. With practice the new type of messaging becomes easier and more natural, and it doesn't take long before we reap the benefits. We may find we have more energy, we remain more open to possibility and allow good things to come in, and we experience a greater sense of well-being. Words have a huge effect on how we feel and how we act. Words have the power to positively transform our lives.

Chapter 17 – Key #2

Embodiment

I love my body. I love that it takes me where I need to go. I love that, through it, I get to enjoy delicious food and hear amazing music and feel the cool water of a lake on a hot day.

Have I always loved my body? No. I spent many of my earlier years not liking it at all. This body part was too big, this one too small... There have been a lot of times when I was disconnected from it, without even realizing it. I was caught up in the flurry of school, work or day to day life to give much thought about my body. I am grateful how the movement practices of martial arts and yoga have helped me reconnect to it.

This chapter and second Key is about embodiment. In essence, we'll be looking at what it is to be connected with our bodies. There's a quote by Pierre Teilhard de Chardin that I enjoy, "We are not human beings having a spiritual experience. We are spiritual beings having a human experience." Sometimes I rephrase this sentiment of de Chardin to say, we are energy beings having a human experience. There's this incredible thing called life, and we are one of many forms of life. Life energy on this beautiful planet expresses in a multitude of ways – as humans, animals, fish, trees, etc. We're all connected as we share the experience of being alive. Life is so profound and full of mystery that we often link it to the spiritual. "Spiritual" is one of those words we sometimes use to give name to an experience that is much larger than ourselves, or to concepts beyond our full understanding. It can make smoke come out of our ears to try to mentally figure out what it is to be a spiritual being, but we can fairly easily look at what it is to be human.

Embodiment involves remembrance. It involves remembering and connecting with our bodies as vehicles for living. A number of us take care of our car, truck or SUV. We change the oil and replace the fluids in our vehicle, keep it fueled up and tuned up, and give it a good washing every now and again. We understand how regular maintenance helps to keep it running smoothly and makes it less likely that we'll end up stranded on the side of the road. Similarly, each of our bodies might be thought of as a vehicle. It's amazing and complex, but the body is an organic machine which also requires fuel and maintenance to work well and get us from place to place. In the often hectic pace of life with work and family responsibilities pulling our attention in many different directions, it's easy to forget that we need to take care of our bodies. Or we may feel we simply don't have the time.

You might take a moment to think about your own body. Notice what thoughts come up around it. Are there some things you like, other things with which you're not so satisfied?

Now take a moment to *feel* your body. Feel your toes and feet. Do they feel firmly planted on the floor? Do they feel weightless because they're propped up? Or warm or cold, or tired? How do your legs feel? Your calves and shins, your thighs? How about your hips? How's your back feeling? The low back, the area between the shoulder blades... are there any aches? How do you feel in your belly and chest? What about the shoulders and neck? Do you feel strong? Is there any discomfort there? Just scanning through your body. How does your head feel? Do you have a headache? Does it feel comfortable?

Now you might take notice how you're standing or sitting. Do you feel slumped forward? Do you feel strong in your core? Overall, how is your energy level? Do you feel sluggish, or low energy, or do you feel energized and ready to go?

How often do you take the time to check in with your body and do a quick scan? If you're like most of us, probably not often. What does get our attention, though, is pain, or when something goes wrong. A lot of time we go through our days not thinking much about our bodies until we've hurt our back, have the flu or experience some other injury or illness. Then it's constantly on our minds.

We have this lifetime to accomplish what we set out to do, to raise a family, to contribute to society, to find direction or purpose, to enjoy recreation, to live this human experience. Our bodies play a huge role in the accomplishment of our goals and our overall happiness. Embodiment, in this context then, is about tuning in to our physical bodies and learning ways to support our health and well-being so that we *can* do what we need to do, and enjoy the journey. In this chapter, we'll explore two primary areas of benefit: movement and food.

MOVEMENT

In the previous chapter, I talked about benefits of increasing awareness around our words and thoughts. Similarly, there is tremendous value in raising awareness around our bodies. A couple ways to raise awareness is by learning more about how our bodies work and understanding some of the factors that affect our health. Some of this information may be familiar, some of it may be new. I find, when it comes to our wellness, even if the information may be familiar, reminders can be helpful.

Our Bodies are Made for Moving

When we look at our bodies, we see they are certainly designed to move. Our skeleton provides a strong framework. The joints allow for a wide range of motion. Our soft tissue – the muscles, tendons and ligaments – work together to move the bones, making it possible for us to move our bodies in a variety of ways.

Movement has an important role in muscle development. The saying is true, "Use it or lose it." To varying degrees, lack of strength-building exercise makes our muscles atrophy. Without strong muscles in our core and throughout our bodies, it is more difficult to keep our skeletal structure in alignment and there is an increase in the risk of injury and pain, including in the neck and back.

In addition, being mostly water, our bodies contain various types of fluid. There's synovial fluid found in our joints, cerebrospinal fluid around our brain and spinal cord, and intracellular fluid, found inside each of our cells. There's interstitial fluid between the cells, lymphatic fluid and, of course, blood. Blood is the only fluid that is circulated throughout the body by a pump, the heart. All of the other fluids are circulated by body movement. With insufficient movement, these fluids are, in a sense, prone to stagnation.

When we think of a puddle or pond that has grown stagnant, we observe an increase in bacteria and parasites. Mosquitoes and other insects begin to swarm around it, and there is a foul odor. We wouldn't want to drink it, because it becomes toxic and would make us sick. Similarly, when the fluids in our bodies don't receive enough movement, sickness or disease can develop.

Movement is Essential for Every Aspect of Health

Movement is key for supporting our health on many levels. Movement is required to circulate lymphatic fluid throughout the body. Like blood, lymph contains white blood cells, the cells of the immune system, protecting the body against disease. The work of the lymphatic system destroys bacteria and impedes the development of tumors and cysts. Moderate, regular movement serves to strengthen the immune system.

Movement also activates important enzymes. One enzyme, lipoprotein, collects fat and cholesterol from the blood and turns the fat into energy while shifting the cholesterol from LDL (the "bad" kind) to HDL ("good").

Though our cardiovascular system has the heart as a pump, exercise that increases heart rate helps the heart grow stronger, aids in the return of blood from the extremities, and pumps more oxygen through the body, stimulating healing.

Exercise helps us lose weight by increasing the amount of calories, or energy, we burn. Movement that gets the heart rate up is especially effective for weight loss.

Weight-bearing and impact exercise stimulates bone formation (increases bone density) and decreases the risk of osteoporosis. Exercise in the form of active stretching has been shown to improve strength, muscular endurance, agility and joint range of motion. Movement improves digestion and helps lower blood pressure. Regular physical activity reduces the risk of heart disease, certain cancers and type II diabetes. Exercise promotes an improved quality of sleep, helping us fall asleep easier and sleep more soundly. Movement influences hormone levels and the release of neurotransmitters, such as serotonin, dopamine and norepinephrine. These neurotransmitters elevate mood, create a natural feeling of well-being and decrease feelings of anxiety and depression. In short, **movement plays a crucial role in keeping our bodies well, and it helps us feel good.**

Indeed, **movement is good medicine.** We often think of medicine as a pill, injection or surgery, as these are often used to treat illness or injury. Yet, movement can also be incredibly potent in treatment and prevention. Regular physical activity can decrease pain and have profound healing effects. It is also something you can do for yourself. Plus, it's inexpensive, readily available, socially acceptable, and when we weigh the risks and benefits, it is often superior to that of drugs and surgery.

Early Movement

If we think what it is like when we are children, we see how being in motion during waking hours is our natural state. Only weeks after birth, infants' arms are constantly waving, hands grasping, head moving, mouth working, exploring their surroundings. At just a few months old, babies learn to roll over and scoot, scoot, scoot across the floor. As they learn to crawl, they really begin covering some ground. Toddlers are always on the go. We put up gates and protective barriers just to keep them contained and safe. Children quickly master the ability to walk and run. They love to climb, crawl, push and pull, do somersaults, twirl and jump. All of this movement is crucial to their brain development and physical, mental and emotional health.

We learn about our bodies through movement. As we grow, we learn the body's abilities and limitations, sometimes through a few bumps and bruises. We also learn how movement can feel enjoyable. Play is fun.

We start off in motion, then what happens? We hear "sit still," "stop squirming," "why are you so fidgety?" Children are often expected to adapt fairly early to a less active world designed by (less active) adults. In school, the structure often requires children to sit still and pay attention for hours with only a few minutes per day for outside play.

Some children and teens have P.E., dance, or other movement-based classes in school. Some do not. Some children have the chance to ride bikes, play sports, play at the park or otherwise be active after school hours. Other children do not, whether it's due to one's living environment, household income or other factors. As adults, **the more we can provide children movement opportunities, the more we can help them succeed and be healthy and happy**.

Children love to move, yet today's youth are much less active than their predecessors. Modern technology is playing a role. Children ages 2-5 years are spending about 25 hours/week in front of a TV. A study from the Kaiser Family Foundation showed that children ages 8-18 are spending more than 7.5 hours a day with electronic devices.

This inactivity, sadly, is contributing to serious health consequences for children. In the U.S., in 5-8 year olds, 40% show at least one heart disease risk factor, including high blood pressure and obesity. The Center for Disease Control and Prevention (CDC) estimates that American children born in the year 2000 face a 1 in 3 chance of developing type 2 diabetes. Type 2 diabetes was previously known as adult-onset diabetes, because it was rarely seen in children. For the first time in recent history, this current generation of children is expected to have a lower life expectancy than that of its parents.

The habits we form as children very often continue into adulthood. As we grow up, we may find ourselves in front of a screen for many hours per day, whether it's the television, computer, tablet or smart phone. We frequently work at jobs that require us to sit for hours per day, or jobs that require hours of standing. Most jobs do not allow us to engage in the varied forms of movement that our bodies need to stay healthy. We find ourselves in the same position hour after hour, day after day, year after year. Or, doing the same, limited, repetitive movement day after day, year after year. The large majority of our jobs are designed for productivity, not designed to support our health. Although, companies that do their research will learn that a healthier employee is a more productive employee, and they would be wise to put resources toward workplace wellness programs.

With this lack of adequate movement as adults, perhaps we find that we are overweight, out of breath when climbing a flight of stairs, facing chronic disease, experiencing neck, back or other pain, and/or feeling anxious or depressed. We wouldn't be alone. Let's look a little more at the overall health of individuals in the U.S.

The Nation's Health - A Look at Some Facts

According to the CDC, obesity and chronic disease are at an all-time high. About 70% of adults are overweight or obese. Individuals who are overweight have an increased risk for heart disease, stroke, certain types of cancer, such as breast cancer and colon cancer, and type 2 diabetes.

It is very likely you know someone with type 2 diabetes, or you may be diagnosed with it yourself. More than 29 million Americans have diabetes. Another 86 million (1 in 3 people) are pre-diabetic. People with diabetes are more likely to develop serious health complications, including vision loss, kidney failure, amputation of feet or legs and premature death.

The CDC also states 610,000 people die of heart disease in the U.S. every year. It is the leading cause of death for both men and women.

Other common issues include back pain, anxiety and depression. The *Journal of the American Medical Association* reveals that just in 40-65 year old workers, back pain cost employers $7.4 billion/year. The National Institute of Mental Health states about 40 million adults suffer from anxiety disorders, and 15 million adults are treated for major depression.

The health issues facing us here in the U.S. are currently being treated, in large part, by medication. The CDC states the most frequently prescribed drug is pain killers, many of which are highly addictive. The next most frequent prescriptions are those used to lower cholesterol and treat heart disease and type 2 diabetes. Following that is antidepressants. Nearly half of all Americans have taken at least one prescription drug in the last 30 days. Approximately 11% are using five or more.

Researchers from the Mayo Clinic and Olmsted Medical Center reveal how these numbers may be even higher. Their findings showed almost 70% of Americans are on at least one prescription drug, and 20% are on five or more. Overall, women and older adults receive more prescriptions. Antidepressants and opioid pain killers are most common among young and middle-aged adults. Cardiovascular drugs are more commonly prescribed in older adults.

In short, many individuals are experiencing moderate to severe health challenges. According to the CDC, collectively, we are experiencing a health crisis.

Why the Health Crisis?

With all the developments and breakthroughs in modern medicine, we might wonder how the health of people in the U.S. can possibly be at crisis level. The answer can be summed up in one word: lifestyle. More specifically, it comes down to physical activity and eating habits.

In addition, the traditional western approach to medicine is primarily focused on treatment, rather than prevention. Heart disease, stroke, type

2 diabetes, and certain cancers, including breast cancer and colon cancer, are some of the leading causes of *preventable* death. In other words, with increased physical activity and better eating habits, these diseases can be prevented.

But ultimately the responsibility rests in our hands. It's like Smokey the Bear says, "Only YOU can prevent forest fires." You are responsible for your health, just as I am responsible for my health.

It's not that we don't *want* to be healthy. No doubt, each of us would rather feel good than not. There are several factors that have contributed to this lifestyle change and decline in health as a whole. Technology was mentioned earlier. The way we work is a major factor. Let's turn the clock back for a moment.

As a culture, our work has shifted from that involving physical labor, which just about everyone did 100 years ago, to the digital age of today. Even 50 years ago, about half of the jobs required moderate physical activity, compared to less than 20% today. Previously, movement was a way of life; we moved to feed ourselves and to survive. We'd be out farming or mucking the horse stall or gardening or building.

Most of the jobs we do today, though, are much less active. The work the majority of us do now is frequently very mental. We can be engrossed for hours on the computer – running reports, doing research, sending emails, watching videos, creating projects, doing online marketing, preparing for presentations, etc. – and our bodies hardly move. In addition to desk jobs, there are other jobs that offer little movement, including dental hygienists, long-haul drivers, accountants, checkout clerks, computer techs, bank tellers, the list is many. Of course, there are construction workers and landscapers and a few other careers today that are active, and this can be a gift.

Modern work has also brought more of us into the cities, which has an impact on our access to the outdoors and how we move our bodies. As of 2010, we've officially become an "urban species." A report released by the United Nations reveals that, globally, more people now live in cities than don't. In North American and European countries, on average, 90%

of our time is currently spent indoors, and another 5% is spent in a vehicle.

Some of us take an opportunity to be active after work hours, maybe working in the yard, going to the gym or cycling on the weekends. Others of us come home from work and just feel like propping the feet up and watching a movie to de-stress from the day. Or, we have to drive to pick up the kids from practice, then make dinner, then help them with their homework, then, feeling exhausted, collapse into bed. The changing nature of our jobs, housing and modern technology means **we now have to be intentional about putting movement back into our lives.**

I'd like to take a break from all these statistics for a moment and share from personal experience. I spent many years, more than a decade, with chronic neck and back pain. This was due, in large part, from doing work that involved sitting for several hours per day. The majority of my time in the office involved working at the computer. There were usually deadlines to be met, and I juggled a lot. I worked quickly, feeling a sense of accomplishment in getting so much done in a short amount of time. I'd just power through, rarely getting up and moving around for any extended period. When I wasn't at the computer, I was usually sitting in a meeting. The area of my back between the shoulder blades often had a lot of discomfort. My neck hurt. My low back and hips ached. When I saw a physician about some of the issues, he stated there wasn't much that he could do and suggested I take ibuprofen to help manage the pain. I made frequent visits to a chiropractor that I trusted. He was skilled and kind enough to make adjustments and also give me tips for easing the pain, such as getting up every 20 minutes to walk and specific strengthening exercises. I did a little here and there, but I never fully followed his directions. I'd soon forget and let things slip by the wayside. After all, I had reports to finish, emails to send and more meetings to attend. Who had time for such things? My body was screaming, but I didn't hear it, or at least I didn't listen.

I then started doing yoga. Yoga helped me gain greater awareness around my body's needs and provided motivation to move on a regular basis. I'll talk more about yoga shortly. The increased body awareness didn't come all at once, though. It was a learning process. I was quite early in my practice and understanding of yoga, and understanding of the various aspects of wellness in general, but I was starting to realize that something needed to shift for me. An insight came to me one morning. I had only just started my day. Sitting at my desk, already my neck, back and hips were on fire. I realized, I *have* to change *how* I work.

My continued yoga practice helped me be able to tune into what my body was saying and *listen*. Though I maintained that type of work for a few more years, I started to change the *way* I worked. Over time, I gained greater core strength so I could more easily sit upright, rather than slouch forward. Rather than wait until my body felt on fire with pain, I'd get up from my chair more frequently. I started incorporating "walking meetings" with my staff. I even brought my yoga mat to work and laid it out on my office floor for short stretch breaks.

Eventually, I listened and understood that I wanted and needed to shift into a different form of working altogether. I changed from working full time to part time, allowing my body more time to move rather than sit. Finally, I stepped away from working for others and jumped wholeheartedly into my own work as a writer and teacher. I transformed the way I work, so that now I create my own schedule, movement is part of my daily life, I no longer feel chronic pain, and I get to share the benefits and joy of movement with others.

Of course, not everyone may choose to completely change his or her type of work. There are often things we can do, though, to change *how* we work, or change up our normal routines. Indeed, there are many simple ways to bring more movement into our daily activities to better support our health, which I'll cover in the next section. Also, it doesn't have to feel like a chore. Just as when we were young, we may find moving our bodies to be enjoyable!

What You Can Do

Step 1: Tune in

How can we maintain (or regain) a connection with our bodies so that we can enjoy a healthy, happy and productive life? Whether we are regularly active – running, cycling, swimming, doing yoga or physically working hard – or are not very active, there is much to gain from increasing body awareness. It opens the door to feeling better physically, mentally and emotionally. It is a pathway to having more energy to do what we love, and living longer.

We can begin by tuning into the messages that our bodies are telling us. "I don't have any energy," is one thing the body might be saying. Or, "I feel heavy," "my back hurts," or "my hamstrings feel tight." Just as it takes practice listening to others so as to provide reflections and ask appropriate open questions, it takes practice listening to what our bodies say so that we get an idea how to appropriately respond. There's always an opportunity for a deeper relationship with our own bodies.

If our back hurts, perhaps we learn we need to not sit for such an extended period, or to not do so much repetitive heavy lifting. Sometimes we can hear the messages and not know what to do. If the body is saying, "I don't have any energy," we may not have the slightest idea where to begin. It's okay, the first step is simply to take notice, to listen to how we feel, to bring greater awareness to our bodies. With that awareness, then, we can begin to take steps towards feeling better. We can put this awareness into action.

Step 2: Add movement

In this chapter, we've seen numerous ways how movement is crucial and beneficial for our health. So let's increase our activity level. One helpful thing to keep in mind – **start small! You can always build on it.** The benefit of starting small is we're more likely to accomplish what we set out to do and stick with it in the long term. I have heard many stories from people who, after years, even decades, of very little to no exercise, decide they must "get in shape." They take a strenuous boot camp class at the gym, or they believe they must hit the ground running and begin a wellness routine by vigorously exercising 2 hours per day, 5 days a week. After a day or two, the person often feels too sore to continue, develops an injury or otherwise loses motivation. It's too much, too soon. Rather than try to eat the whole watermelon at once, savor the sweetness of small, refreshing bites. The key is to pick something very simple, something to which we are willing and able to commit. There's an incredible amount of satisfaction and joy that comes when we accomplish our simple goals. It's nice to start there, and then *gradually* add to it when we feel ready to do more.

In addition to starting small, here are a few more helpful tips:

- **Be specific.** Maybe it's walking for 15 minutes on the treadmill on Mondays. Or perhaps it's taking the group exercise class that meets at 9:00am on Wednesdays. Or walking for 30 minutes through your neighborhood on Tuesday and Thursday evenings after dinner.

- **Put it on your calendar.** Just like a doctor's appointment or any other important reminder, schedule in your movement activity. It is time you are setting aside for your health and well-being. If it's not on the calendar, it's much more likely it will get crowded out, pushed aside and neglected for other activities.

- **Be consistent.** Engaging in a little physical activity three times per week is more beneficial than doing a lot of exercise three times per year. Our bodies are best served by regular physical activity.

- **Find a friend.** Having a friend or family member to share in the exercise can help keep us motivated, as we receive support and encouragement and are able to assist in holding each other accountable to the commitment. It can also simply be more fun!

Let's look now at a couple specific types of physical activity which provide our bodies the benefits of movement. Doing just these two things can go far in increasing our health and well-being.

Walking

Many of us have access to walking, which makes it one of the easiest and primary ways in which to add more movement into our lives. This might involve walking around the neighborhood, walking during your lunch break at work, walking on a treadmill or enjoying a nature hike. If you have the opportunity to walk in nature, such as parks, trails and other green spaces, the benefits are even greater. Compared to walking in an urban environment or indoors, walking in nature is more effective at reducing stress and increasing feelings of well-being. It also helps remind us of our deep connection with, and dependence on, the natural world. Finding various levels of intensity is helpful as well, such as adjusting the incline on your treadmill or walking up and down hills.

You might set an intention, such as: "I will walk briskly 45 minutes 2 times per week." Remember to pick specific days and add it to your calendar!

Yoga

It is worth noting that there are many different types of yoga, and each teacher has her or his own approach. I teach a Vinyasa style called Prana Flow®. I will speak on my experience of yoga, as I learned it from world-renowned instructor, Shiva Rea. I also have my own approach that blends the teachings from Shiva, my years of experience working in the area of preventative health and wellness, and my personal embodiment of the practice.

Unlike running or cycling, yoga is not a single set of movements. It offers a **variety of movements** designed to strengthen each of our muscles, as well as increase flexibility. As mentioned earlier, most of us do not receive the variety of movement our bodies need to stay healthy through simple day-to-day activities. For instance, there's often too much sitting, too much standing in place, not enough strengthening activities for our core, or overuse of certain areas of our bodies. In yoga, there are movements to strengthen the abdominals, the back, shoulders, neck, legs, arms, etc. There are movements to increase flexibility in the hamstrings, hips, shoulders and throughout our bodies. When we receive the varied strengthening and stretching we need, we become more balanced, and our bodies can function more like they are designed to function.

Yoga has, in fact, a number of features. There is a focus on structural, or skeletal, alignment and proper body mechanics, which helps reduce the risk of injury. Yoga supports a healthy spine, which can decrease or eliminate pain in the back and neck. There are times when yoga can be very active, providing cardiovascular benefits, and there are times for rest and rejuvenation. Yoga provides techniques to reduce the harmful effects of stress and experience greater peace of mind. It can give us more energy. It's a way to gain more awareness about ourselves – our physical bodies, as well as our thoughts and emotions. It includes a deeper awareness of and connection with the breath. Yoga is not a religion, but some individuals also find a sense of spiritual fulfillment through the practice. It offers different things for different people and can be whatever you want it to be.

An activity that connects with the needs of body, mind and spirit often leads to a deeper feeling of satisfaction, joy and well-being than an activity that touches on only one of these areas alone. Yoga provides that whole-body connection.

The movements and techniques can be adapted to meet the needs of the beginner, as well as provide a challenge for the most seasoned practitioner. Each person is encouraged to start where he or she is. Yoga is a means to educate ourselves about how our bodies work and for staying well.

It sounds like yoga encompasses a lot, and it does. To put it simply, **a regular yoga practice can help us enjoy a healthy, more vibrant life**.

I've been teaching yoga for 9 years. When someone learns that I teach yoga, one of the things I hear the most is, "I'm not flexible enough to do yoga." I find there are a number of misconceptions about the practice, and one is that we need to be flexible to do it. Nope, you don't have to be flexible. Yoga helps to increase flexibility over time, and there is no expectation, ever, that you have to be able to wrap your feet behind your neck! Various movements in yoga are designed to increase strength, which many of our bodies need (often more so than flexibility). So in addition to providing ways to gain flexibility, there is a focus on building strength. As mentioned, too, a primary aspect of yoga is increasing awareness. It serves to reconnect us with our bodies, to truly feel and experience our bodies, to live an embodied life.

Another misconception is that if you do yoga, you will have to start drinking green juice, stop shaving your armpits, or only eat tofu. Truth is, you get to do what you want to do. Of course, green juice can also be pretty darn good. The point is, you get to be yourself. Yoga has tremendous practical value and is one of the most effective ways to increase our health on many levels.

Yoga is an age-old practice that has been adapted to modern life, and it is becoming more and more popular as people understand its many benefits. Doctors are recommending it, professional athletes are doing it. Yoga is proving helpful for individuals doing any type of work – construction workers, executives, artists, nurses, customer service reps, attorneys, physicians, housekeepers, grocery clerks, realtors – for anyone and everyone, including mothers, fathers, youth, older adults and everyone in between.

Working with a skilled instructor is important. The instructors from whom you will gain the most benefits, I feel, are those who: 1. Have an in-depth understanding of body mechanics and alignment, 2. Utilize movements that meet our bodies' need for both strengthening and flexibility, 3. Incorporate relaxation and stress-management techniques and 4. Demonstrate practical applications. That is, the instructor will help you find ways to apply what you learn in yoga to your daily life.

With the various styles of yoga and instructor approaches and personalities, it may take a few tries to find a class that works well for you and that you enjoy. In addition to yoga studios, most gyms and local Ys offer classes. Yoga videos are also an option and offer the convenience of doing yoga at home.

Some of the benefits gained in yoga can also be obtained from other movement practices, such as Pilates or dance, especially when they are taught by experienced instructors. Yoga is unique, though, in that it intentionally seeks to work with individuals in a holistic sense – body, mind and spirit.

You might set an intention such as: "I will take 1 yoga class per week." Again, remember to pick a day and time and include it on your calendar.

I've talked a great deal about yoga, but this section is about adding more movement into our lives in general. In my experience, walking and yoga are two of the best medicines we can give ourselves. However, feel free to find ways of moving that are of interest and enjoyable to you, whether it's playing sports, dancing, rock climbing, aerobics classes, kayaking or working in the garden. Swimming is also an excellent way to increase and maintain a healthy body.

The greatest benefit comes not just from movement, but **movement with awareness**. For instance, a construction worker is moving constantly, but he can easily be injured, perhaps from repetitively lifting heavy objects or shoveling and twisting. An executive might stay active by running 5 miles every evening after work but find that she has constant neck pain or shin splints. The more we can increase awareness of our body as a whole, as a system, the more we can contribute to our health.

It becomes easier to tune in to our bodies with practice. A construction worker who has gained greater awareness about his body is more likely to find other means for lifting heavy objects, such as recruiting the help of another, or using equipment rather than pure physical force, *listening* to his body's needs. An office worker might use this greater body awareness to incorporate some neck stretches throughout the day or step away from the computer more often. A runner might listen to her body and lessen the number of miles she runs so as to allow her body to heal.

In some cases, awareness involves reducing or changing the type of movement.

Integration, integration, integration is key. Integration means we incorporate movement into our daily lives. This is how we receive the optimum health benefits. With reminders and practice, over time we learn the importance and value, and, yes, even joy, of including activities throughout the day which serve our bodies' need for movement.

If we approach movement thinking we have to change how we do *everything*, it's easy to feel overwhelmed. What do we do when we feel overwhelmed? Often, we throw in the towel. Perhaps we feel down on ourselves. Or, my personal favorite, I want to hide in a cave in the hills with just my journal and some hot ginger tea. Okay, let's take a deep breath... inhale... exhale... It can be quite simple.

We don't have to change everything, and certainly, we don't have to change everything all at once. **Small changes over time lead to sustainable results**. Small changes are manageable, and they have more sticking power. Here are a few ideas how you might integrate more movement into your daily activities. You may choose one or two on which you'd like to focus at a time. If you forget, it's okay! Simply take a deep breath and begin again. You can put post-it notes on your fridge or bathroom mirror to help remind you, if you like. Or, mark this chapter in the book. I've left two blank spaces in case you think of a couple things you'd like to add.

- Take the stairs
- Go for a stroll at lunch
- Park further away from the entrance when doing shopping
- Add some squats to your laundry routine
- Step away from the desk and walk for a few minutes, frequently
- Alternate using both hands while gardening or doing yard work

- Add some forward folds and thigh stretches while dinner is cooking
- Do a few shoulder rolls while you're waiting at a stop light
- Play *with* the children at the park
- Follow along with online yoga or fitness videos
- Walk, walk, walk
- _____
- _____

Remember, staying in motion helps us feel good and keeps us healthy!

FOOD IS OUR FUEL

You might notice I have a lot of emphasis and passion in the area of prevention. There may be dark clouds looming over the health of the nation, but there is also a bright side... with a really cool rainbow, and that is this: **many of the injuries and illnesses that we face can be prevented or alleviated through movement (conscious, varied) and what we eat.**

Food, or nutrition, is a second way for us to gain a deeper connection with our bodies and support our overall health. This section provides a few simple concepts around food that I hope you find beneficial in your wellness journey.

There are many perspectives when it comes to nutrition and what constitutes a healthy diet. Everybody has an opinion. There are celebrities, doctors, nutritionists and athletes each promoting their version of a healthy diet. There's the "caveman," or paleo, diet, the Mediterranean diet, South Beach diet, McDougall diet, the gluten-free diet, vegetarian diet, vegan diet, raw food diet... With all of these various perspectives, how is a person supposed to know what to do for his or her health? The information I put forth in this section is but one more perspective. Perhaps it will resonate with you, perhaps it will not. My approach is not to focus on a specific diet, per se, but on *increasing awareness* around what we eat. It is a way to be more conscious about our food and how it serves our bodies and the planet.

Food is our fuel. Part of taking care of the vehicle we drive involves providing it fuel. Where our car uses gasoline, or electricity (or hopefully additional alternatives in the near future), our bodies are fueled by food. If we put a low-quality fuel into the gas tank, or maybe dump some sugar in there, the car won't run very efficiently, if at all. Automobiles are designed to run on a certain type of fuel. Similarly, our bodies are designed to run on certain types of fuel. When our bodies don't receive sufficient high-quality fuel, and/or an excess of low-quality fuel, disease can result.

Food is also energy. We know this on an everyday level, such as when we're hungry and it feels like we're running out of steam. We can feel like we're running low on energy physically, and also mentally, not thinking as clearly. We eat a good meal, and soon find we have the energy and focus to tackle the next project. That is what one's body does with food. It converts food to energy that we then use to work, play, analyze, create, and everything else that we do in life. For practical reasons, we measure this energy in calories. However, this section is not about counting calories. Rather than focus on calories, it is more beneficial to focus on the types of food we eat.

In this exploration of food, it can be helpful to think about our animal nature, as it provides insight on the types of food our bodies are designed to eat and use as energy. Humans are but one species among many here on earth. We are mammals, bearing live births and nursing our young. We are categorized as primates. In the tree of life, humans share the limb with the other great apes – chimps, gorillas, orangutans. We know our consciousness is evolving, and through technology, our lives are rapidly changing, but we are also just a bunch o' apes. Humans and chimps share approximately 98% of their DNA. Humans have accomplished complex tasks like sending a probe 3 billion miles to fly past Pluto and beyond our solar system and send back amazing photos, but if we look at the research or have simply viewed the nature discovery shows about chimps, we can see many similarities with humans in anatomy, social bonds and behaviors. Not only does this explain why I think bananas are just about the perfect food, it offers a glimpse into our animal bodies' needs. Of course, our bodies are not *exactly* like a chimp's, and our needs may not be *exactly* the same. But the comparison may be helpful in remembering that we, too, are animals, our bodies have foundational needs, and these needs are closely connected with nature.

Chimps are omnivores, like us, eating vegetation and meat. In the wild, you're not likely to find a chimp foraging for soda, beer and nachos. Through scientific observations in nature, a chimp's diet has been revealed as the following:

59% fruit

22% leaves

5% nuts & seeds

4% blossoms/flowers

4% insects

1% meat

5% other

Approximately 95% of their diet is made up of plant-based whole food. Some primate researchers state as little as 2% of a chimp's diet consists of meat or insects, leaving 98% to be plant-based. Though there are some obvious differences between humans and chimps, our bodies function in extremely similar ways.

We are an intrinsic part of nature. Our true food, or fuel, is what comes from the earth – what sprouts from the ground and grows from the trees. This is what our bodies are designed to ingest, digest and convert into energy most effectively. Instinctively, we know this well. It is so satisfying (and delicious!) to pick some squash or leafy greens from the garden and eat them for dinner, or pick a juicy, sweet apple or apricot right off the tree and enjoy a nice snack. Our bodies are not designed to survive, and most certainly not thrive, on items like sodas, energy drinks, chocolate croissants or Grande Caramel Frappuccinos. Sometimes I refer to items such as sodas, which are developed by humans rather than grown by nature, fake food. They're created in a laboratory and filled with artificial flavors, colors, sweeteners, etc. More naturally-occurring beverages, such as water, fruit and vegetable juice, and tea are some healthier alternatives.

As far as beverages go, water is what we need the most. The majority of our bodies are made up of water, and drinking water is vital for keeping our bodies alive, well and in motion. Unfortunately, much of city tap water is not desirable for drinking. Also, a large amount of bottled water is just filtered tap water, which frequently seems to have no taste and lack the feeling of being refreshing. Good water is not always easily accessible. There is some bottled water that comes from natural springs, and it maintains more of the minerals our bodies need. It also tends to taste better and has more of that thirst-quenching quality. If you're lucky enough to get good water from a well on your property, even better. There are also water filtration systems that can add minerals back into the water. Wherever we get our water, at some point it was snowed or rained down, maybe flowed from a spring, or held in an alpine lake or aquifer, then drawn up for us to drink. Nature provides. Some water remains pure. Much of it does not, due to pollution, additives and other factors. Regardless, our bodies need water.

This is not to say that we can *never* enjoy a drink at Starbucks. This is merely an invitation to think about our eating *habits* and how these habits relate to our bodies' needs and how we feel. Habits are what we find ourselves doing on a regular, perhaps daily, basis. Here are a few questions that you might find helpful in this self exploration around food:

Do I feel like I need caffeine to have energy?

Do my food choices make me feel heavy?

Do I feel satisfied after I eat?

Does my diet help me feel balanced?

In our goal to eat healthier, it can be incredibly helpful to **start small**. Just like adding more movement into our lives, in regard to food choices, small changes over time are more manageable (less overwhelming) and easier to sustain long-term.

It comes down to choices. For instance, we might choose to eat a Hostess brand apple pie snack, or a container of apple sauce, or a fresh apple, or an organic fresh apple. The Hostess apple pie contains things like partially hydrogenated vegetable oil, artificial colors, artificial flavors, lots of sugar, high fructose corn syrup, beef fat, locust bean gum and dozens of other ingredients, some of which I have no clue as to what they are or why they are in there. It's considered a highly-processed, packaged food. Obviously, out of these 4 choices, it is the least healthy. It's also furthest away from food in its natural state. The closer we can stay to nature in our food choices, the better we will feel, short-term and long-term.

Over time, it is advantageous to reduce the amount of highly processed foods in our diet, which often contain large amounts of processed sugar, salt and/or saturated fats, and increase the amount of whole foods. Whole foods are nature-based, infused with life and provide our bodies what they need. Indeed, whole foods might also be considered a powerful medicine, as they help keep us healthy and well.

Sometimes you'll hear someone say, "Eliminate processed foods from your diet." For the large majority of us living our modern way of life, it would be next to impossible to completely eliminate processed food. If we were stranded on a deserted tropical island with only fresh water, bananas, coconuts and fish to eat, then perhaps we'd be able to live without processed foods. Even if we have a huge vegetable garden and fruit trees, we still likely process food in the form of canning in order to preserve it. Of course, doing the work ourselves, we'd at least know what ingredients were put into the canning. Not all processing is "bad." Processed foods surround us on a daily basis – cereals, canned goods, sausage, milk (pasteurization is a form of processing), cookies, pasta, etc. It's much more manageable to think about *reducing* highly processed foods, and continuing to reduce over time. We might work to choose foods that are minimally processed (a good rule of thumb is you know what the ingredients are). For example, our applesauce with the ingredients of apples, concentrated apple juice, cinnamon and ascorbic acid (vitamin C) is less processed than our Hostess apple pie treat. The goal is to **gradually incorporate more whole foods**. Plant-based items, such as vegetables, fruits and nuts are nutrient-dense food that gives us the energy we need and allows our bodies to thrive.

In addition to reducing highly processed foods, we might also consider reducing the amount of wheat–based products that we eat. For many of us in the U.S. and other industrialized nations, our diet consists of a lot of bread, pasta and other items made from wheat flour. For instance, one might have a bowl of cereal or piece of toast in the morning, a sandwich at lunch, pasta for dinner and cookies for dessert. Though wheat is a plant, specifically a grass, our bodies are not designed to adequately process it. We're more like the ape foragers of the jungle than the grazing animals of the plains.

Wheat contains gluten. Gluten seems to be the talk of the town as of late, and gluten-free products are flying off the shelves. What is it and why all the buzz? Gluten is a protein composite of gliadin and glutenin found in wheat and certain other grains, including rye, barley and spelt. According to Allessio Fasano, a world-renowned specialist in gluten-related disorders and the Medical Director for The University of Maryland's Center for Celiac Research, no one can properly digest gluten. He states, "We do not have the enzymes to break it down." Unlike fruit and vegetables, which humans are designed to eat, these grains have a way of working against our bodies. During digestion, peptides are released which are seen as an enemy, like a bacteria, and our immune system prepares an attack.

"For the vast majority of us," Fasano states, "there is a controlled reaction, the enemies are defeated and nothing happens." A few people lose the battle and develop celiac disease, gluten sensitivity or wheat allergy. For those with celiac disease, a completely gluten-free diet is a medical necessity.

In addition to the 3 million reported to have celiac disease, up to 20 million people are believed to have non-celiac gluten sensitivity. These individuals might experience bloating, abdominal pain and other digestive distress after consuming products that contain gluten.

I've observed that we have a tendency to fixate on just one aspect of our diets through the decades. In the '80s it was red meat, the '90s, trans fats, now gluten. Wheat and gluten are currently being blamed for a number of health issues, from joint pain, to fatigue, to skin rash, though the scientific evidence does not yet support all the claims. Continued research is being conducted in this area, which may soon shed more light on the subject. However, if symptoms go away upon reducing or removing wheat-based products from one's diet, then there is certainly an advantage in taking that step.

Wheat also raises blood sugar. Cardiologist, Dr. William Davis, noted in his book, *Wheat Belly: Lose the Wheat, Lose the Weight and Find Your Path Back to Health*, that the glycemic index of wheat is very high. Two slices of whole wheat bread can increase blood sugar levels higher than a single candy bar. He states that too much wheat can also result in "deep visceral fat," which grows around the inner organs and spells trouble for our health. It increases the risk for heart disease, stroke and diabetes.

Again, this is not to say you can never enjoy a delicious slice of sourdough. The variety of food is one of the joys of life. Rather, it is about continuing to increase awareness around what we eat, particularly in regard to quantity and habits.

Fresh is best. Whenever possible, it best serves us to eat food that is fresh. For instance, fresh green beans maintain more of their vital nutrients than frozen or canned green beans. Fresh generally tastes better, as well. Farmers' markets are a great place to pick up seasonal fruits and veggies.

Whenever possible, go organic. Organic food is becoming more readily available as people understand the benefits. Where it used to be available only in "health food stores," large grocery store chains are now carrying more organic products. The higher monetary cost of organic food can make us want to veer away from organic for more conventional products. Some stores charge more than others, so it's helpful to shop around. I believe if there is one thing to spend extra money on, it is good food. What we put in our bodies has a direct impact on our overall health, and higher-quality fuel leads to more positive results.

I saw an amusing bumper sticker that read, "Eat organic. It's what our grandparents used to call... food." For most of agricultural history, crops were grown using practices we would call organic. It was not until the second half of the 20th century that the use of synthetic fertilizers, pesticides and toxic herbicides (weed killer) became common. Harmful consequences have resulted from these chemicals in our soil, air, water and our bodies. Organic farming produces safer, more nutritious and often more flavorful foods while protecting our natural resources for future generations. It's good for people and planet.

Expanding out again to view the big-picture, there is indication that there is a wave of change occurring in regard to food choices. We're just at the beginning of that wave, but it has momentum. More and more of us are becoming aware of the importance and benefits of eating organic. The market for organic food was $63 billion worldwide in 2012. In 2014, it was $80 billion and continuing to grow. The U.S. is currently the world's largest organic market. Our food-buying dollars are a powerful force for change in the food industry. Consumer demand has a huge impact on food production. The more we choose organic, the more farmers will convert to organic growing methods. This will help bring down prices, provide us healthier food options and preserve the planet.

We've talked about plant-based food, now let's talk about meat and animal-based products. Individuals in the U.S., and in many other places around the world, eat a lot of meat. Meat and dairy is another area where becoming more conscious of our choices is greatly beneficial.

Meat consumption in the U.S. has risen dramatically over the last few decades. In 1950, we consumed about 17 billion pounds, according to the Earth Policy Institute. In 2012, we were at 52 billion pounds. The last handful of years, we experienced a slight decrease in meat consumption. However, according to the Food and Agriculture Organization of the United Nations (2010), at 270.7 pounds of meat per person per year, we still eat more meat per person here than in any other country on the planet except one (Luxembourg).

Earlier it was mentioned how food is energy. Energy is also linked to food in the sense that it takes energy to produce food. Meat has more of an impact on the environment than any other food we eat. This is because livestock requires considerably more food, water, land and energy than plants to raise and transport. According to the *Journal of Animal Science*, to produce one quarter-pound hamburger, it takes 6.7 lbs. of grain for feed, 52.8 gallons of water for drinking and irrigating feed crops, 74.5 sq ft of land for grazing and growing feed crops, and 1,036 Btu of fossil fuel energy for feed production and transport. Another way of looking at it is industrial feedlot meat production requires about 16 times more fossil fuel energy and generates about 24 times more greenhouse gases than producing the same number of calories of vegetables and rice.

Many of us are familiar with the often atrocious conditions that animals in factory farms experience. Instead of the small family farms that were commonplace at the time of our grandparents, we now have huge factory farms working to raise as many animals in as little space as possible in order to meet the demands of our meaty appetites. That generally means unhappy animals, to put it mildly. Many are raised in crates, leaving them unable to move and have their bodies normally develop. In conventional meat production practices, the animals are usually given hormones and regular, sub-therapeutic doses of antibiotics to help keep them "healthy" in the confining and crowded environments. The antibiotics create more resistant strains of bacteria and make infections in humans more difficult to treat. A great deal of animal waste is produced, which can pollute water sources. Also, large amounts of chemical fertilizers and toxic pesticides are used to grow the animals' feed. What goes into their bodies eventually ends up going into our bodies. These same circumstances exist in the production of conventional dairy products as well, such as milk, cheese, yogurt and butter. You are encouraged to learn more about factory farming.

In thinking about dairy, it's also interesting to note how, out of all the mammals, humans seem to be the only ones that regularly drink or ingest milk beyond infancy and childhood. Humans are also the only ones who regularly drink milk of another species. Infant mammals can drink their mother's milk because the lactase enzyme, which digests lactose (a sugar found in milk), is active in early development. When the mammal gets to be a certain age, that enzyme gets turned off, in a sense, and the mammal can no longer adequately digest milk. It's part of the animal's natural course of development.

The majority, approximately 65%, of the human population around the globe has a reduced ability or inability to tolerate lactose as adults. For these individuals, ingesting milk causes abdominal pain, diarrhea or other digestive distress, as they no longer produce the lactase enzyme. For some populations, such as those of East Asian descent, more than 90% are lactose intolerant. It's been fairly recent in human history that some people have been able to keep producing the lactase enzyme into adulthood, an adaptation in our evolutionary journey.

In addition to potential digestion issues, milk is a mucus-producing and inflammation-inducing food and has been linked to sinus congestion, headaches, recurrent ear infections, strep throat and more. Removing dairy from the diet frequently resolves these conditions.

Some people choose to become strictly vegetarian (no meat) or vegan (no meat/no dairy) based on ethical, environmental and/or personal health reasons. One might see the many benefits to doing so.

We've heard for a few decades now how excess meat consumption, particularly of red and processed meat, leads to an increased risk of obesity, heart disease, stroke and type 2 diabetes. Bacon, sausage, hot dogs and other processed meats are now ranked as high as cigarettes and asbestos as known carcinogens and in terms of causing cancer, the World Health Organization recently announced. These meats have been found to cause colorectal cancer and create a much higher risk for stomach, bowel, prostate and pancreatic cancer, and early death. Whereas, diets high in vegetables, fruits, beans, legumes, nuts, seeds and some whole grains can help prevent these conditions. Reducing the amount of meat in our diets and incorporating more plant-based food promotes greater health.

The majority of people choose to consume meat or dairy products in varying amounts. For those of us who do, there are ways to be more conscious in doing so. **We can reduce negative health and environmental impact through our meat and dairy choices.** When buying meat, we can look at the type of meat we get, for example beef or chicken, and how the meat was produced. Choosing chicken or fish is generally a healthier option than beef or pork. Also, the larger the animal, the larger the environmental impact. Beef has the largest environmental impact. Pork has less of an impact than beef. Chicken has less than pork, fish less than chicken. Plant-based food has the least environmental impact.

Organic is a better option. You might look for meat and dairy products that bear the USDA Organic symbol. This is the strictest and most regulated label. Animals must be fed a 100% organic diet, and they are never to be given hormones or antibiotics. They are not exposed to synthetic pesticides. Cattle may be pasture fed or fed a combination of grass and organic grain in smaller, less crowded herds. Hens are not caged and must have outdoor access. Regulations require that all animals be raised in living conditions that accommodate their natural behaviors, such as the ability to graze on a pasture or flap their wings. It may not be ideal, some things may slip through the cracks, but the negative impact is reduced, and that's a significant step.

Whole Foods is a grocery store chain that has a 5-step animal welfare rating system. Fresh turkey, chicken and beef in their meat department must achieve at least a Step 1 rating, which requires the farmers to meet more than 100 animal welfare standards. It also often sells products from local growers and farmers and offers numerous organic options.

I have a recipe book that I like called, *The Earthbound Cook: 250 Recipes for Delicious Food and A Healthy Planet* by Myra Goodman. Myra is also the author of the cookbook, *Food to Live By*. She and her husband founded the very successful Earthbound Farm, which started as a backyard operation to become the largest grower of organic produce in the country. Their organic salads and products are now found at Costco, Whole Foods, Safeway, Albertsons, Sprouts and many other stores. The book offers a variety of recipes, including vegetarian options, has that warm-hearted, down-home feel, and you can find more wonderful information about organic farming and other Earth-friendly tips.

Each of us may be personally responsible for our health, but we are collectively responsible for the health of the planet and future generations. As individuals we can make changes, big or small. When many of us make even just a small change, it can have big, far-reaching results. We each can take steps which lead to greater health and sustainability. That's a win-win for all.

Remember, increasing our health and finding ways to be more environmentally friendly is a process. There is no guilt necessary. Be patient and non-judgmental of yourself and others. You're still a good person if you give in to a craving and eat ice cream, or if you buy conventional apples instead of organic.

One of the most helpful things is to **have healthy options around the house**. When nutritious food is easily available, we're much more likely to eat it. Likewise, when sugary or high-fat snacks are around, we're likely to munch on those. Here are a few things I like to keep around the house, or pack to go, to have as a quick, healthy snack:

- Baby carrots and hummus
- Sliced apple and peanut butter
- Variety of fresh fruit
- Organic sweet potato or rice chips

- Mixed nuts
- Green salad fixings (topped with thinly sliced pears or apples, dried cranberries and almonds)

Many of us may not think about chronic disease such as diabetes, cancer or heart disease until the doctor breaks the news of the diagnosis, but in my work, I've found that just about everyone would like to lose a few pounds. **The best solution for losing weight and feeling great is a _combination_ of increased physical activity and choosing healthier food options.** Cardiovascular exercises, such as walking, hiking, running, cycling, and swimming are most effective for weight loss. They get the heart rate up and burn off lots of energy (or calories). Substituting healthier food options in place of unhealthier ones provides the body more of what it needs and utilizes, and less of what weighs it down, compromising our health. You might choose a green salad instead of lasagna, or substitute salmon in place of beef, or choose rice pasta over wheat pasta. It may feel like a challenge at first, but like creating any new habit, it gets easier with time and practice. Small steps.

The Natural Eating food pyramid below represents the food, or fuel, that our amazing bodies utilize best, supporting our health and well-being (find a larger, full-color version of this pyramid [which you can post on the fridge] at www.kristibowman.us/a-butterfly-life). Stay close to nature, eat well and enjoy life!

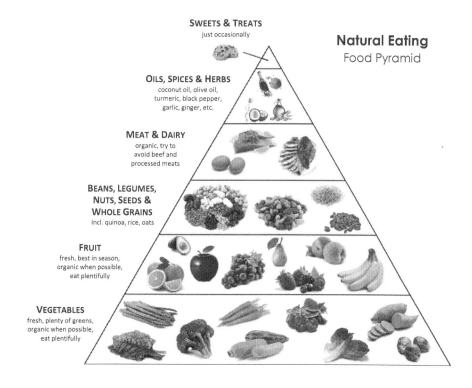

Natural Eating
Food Pyramid

TO SUMMARIZE:

Food is our fuel
Start small
Choose more whole foods
Be conscious of meat and dairy choices

Go organic when possible
Fresh is best
Remember it's a process

Simple things you can do:

Keep a bowl of fresh fruit in the kitchen
Pick up a fresh, organic veggie for dinner
Go meatless Mondays
Drink more water
Add beans and lentils to your soup for extra protein
Make fruit smoothies for a refreshing, sweet treat
Use almond, soy, rice, coconut or other non-dairy milk
Enjoy more green salads
Choose meat that has less impact

Chapter 18 – Key #3

Be Do Have

S o far in this Butterfly section, we've looked at ways to gain greater happiness and satisfaction in relationships and ways to increase our health and well-being. In this chapter, we take a look at work and the third Key.

Often, one of the first questions we ask when meeting someone new is, "What do you do?" This is not surprising, considering most of us adults spend many of our waking hours at work, and work may even feel like a part of our identity. Undoubtedly, our work, or career, is a big part of our lives. It's also a big area in which people often struggle. We may struggle in the sense that we're not happy doing what we're doing and/or feeling like we don't know which direction to go.

In the past, I certainly experienced some struggles in regard to career. From the outside, it might seem I lacked direction. I've taken a number of detours. I originally was in a doctorate program to practice as a Clinical Psychologist. Then I decided to withdraw from the program and veered over to non-profit management. I worked as a leader with the Y for many years. I veered again to focus on supporting people's health and happiness in other ways.

During this process of figuring out what it is I "do" in the world, I've often felt lost. Through the previous 15 years or so, I've had times, sometimes long times, of confusion, boredom, and distress around work. I've also experienced intense work challenges, such as the situation with the local Y. Work hasn't always been a walk in the park. For the most part, I did enjoy what I was doing and felt dedicated to it. It has had its ups and downs, and I've ridden the waves. I'm grateful to now find myself doing work that brings me immense happiness and a sense of fulfillment.

It seems that relationships, work and health are the areas of greatest challenge for many of us. I've seen these three areas come up time and time again in my coaching work, which is why I wanted to address each of these areas in this final section. We're often looking for a loving, caring, supportive partner or a job that pays well and doesn't feel soul-sucking, or looking to lose weight and have more energy, or all of the above. Listen First is an avenue to finding happiness in relationships. Movement and what we eat are the guiding posts to greater wellness. But what is the secret to finding fulfillment in our work and career?

Before getting into specifics, it's helpful to first be open to the possibility that we *can* find fulfillment in what we *do*, just as we can achieve greater health and enjoy more satisfying relationships. Indeed, many people are doing it. Secondly, it's no secret. The answers are already within us. As with most things, it comes down to this inner work. Let's do a little personal exploration and see what we find.

START WITH BEING

As we think about work, it can be helpful to ask ourselves a couple questions. If you have a paper and pen nearby, you're welcome to jot down some notes.

First, when we think about the things we want in life, what comes to mind? Here I'm referring particularly to the tangible and material things. As we ponder that, a list emerges that might look something like this: a newer car, a house, new technology, a romantic partner or spouse, children, health insurance, quality childcare, jewelry, better job, retirement savings, recreational vehicle, a remodeled kitchen, college education, vacations. There may be other things you would add, as well.

Now, *why* do we strive for these things? After thinking for a bit, perhaps another list emerges. We often find it is to experience happiness, or feel a sense of security, freedom, vitality, success, comfort, love, fulfillment, appreciation, enjoyment, etc.

As we think about these two lists, are there people who have a nice house and new car who are not happy? Of course. Likewise, there are individuals who feel fulfilled and secure who don't have things on the first list. Though there may be some overlap, there is no direct causal connection between the two lists.

When you boil it all down, what each of us essentially wants in life is to be happy. Aristotle went so far as to say, "Happiness is the meaning and the purpose of life, the whole aim and end of human existence." The kicker is we often forget that happiness is part of our nature. It wells up from within us. Instead, we're frequently looking outside of ourselves – to a relationship, career or material items – to find happiness. Sometimes we work very hard, striving towards those outward perceptions of "success," such as money, title, a big house or an expensive car, thinking this will make us happy. But these things can still leave us feeling empty.

There are a few different ways to look at life and work that can have a big impact in how we seek happiness. Below are three perspectives. I first became familiar with these from a book called *Relationships That Work: The Power of Conscious Living* by John B. Wolf, Ph.D. I find these concepts can have application, not only in our personal relationships, but in our relationship with work.

The first is called Have-Do-Be. It's a way of thinking such as, "If I just could *have* one million dollars, then I could *do* what I want and I'd *be* happy." Or, "If I just had a better boss/job, then I'd work harder and be appreciated." "If I had the right man/woman in my life, then I could do things that couples do and I'd be complete." "If I just had more time, I'd go to the gym and I'd be healthier." In this way of thinking, our experience is dependent on having. It's based on inactivity. There is a passive waiting for something to come to us before we believe we can enjoy happiness, love, health, etc.

Another perspective is Do-Have-Be. In this way of thinking, we believe that if we could just *do* what we want, then we will *have* what we want, and we'll *be* happy, appreciated, loved and so on. "If I work a lot of overtime, then I can have a new car and I'd feel successful." "If I join this group, I'll have community connections, and I will be respected and valued. The to-do list is another way of looking at this approach. "If I could just complete my to-do list, I'd be peaceful and content." In this perspective, our experience is dependent on activity.

There is no judgment towards these two perspectives. In fact, there is much to be said for hard work helping us feel a sense of accomplishment and contentment. Effort certainly plays a key role in meeting our goals. But we are not human *doings,* we are human *beings.* Let's look at it from another angle.

A third perspective is Be-Do-Have. Here, experiencing balance, happiness, freedom, a sense of vitality, contentment, etc. is not dependent on having or doing. Rather, it is considered that these things are part of who we are, aspects of our true self. These qualities reside within us. It's worth noting that Be-Do-Have does not lack doing or having. On the contrary, it is believed there is a richness and greater potency in what we do and have *because* it flows naturally from our being. Being bold and confident, we naturally do things that bold and confident people do, and thus have what bold, confident people have. Being compassionate and joyful, we do things that compassionate, joyful people do and have the things that compassionate and joyful people have.

This goes both ways. If I am being angry, depressed and jealous, I will do what angry, depressed, jealous people do and will have the sort of relationships and life results that angry, depressed, jealous people have.

Throughout my life, I feel I've put a lot of effort in the area of personal development, striving to be more conscious in my thoughts and actions. As I've gained this greater understanding of myself, I still have often been confronted with the question, what am I supposed to *do*? I've wrestled with it. In fact, I wrestled with it until just a few years ago. Am I supposed to go back to grad school? Am I supposed to be a psychotherapist? Should I work for the Y? What? My mind would go round and round. Working for the Y would mean having a great deal of responsibility, a good salary and benefits. I enjoy non-profit work. Likewise, going back to grad school and getting licensed as a therapist would provide a sense of completion in my formal education, lend support for job security and provide a comfortable income. I'd be helping people on a deep level. In both of these roles, I'd be doing something good for the community. Certainly, they are worthwhile endeavors. Though there was a lot of time when I felt passion for working as a Y leader or passion to provide therapeutic support, I got to a point where it was no longer the case. The passion subsided. Something else pulled on me, and yet I wasn't exactly clear what it was. So I continued to wrestle, what do I *do*?!

Then one day I heard that inner voice of wisdom. It responded to my question: *Do what comes naturally.* I wrote the phrase on my dry erase board so I would see it every day as I passed by it.

I remembered Be-Do-Have. *Okay*, I thought to myself, *as a vibrant, successful, happy, creative, confident person, what naturally follows?* As I gazed at the white board and pondered the message, I realized the answer was literally right there in front of me. There was a note that I had written on the board a few days prior reminding me to email my yoga students, another note to finish the flyer for an upcoming workshop, and another note indicating my weekly writing schedule. *I am already doing it. I am writing, teaching, helping others.* Writing and yoga feel like the most natural things for me, a natural extension of my soul. I laughed out loud as the answer, so sweet and simple, stared me in the face. And I felt such a huge sense of relief. It was as if the universe was giving me permission to simply be... and to *do* what naturally flows from that being.

So one way to find greater fulfillment in our work or career is to start with *being*. That is, *be* who we inherently are – strong, creative, joyful, balanced, worthy, loving, free, powerful, wise, beautiful beings. This means letting go of the insecurities and feelings of unworthiness we carry around. Letting go of the need to control, or the desire to be small and hide. It means putting aside the masks we sometimes wear to help us feel important or safe. It means getting down to our true selves. Also, it is about being open to possibility, leaving the door open for more good things to come into our lives. What we *do* will then be a natural expression of who we are.

You might be saying, "Easier said than done." Right? Perhaps it is easier said than done, but being who we authentically are is absolutely doable, and rewarding. It is possible for us to increase awareness of our thoughts and feelings around work and about ourselves. Our level of awareness influences our beliefs and actions. Sometimes it's helpful to work with a therapist or coach. Someone with an outside perspective can be valuable in helping identify areas where we're holding ourselves back. As we grow in this awareness, we can disregard those things that are not truly us, and be our genuine selves.

I find we can also use our own bodies as a compass to help guide us back to who we are at the core. Sometimes we experience anger, fear, jealousy, depression and insecurity. You might take a moment and imagine when you feel angry, depressed or jealous. You may notice how your body feels tense and overheated, like you're going to explode, or possibly heavy, weighed down. Or maybe it feels like you're tied up in knots, blocked, or stuck. Perhaps there is a sense of darkness or discomfort, or you even feel sick.

On the other hand, if we tune into our bodies and imagine what it is like to feel joy, love, contentment, you might observe a lightness in your body, a gentle warmth. Perhaps a smile spreads across your lips, or laughter, or you experience a sense of calmness. These experiences feel good, contribute to enjoyment of life, and help us to thrive.

Let's look at a couple scenarios and see how one might apply the concept of Be-Do-Have in regard to work:

Scenario 1: Roger has been a checkout clerk at a supermarket for 10 years. He's generally happy, but feels like it's time for something different in life. From the perspective of Be-Do-Have, Roger begins with connecting in with his innate qualities. From an understanding of himself as personable, capable, energetic and innovative, Roger decides to quit his job and open a small, family-owned and operated deli. He gets to spend more time with his family, feels a greater sense of independence and excitedly buys himself a new fishing reel for an upcoming camping trip.

Scenario 2: Linda works in the field of Information Technology and enjoys the responsibilities of a computer tech. With a recent change in management, her work environment has shifted to one of unreasonably strict deadlines, mandatory overtime and resistance whenever she requests funding for necessary equipment. She begins to feel frustrated, stressed out and disheartened. As a person who knows herself to be responsible, skillful and worthy, she decides to leave the company and work for a different organization in IT where the requirements feel to be more reasonable and balanced. The pay and benefits are the same. She enjoys greater peace of mind and has time after work to go out with friends.

DO WHAT YOU ENJOY

You might take a moment and imagine enjoying what you do. As you imagine, does it bring a smile to your face? Does it feel freeing? A person can range from not enjoying his or her work at all to enjoying it somewhat to enjoying it a lot. What would you say is your level of enjoyment?

In work, there seems to be a lot of focus on the concept of "success" and what that looks like. As material items can still leave us feeling unfulfilled, **perhaps a better gauge of success is simply happiness**, finding enjoyment in what we do. Let's look a little more closely at work and job satisfaction as a whole.

One obvious thing about work is that it provides money. With this money, we are able to pay for food, shelter and other items and services.

Humans didn't use to be dependent on money. Indigenous people simply utilized the resources around them to take care of their needs. Work involved building shelter, protecting the village, fishing, hunting and foraging for food, meal preparation, making clothing and child rearing. There are still a few today who live in this manner. But for the large majority of us here in the 21st century, money is a rather significant part of our lives. Work is no longer directly related to meeting our needs. Instead, we work to make money, and then use that money to pay for what we need and want.

I've often wondered how this separation, this gap, between work and experiencing its direct results in our lives may contribute to the level of dissatisfaction that many individuals feel in regard to work. When we look at workers in the U.S., we find more than half are unsatisfied with their jobs. According to the 2014 edition of The Conference Board Job Satisfaction survey, only 47.7% of American workers are reportedly satisfied.

Similarly, a 2013 Gallup report revealed that only 30% of the U.S. workforce is engaged in their work. In other words, they're passionate about their work and feel strongly committed to their employers. It has been shown that engaged workers are most likely to build new products, create new services, attract new customers and drive innovation. The remaining 70% of American workers are either "not engaged" or "actively disengaged" in their work. These are the ones who are "checked out," putting in time but not much energy or passion. Those who are "actively disengaged" tend to act out on their unhappiness, taking up more of their managers' time and even undermining what their coworkers accomplish. According to Gallup, active disengagement costs U.S. companies $450-$550 billion per year.

It may be relieving to know that, as workers, we can raise our level of satisfaction. Research conducted by Brent D. Rosso, Ph.D. and colleagues has shown that finding *meaningfulness* in one's work increases job satisfaction, motivation, engagement and personal fulfillment. When I first came across this research, it provided an answer to my wondering about the gap. One might say that modern work has lost much of its meaning. However, we can bring meaningful work back into our lives.

Meaningful Work for Greater Satisfaction

There are a few specific ways we can create more meaningful work. One way to do this is by **reframing our view** of work. To illustrate, there is an old tale of three bricklayers (which I've updated slightly). When asked what they are doing, the first bricklayer responds, "I'm putting one brick on top of the other." The second replies, "I'm making $14 an hour." The third says, "I'm building a hospital." All three are doing the same work. However, the third bricklayer is likely to find the most satisfaction in his work because of the meaningfulness he attributes to it; he is looking at the bigger picture.

I do wish to note that this does not give someone in management justification for not allowing someone to rise up and gain new skills and experience, because he or she "should be satisfied" being a bricklayer. This illustration is for the individual worker only and understanding different perspectives of work.

In addition to reframing our view, there are other factors that play an important role in regard to meaningful work and greater job satisfaction. The research conducted by Rosso and team has looked at these factors in depth. I have summarized the information into 4 key areas.

I find that much of what I do when working with others is simply remind people of what they already know. As mentioned at the outset, the answers are already within us. As you read through the following paragraphs, some of the information may be familiar. Perhaps you feel a sense of recognition on a deep level. In a way these concepts help us stay connected to what it is to work and be human. For some of us, these concepts may seem new. Regardless, these 4 areas can be powerful for helping to transform our work into that which brings a greater sense of satisfaction and happiness.

1. **Authenticity.** Authenticity can be thought of as having a sense of alignment between our behavior and how we perceive the true self. It involves behaving consistently with our interests and values. An example of this in regard to work might be how an individual who values social responsibility is likely to feel more fulfilled when working for an organization that acts in socially responsible ways. Another example: a person who sees herself as dedicated and organized and has a passion for the environment may find satisfaction as an environmental attorney. Or, an individual who recognizes himself as personable, caring and likes to stay busy might find enjoyment working as a nurse. Mahatma Gandhi expressed it well, "Happiness is when what you think, what you say, and what you do are in harmony."

2. **Making a contribution.** This is about doing something that is greater than oneself. It includes believing that we have the power and ability to make a difference. It may also involve having skills that are useful and contribute to a larger goal. It is beyond the ego. Rather than "What's in it for me?" it is "What can I do to help?" An example is an electrician who uses his skills to contribute to the construction of a house. Or, an accountant who works for a community college who finds her work meaningful, not simply through balancing the books, but because she feels her work allows others to advance themselves through education. Or, a childcare worker who feels he or she is making a positive difference in the lives of children and future generations.

3. **Purpose.** Work experiences which reinforce a sense that our actions are purposeful or move us closer to a desired goal are likely to be viewed as especially meaningful. Here, there is a sense of directedness and intentionality in life. This may involve internally-driven motivations or an external or spiritually-driven sense of purpose that one feels called to fulfill. The minister who feels it is her calling to provide spiritual support to others is an

example. Or, the zookeeper with a college degree, making $29,000 year, who is able to find satisfaction because he is not only working to care for individual animals, but helping to educate people and preserve an entire species.

4. **Sense of belonging.** Greater meaning and job satisfaction are also found in having positive, significant, long-lasting relationships. It very well may be our coworkers, which can become our friends or even feel like family, that keep us at a job year after year. Coworkers can provide a great deal of support and be a strong community connection.

Additional research by Michael G. Pratt, Ph.D., a professor of management and organization at Boston College, has shown that certain types of work may feel more meaningful than others. Craftsmanship, service and kinship types of work are especially likely to be meaningful, Pratt says. People with a craftsmanship orientation take pride in utilizing their skills and performing the job well. Individuals with a service orientation find purpose in the ideology or mission behind their work. Others draw meaning from the sense of connection they experience with coworkers.

You might note that each of these areas point to something beyond the individual. **Work that is bigger than oneself is often found to feel more meaningful.** How interesting and wonderful to know that when we provide a service, or work for the greater good, it actually makes us feel good, too!

Doing Involves More Than Work

Another way to gain more satisfaction from what we do is to remember *doing* encompasses more than just work. In other words, what we do can extend beyond what we get paid to do. Authenticity, making a contribution, having purpose and a sense of belonging apply in other areas of life as well. These areas might be volunteering or social groups or hobbies. Even if the paid work we do does not bring us the amount of satisfaction we desire, we can find enjoyment and fulfillment through other avenues.

Volunteering has a number of benefits, both personal and in the community. A Harvard Health Publications article noted that volunteering helps people feel more socially connected, which can lessen feelings of loneliness and depression. People who give of their time also have been shown to have better physical health, including lower blood pressure and longer life. Volunteering can reduce stress and help a person be more active.

Volunteering can help us stay motivated and feel a sense of accomplishment. It has been shown to increase self-confidence and self-esteem. When we share our time and talents, we can help improve lives, find new interests, gain new skills and experience, strengthen communities, solve problems, meet people, broaden our support network and transform our own lives. Volunteering may provide a renewed sense of creativity and vision. It can bring fun and enjoyment into life, as well as provide a sense of purpose. Many of the benefits overflow into our personal and professional lives.

A person's interests can be matched with opportunities. For instance, if you like performing arts, you might volunteer as an usher at the local community performing arts center. Like to be outdoors? Volunteer to help clean up a local park. Love animals? Volunteer at the local shelter or wildlife center. Like helping youth? Volunteer at a youth organization, coach a sports team or help out with other after-school activities. If you're part of a church or spiritual community, you can volunteer at an annual picnic or a fundraiser event. Enjoy leadership? Volunteer as a Board member of a local charity.

Researchers at the London School of Economics examined the relationship between volunteering and measures of happiness in a group of American adults. They found the more people volunteered, the happier they were, according to a study in *Social Science and Medicine*. Compared with people who never volunteered, the odds of being "very happy" rose

7% among those who volunteer monthly. Among weekly volunteers, the odds rose 16%.

Hobbies can be another avenue through which to find increased satisfaction in what we do. We can engage in hobbies alone or with a group. When we explore our hobbies with others, we also reap the benefits of community. There's an opportunity to make genuine social connections and feel a sense of belonging. We are social creatures. We need each other to help us stay healthy and happy.

You may search your local area for interest groups. The library, local Y, community center, senior center or even coffee shop may have postings on activities. A helpful way to connect with others with similar interests is through an online platform such as meetup.com. There you can search your geographical area and find others interested in activities you enjoy, such as photography, book clubs, golf, gardening, movies, hiking, biking, crafting, cooking, building, healthy eating and more. Or, you can start your own group.

This chapter has provided a number of concepts that can positively transform our work and help us find greater fulfillment in what we do. It begins with being. As we allow ourselves to be authentic, remember the big picture, and connect with others, what we do will have greater meaning and joy.

HELPFUL TIPS:
- Remember your true self
- Be-Do-Have
- Do something bigger than yourself
- Create meaningful connections with others
- Do what you enjoy

Chapter 19 – Key #4

Remember Love

"I want to think again of dangerous and noble things.
I want to be light and frolicsome.
I want to be improbable, beautiful and afraid of nothing,
as though I had wings."
– Mary Oliver

*J*t feels like we've been on a journey together, you and me. Perhaps less a journey than a process, a process of transformation. After all, this story is ultimately about Butterfly. I hope through sharing about my personal experiences and introducing the various tools, that I've offered you something of benefit for your continued transformation, health and happiness.

There is one Key yet to talk about, though. Frankly, everything else rests on this one. You know what I'm going to say – love. I'm not talking about the let's wear our flowing dresses, take silk scarves in hand and twirl around kind of love. I'm talking about the warm hearted, grounded in action, what makes us human kind of love.

When we connect with this kind of love, we feel better about ourselves, we're able to make choices that support our own and others' growth, and we enjoy a greater level of happiness and fulfillment in life.

Love is directly linked to our life energy, and an environment of love allows one to thrive.

You won't see stats and figures in this chapter. I mentioned previously how it feels like much of the work I do is helping others remember what they already know. Love is something we all know, but often forget. Love connects us and is as available to us as the air we breathe. There's another quote that I enjoy from Pierre Teilhard de Chardin that says, "Love alone is capable of uniting living beings in such a way as to complete and fulfill them, for it alone takes them and joins them by what is deepest in themselves."

Love is the water in the ocean of life. Just as it is difficult to jump into water and not get wet, as we immerse ourselves in the experience of love, it's difficult to not be changed. More than anything else, love has the power to transform lives in beautiful and profound ways. This is true individually, in relationship, with family, friends, community and globally.

What is love? When I speak of love, I am primarily referring to unconditional love. That is, a way of viewing ourselves and others without judgment. There is a purity to it, like water at the source of a spring, before it is filtered, polluted or has chemicals added to it. It comes straight from the heart, before the mind has had a chance to put limitations on it.

Even more than a feeling or emotion, love is an experience. A simple way to connect with the experience of love is through visualizing someone or something that wells up love within us. You might imagine yourself in a room, comfortably seated on a cushion or chair. The room is painted in warm colors. There are large windows which let in the light. The furniture in the room is tasteful, relaxing and homey. Perhaps there is the smell of soup cooking on the stove or soft music playing in the background. The door in the room opens and in walks a loved one. Imagine someone you care about very much. It may be a child, a partner or spouse, a family member, a dear friend, or even a beloved pet. Immediately your eyes light up and a beaming smile spreads across your face. Your loved one comes straight to you, and you embrace him or her, not with one of those perfunctory one-second hugs that we often exchange in life, but with a hug that shares the warmth from your heart. During those brief moments in that embrace, there are no worries, there is no anger, no hate, no hurrying... There is no room for anything else. There is only love.

Visualizing someone we care deeply about and noticing how we feel when with that person or pet may give us a glimpse of what love is. It can help us remember. A lot of the time, we're not fully in the experience of love. We're preoccupied with the tasks of life, or complaining, or feeling stressed, or weighed down by sadness, grief, frustration, blame, anger, or swept up in the pursuit of "stuff."

I'm not saying that it is necessary, expected or even desirable that we live in that experience of warm-hearted, big-smile love every second of every minute of every day. Life flows, and it's natural to have a variety of feelings and experiences. However, **it supports our own and others' growth and happiness to be able to feel and act from a place of love at will and when the situation calls for it.** You might think of love as an undercurrent to our existence. It's there, within us, maybe not always seen in its full expression, but it continually courses through us and is ready to be utilized.

To illustrate, at home alone folding laundry, or filling the tank at the gas station, we might not feel immersed in the experience of love. Rather than twinkly-eyed and beaming, we may simply be in a zone, busy with thought or daydreaming as we perform a routine task. Then, a thought comes to mind that is belittling to oneself, "I'm lazy and overweight and no one is going to want to be with me." Here is an opportunity for love.

Connecting with love in this instance means loving oneself, speaking kindly to oneself. As discussed in the Listen First chapter, it helps to bring greater awareness to our thoughts. As we do, we can learn to build ourselves up rather than tear ourselves down with our words. **Know that you are worthy of love**. From this foundation of love, then, it's easier to change the message from that of, "I'm lazy and overweight and no one is going to want to be with me" to something more encouraging, such as, "I want to take steps to improve my health and feel better about myself."

A second example: you're engaged in conversation with your romantic partner. Your partner is upset and is beginning to take some frustration out on you. Your immediate reaction may be to want to get defensive and start spewing frustrations right back. Now is a great opportunity to pull something loving out of your back pocket. Rather than jump into conflict, you might pause for a moment, and ask yourself, "How can I respond in a more compassionate way?" This simple pause and moment of increased awareness can alter the course of the conversation. Instead of going blow for verbal blow, you can choose to respond in a gentle tone and reflect, "I see you're feeling frustrated." This is the work of remembering love.

There could be a number of reasons why we're not fully dialed into and acting from a place of love each time we could be. A lot of it simply has to do with awareness. It's easy to get caught up in the drama or details of a situation. Being aware requires that we consciously take a step back and view the bigger picture. Or, maybe we didn't experience unconditional love during those formative years of youth and so do not yet know how to truly express it. Individuals neglected or abused as children may particularly have a difficult time understanding what love is. This is also true with individuals who grow up surrounded by drug abuse and violence. They often develop survival and coping strategies to simply get by, and those strategies are not always looked upon favorably in society. They may include lying, manipulation and addiction. There might also be mental health issues and criminal activity. One can imagine how their view of the world, and of love, may be affected. Not having felt and experienced love that is compassionate, protective, caring, empathetic and supportive of growth, it can be a real challenge for them to share that with others.

However, even when coming from difficult circumstances, each of us seems to recognize unconditional love when we see it. We recognize it at a soul level. If we are so fortunate to have someone come into our lives who demonstrates care and compassion, patience and dedication, it feeds something deep within us. It's as if this love is the state we rested in before we were born, and the state we longingly hope to rediscover in life.

We also respond positively to love. From my experience with Maddie, I came to see this in a powerful way. Shortly after Maddie and I got reacquainted in 2013, she expressed how it seemed like no one cared whether she lived or died. When she said that, I felt compassion in my heart, and I communicated to her that I cared. After she stole the red Blazer, I could have closed off from feeling love, mentally justifying it. It was an emotionally intense experience and a breach of trust. I could have said, "No, I can't help you." But I allowed my heart to stay open. I remembered the tests I put my therapist through when I was in my 20s, all in an attempt to get her to abandon me, to prove I wasn't really loved. That is often what people who have experienced severe trauma do. They test others, searching and wondering, will *this* person stick by me? I saw this young woman in a state of crisis, and with old wounds not yet healed. I felt love, and I committed to providing the support she needed. Neither of us knew what all that would entail. Neither of us knew how many obstacles would crop up and challenges there would be. But it didn't matter. Love is consistent. It does not give up. During the first couple years of supporting Maddie in her recovery, there was practically an expectation on her part that I would abandon her, as if any day I would say, "Okay, I'm done now." It took her years to realize I was there to stay. In an environment that is nurturing and loving, growth happens. I truly feel love is the foundation for Maddie's incredible transformation. It nourished her and inspired her to make better choices for herself. When we feel someone truly cares, it can change everything.

Love, or I should say, "love," is one of those things that we often ascribe only to close personal relationships, such as a spouse or family member. What would happen if we loved our neighbors, or the addict, or the homeless man? We sometimes get hung up on the word love. So I'm going to start talking about kindness. The feelings and actions are what are more important. Kindness, too, comes from the heart. Within kindness may be found compassion, caring and encouragement.

We can act in loving ways without calling it as such. We can be kind. Ellen DeGeneres says it at the end of all her shows. "Be kind," she says, her way of rippling out some positivity. We can ripple out positive vibes, too. It is possible to love our neighbors and the addict and the homeless man, and we can show that through caring and acts of kindness. These acts can be simple or complex: Assisting the neighbor with a gardening project. Making eye contact and giving a warm smile to the addict. Volunteering on a community task force to help reduce homelessness.

As we increase our awareness, we realize we can choose our responses. We can choose to ignore and not feel, or we can choose to draw from that undercurrent of love, keep our hearts open and care. From this open-hearted place, we may feel compelled to act in a kind, empathetic manner. Through the process, we may change our own life and/or that of someone else. With each of us rippling out the positivity, might we even change the world? I am optimistic.

I appreciate these words from philanthropists, Bill & Melinda Gates, "Optimism... isn't a passive expectation that things will get better; it's a conviction that we can make things better – that whatever suffering we see, no matter how bad it is, we can help people if we don't lose hope and we don't look away."

There may be some who hear me talking about love and kindness and say, "Ah, this is about spirituality," which can lead the more secular-minded individuals to close off. For some reason such grand concepts as love and kindness often get relegated to the realm of the spiritual, as if they have no place in all other aspects of life. Quite simply, this is about humanity. Not only is love very much a part of what makes us human, it is the strongest force for being able to work together collaboratively in community so that we may thrive. Kindness makes the world go round. I enjoy what the Dalai Lama XIV said, "There is no need for temples; no need for complicated philosophy. Our own brain, our own heart is our temple; the philosophy is kindness." Kindness is an expression of humanity at its best. It also contributes to our own happiness. It does good for others and makes us feel good, too.

There are countless ways we can demonstrate kindness in our daily lives. Communication is a big one. First, we can speak more kindly to ourselves – giving ourselves positive messages to replace negative ones, those that deflate us. It might be helpful to differentiate between our thoughts and what I refer to as our inner voice of wisdom. Our thoughts float along the surface of our awareness, moving from topic to topic, like a feather blowing in the wind. These thoughts may be helpful or harmful, true or untrue. Our thoughts have been deeply influenced by the messages our parents or early caregivers conveyed to us, through their words and actions. Over the years, we've likely adopted many world views, attitudes, and even unhealthy patterns from others. These, then, get incorporated into our thoughts. By contrast, our inner voice of wisdom comes from the deepest, truest part of ourselves and desires only to support growth. It is stable, like a tree with firm roots. This voice comes with a pure, loving intent. It is where wisdom lies. This voice is patient and compassionate. The more we can learn to listen to our inner voice of wisdom, and let that voice replace the thoughts that put down and deflate, the more we will be able to be happy, live our potential and shine.

Secondly, we can communicate with others in a more kind and compassionate way, such as by using the skills of Listen First. We can bring more awareness to our choice of words and tone of voice, recalling how words carry energy.

It happens through day-to-day life. Similar to how we want to gradually integrate more physical activity and healthier food, the key is to integrate small acts of kindness into our daily habits. Each day there are opportunities to be kind through words and actions. The biggest impact of kindness in our personal lives occurs in the relationships closest to us. It begins with the relationship with oneself. Then, our family and close friends – our spouse or partner, our mother, father, daughter, son, brother, sister, grandparent, aunt, uncle, nephew, niece, cousin, grandchild, stepchildren, in-laws, close friends, coworkers and so on. Simple things, a considerate phone call to your partner, "I'm on my way home, is there anything you need at the store?" Or an offer to lend your child a hand, "Would you like some help with your project?" Giving a loved one a hug. Remembering to say "thank you" and "please." Speaking words of encouragement rather than putting the person down. Sharing a smile. Being generous. Demonstrating we care. Asking, rather than ordering. "When you have a moment, can you please send over that file?" Each of us appreciates being treated in a kind, respectful manner, and we respond to it quite favorably. The ripple of kindness can extend beyond our inner circle. We can be patient with the woman at the counter mailing our package. We can choose to not get angry and blare our horn at the driver in front of us. We can be kind to others on our vacations and in our world travels.

In addition, being kind makes us happier. Rather than being weighed down by negative thought or speaking negatively to others, we're sharing something that uplifts. It is uplifting to both the receiver and the giver.

One of the most challenging things may be to demonstrate love or kindness towards someone who has jilted us in some way. This may be particularly true for an individual close to us, such as a friend or member of our family. This person may have done or said something that pained us. Holding resentment can be so easy. The kind thing might be to speak with him or her about it. This gives you a chance to voice your thoughts and feelings, and gives the other person the opportunity to hear how his or her actions affected you. When one or both individuals are able to listen and reflect, communicating can go far in helping to mend rifts. Or, the situation may call for creating healthy boundaries, which is a way to be kind to yourself. At times it is necessary to have distance or limits with others in order to maintain our well-being. Regardless of the outcome, kindness can be shown by letting go of resentment. The resentment is held in our bodies and can weigh us down. Letting go frees us to connect with more of our vital energy.

It may feel very challenging, too, to show kindness to individuals who are different from us. The world is full of people with various personalities and different life circumstances. Humanity is made up of individuals of different ethnicities, nationalities, and people who adhere to different religious or political beliefs. In our families and communities, there are those with different sexual orientations, physical and mental abilities, and socio-economic status. Kindness can be expressed through tolerance, not judging, not thinking ourselves to be superior. Kindness can be demonstrated by making an effort to better understand those who seem different from us. Very often, when we do, we find we have more in common than not. We're all members of the human race with the same basic needs, including the need for love.

Kindness is an indicator of our evolution of consciousness. As we increase our understanding and learn to be more compassionate with ourselves and others, and as we learn how to work together cooperatively and collaboratively, we grow stronger. We can choose to share resources and create solutions that benefit the whole. Together we can accomplish more than any one of us can do alone. Kindness provides humanity the opportunity to reach new heights. Through kindness, we can thrive.

I am always touched by the kindness of others. I see it in simple, everyday ways, such as how Tony communicates with me with love and respect. I've seen it in big ways. For instance, when Maddie was still new in her recovery and transitioning from being homeless to needing a place to live, two of my friends said they wanted to help and opened up their home to her. An act from the heart. They had never met her. They just trusted. Their generosity and caring helped Maddie move forward. I've seen the kindness of strangers – the person who holds the door for another, and members of the community who immediately step up to provide food, shelter and other aid to victims who've lost their homes in a fire.

There are so many opportunities to be kind. Until it becomes habit, we may have to be intentional with our acts of kindness. You might think of one person or one situation that you can approach with more kindness starting now.

Practicing kindness increases our ability to be empathetic. It helps keep our hearts open. And that, truly, is the best way to live.

I can't have a chapter about love without talking more about Tony. Plus, it's only fair to you that I catch you up on the latest developments in the area of our romance, in case you are wondering.

Where did I leave off? Oh, yes. We jumped off, hand in hand, into the great unknown. After moving in with Tony, some neck and back issues that he was experiencing created a catalyst for a shift in his work and he quit his job. For us both, our work was in a stage of transition. We trusted the process. We took one day at a time, and remembered to breathe.

In time, Tony gained a closer connection with his body and initiated a renewed focus on his health. Now, stronger, healthier and maintaining a greater level of awareness, Tony is working again full time. He has a new career that he enjoys. Turns out, he's also making more money than he ever has. Be Do Have. There are aspects of his work that he finds challenging or stressful at times. Challenges are part of life. However, he is learning how to unearth the gems from the day, finding things to appreciate: having an opportunity to teach someone a new skill, being able to work outdoors in beautiful settings, or feeling the satisfaction of finding an innovative solution to a problem. Tony is also finding balance in work and life. He integrates healthy movement throughout his day, he takes time to rest and replenish, and he's known to excitedly get swept up in personal creative projects when inspiration strikes.

Tony and I continue to support others through the Center for Sacred Movement. We help individuals and groups enjoy greater health and well-being through yoga, outdoor adventures, workshops, coaching and community connection. It's thoroughly satisfying to be of service in this way, not to mention a lot of fun.

With things feeling more settled, we decide to take another trip to Hawaii in 2014. Tony fell in love with island life while we were there in 2010. For this upcoming vacation, we plan to spend some time on both Oahu and Maui. My former karate Sensei and friend, Mike, and his wife,

Cathy, now live on Oahu, and it's been several years since I've seen them. It'll be nice to catch up, and I'm excited to introduce them to Tony.

Two weeks prior to our departure, I have an idea. Hey, why don't we get married in Hawaii? Tony and I had been casually talking about it for a few months. Neither of us really felt any need to get married. We figured as long as we wanted to be together, we'd be together. I suppose we are not very traditional when it comes to such things. But the idea was in our minds. We've been together now over 4 years, and we both find Maui to be a special place. So we decide to do it!

In the following days, arrangements are quickly made for the marriage license, wedding officiate, beach permit, flowers, etc. It will be a simple ceremony.

Tony and I choose to keep it a secret from family and friends (yes, we were a little sneaky), with a couple minor exceptions. Since we'll be staying at their place the first 3 days of our vacation, I write Mike and let him in on our plans and invite them to join us on Maui for the ceremony. They are excited to be a part of it. I also write my Uncle Milo and Aunt Debbi who live on the big island of Hawaii and invite them. They're elated, too, and make arrangements to attend.

When the special day comes, we gather at one of our favorite beaches, Po'o'lena'lena, on the south side of the island. It is a beautiful morning in the tropics. The sun is shining, the sky is an amazing blue, and the clear, turquoise water is gently lapping on the sandy shore. The officiate is a local minister dressed in traditional Hawaiian garb, complete with kukui nut bead necklace and a boar's tusk. Tony is wearing a blue, Hawaiian, button-down shirt and white shorts. I'm wearing a white blouse with a small sequined diamond at the heart, a couple feathers in my hair, and white yoga pants. Yep, yoga pants. We are gifted with beautiful flower leis and seashell necklaces. With our bare feet in the sand, the officiate blows the conch shell to begin the ceremony. He sings beautiful traditional Hawaiian songs and talks to us about love. Family and friends scurry about to capture the moments on camera and video. Tony slips the ring onto my hand. We gaze into each other's eyes and exchange vows, speaking words of commitment and promising to cherish one another. Pronounced husband and wife, we share a kiss as the conch shell blows. Married on Maui in May.

A few weeks after returning home, we have a wedding reception at beloved Diego Park. It is a blessing to feel the love and support of family and friends, near and far.

We enjoy living in our house on the hill. Redwood, apple, oak and other trees share the land, and sweet deer visit daily. Some mornings, the coastal fog blankets the valley below, leaving the surrounding mountains to rise up like islands amidst the sea. Natural beauty abounds.

People say home is where the heart is. With this kind and loving man, I am home.

As I'm writing this last chapter, coming to the end of the story, I receive some interesting news. First of all, let me put your mind at ease. I'm not pregnant.

No, this news has to do with work, previous work. As of October 1st, 2015, John Smith no longer works for the Y. The Board of Directors made their choice. Change may take time, but it does happen.

We're all butterflies, in various stages. Sometimes people frustrate us, or we have a difficult time understanding why they do what they do. When I'm feeling that way, I try to remember we're all on a journey, all of humanity, on an evolutionary journey.

It wouldn't make sense to squash the caterpillars. Instead, can we approach these individuals with compassion and patience? Maybe a hundred, or two hundred, years from now humanity will be in a much different place, a more positive place as a whole. Maybe we'll get there through acts of kindness. It's up to us.

Let's focus on what we can do today. We can practice our listening skills. We can strive to speak and act from that deep, authentic aspect of ourselves and not worry so much about money, "getting ahead" or stuff. We can add more movement and pay attention to what we eat, so we feel good, support our health, and have the energy to do what we want to do. We can remember we're human. We are connected with nature. The earth holds the water we drink, grows the food we eat, and supports the air we breathe. We can be more conscious about our choices.

Yes, within each of us lies a unique and beautiful butterfly. This is the time of our transformation. Be kind. Choose love.

With the help of the sun's radiant warmth,
her wings have dried
and become much lighter.
"Oh! They're so delicate!" she exclaims,
noticing for the first time how little they do weigh.
She slowly begins to open them,
feeling into this strange, new movement.
It takes some getting used to.
She finds herself so very present in this moment,
and utterly transfixed by her wings.
Open, close... she practices... open, close...
open, close... open, close.
"And the colors!" she observes, "So vibrant!"

She is so different from her old self,
yet this new state feels familiar.
It's as if it has been her true self all along,
simply hidden, not yet revealed.

She looks around and sees
through new eyes,
no longer as a caterpillar,
but as Butterfly.
She takes it all in.
All the beauty.

Butterfly gazes towards the sun.
Feeling energized and ready to meet whatever lies ahead,
she spreads her wings
and takes flight.

About the Author

Kristi Bowman is a nationally-acclaimed Wellness Coach & Consultant and is the Co-Founder and Director of the Center for Sacred Movement (CSM) in the San Francisco North Bay, which supports greater health and well-being through yoga, outdoor activities and community connection. Kristi speaks and teaches across the U.S., and she is most recognized for her Listen First workshops and inspiring people to get up and move.

Prior to co-founding CSM, Kristi enjoyed a successful career with the YMCA, working as a change agent and National Coach & Consultant, helping to transform organizational practices and support communities across the country in healthy living and chronic disease prevention.

An experienced Yoga Instructor trained by world-renowned teacher, Shiva Rea, Kristi believes a holistic approach to wellness – addressing body, mind and spirit – is most effective for enjoying a healthy, happy, fulfilling life. She enjoys helping individuals of all ages experience the many benefits and joys of movement.

Kristi is the author of *Journey to One: A Woman's Story of Emotional Healing and Spiritual Awakening.* You can find *Journey to One* at your local bookstore or favorite online retailer.

She lives with her dearest love, nestled in the hills of northern California. You're invited to find out more about Kristi and her wellness offerings at www.kristibowman.us

Made in the USA
Columbia, SC
28 October 2020

23615166R00195